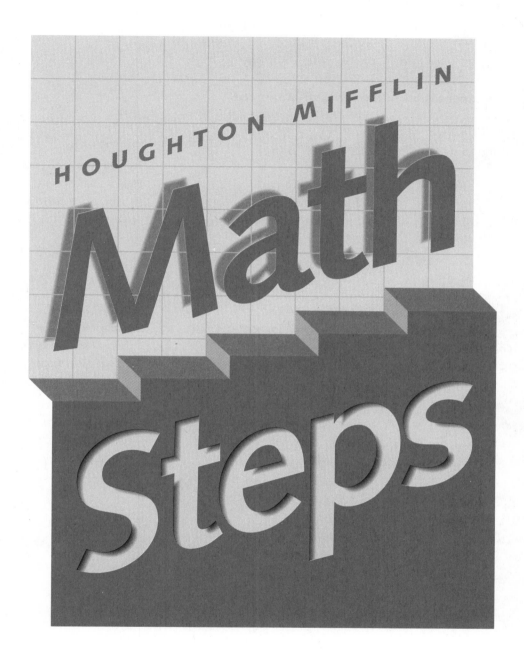

HOUGHTON MIFFLIN

Math Steps

HOUGHTON MIFFLIN

Boston • Atlanta • Dallas • Denver • Geneva, Illinois • Palo Alto • Princeton

Grateful acknowledgment is given for the contributions of

Student Book

Rosemary Theresa Barry
Karen R. Boyle
Barbara Brozman
Gary S. Bush
John E. Cassidy
Dorothy Kirk

Sharon Ann Kovalcik
Bernice Kubek
Donna Marie Kvasnok
Ann Cherney Markunas
Joanne Marie Mascha
Kathleen Mary Ogrin

Judith Ostrowski
Jeanette Mishic Polomsky
Patricia Stenger
Annabelle L. Higgins Svete

Teacher Book
Contributing Writers

Dr. Judy Curran Buck
Assistant Professor of Mathematics
Plymouth State College
Plymouth, New Hampshire

Dr. Richard Evans
Professor of Mathematics
Plymouth State College
Plymouth, New Hampshire

Dr. Mary K. Porter
Professor of Mathematics
St. Mary's College
Notre Dame, Indiana

Dr. Anne M. Raymond
Assistant Professor of Mathematics
Keene State College
Keene, New Hampshire

Stuart P. Robertson, Jr.
Education Consultant
Pelham, New Hampshire

Dr. David Rock
Associate Professor,
Mathematics Education
University of Mississippi
Oxford, Mississippi

Michelle Lynn Rock
Elementary Teacher
Oxford School District
Oxford, Mississippi

Dr. Jean M. Shaw
Professor of Elementary Education
University of Mississippi
Oxford, Mississippi

Contents

UNIT 1 • TABLE OF CONTENTS

Place Value and Addition and Subtraction of Whole Numbers

Dear Family,

During the next few weeks, our math class will be learning about comparing, ordering, adding, and subtracting whole numbers.

You can expect to see homework that provides practice with comparing whole numbers. Here is a sample you may want to keep handy to give help if needed.

Comparing Whole Numbers

To compare whole numbers such as **607,760** and **608,706**, first align the numbers.

607,760

608,706

Then, beginning at the left or at the greatest place value of each number, compare the digits until you find two digits that are different.

↓

607,760

608,706

Since **7** is less than **8**, 607,760 is less than **608,706**. Because the symbol < represents "is less than," we can write **607,760 < 608,706**.

During this unit students will need to continue to practice comparing whole numbers.

Sincerely,

Place Value Through Billions

There are many ways to express a number such as **4,367**.

Standard Form: 4,367

Expanded Form: 4,000 + 300 + 60 + 7

Word Form: four thousand, three hundred sixty-seven

Place-value Chart			
Th	H	T	Ones
4	**3**	**6**	**7**

- - - - - - -

The place-value table below shows **398,412,567,103**.

Billions			Millions			Thousands			Ones			
Hundred Billions	Ten Billions	Billions	Hundred Millions	Ten Millions	Millions	Hundred Thousands	Ten Thousands	Thousands	Hundreds	Tens	Ones	← Place Values
3	9	8	4	1	2	5	6	7	1	0	3	← Digits

← Periods

398 billion, **412** million, **567** thousand, **103**   ← Short Word Form

Read: Three hundred ninety-eight *billion*, four hundred twelve *million*, five hundred sixty-seven *thousand*, one hundred three.   ← Word Form

The number has been separated into **4** groups of **3** digits each, called **periods.** When you write a number in standard form, separate the periods with commas.

Separate each number into periods with commas. Then read each number.

1.	4 5 0 6 1	2 8 3 0 3 7 5	7 8 2 9
2.	1 0 0 0 0 0 0 0	6 0 0 0 0 0 0 0	3 0 0 0 0 0
3.	2 0 0 0 0 0 0 0 0 0 0 0	8 0 0 0 0 0 0 0 0	4 6 3 9 5 2 1
4.	2 6 9 4 5 0 6 1 6	6 0 0 0 0 0 0 0	1 0 0 0 0 0 0 0 1
5.	1 4 6 2 7 2 9 1 5 4 1 2	6 8 3 9 0 0 3 0 0 5 0	2 0 0 0 0 2
6.	6 2 7 2 9 1 5 4 2	7 8 9 3 8 9 6 8 5 0 0	1 5 0 0 0 0 4
7.	7 6 9 1 0 0 0 4	1 0 0 0 0 0 0 0 0 0 0	9 8 0 0 0 1 2 3

Complete.

8. In the number **916,853,274**

the ____ shows the number of hundred thousands

the ____ shows the number of millions

the ____ shows the number of tens

the ____ shows the number of ten millions

the ____ shows the number of hundred millions

Write in standard form.

9. Ninety thousand, four hundred eight _____

10. Nine hundred thousand, five hundred five _____

11. Seven million, twenty-two thousand, two hundred _____

Write in words. Use commas and hyphens.

12. 38,492 _____

13. 276,023 _____

14. 28,005,010,035 _____

Write in expanded form.

15. 45 = _____   333 = _____   527 = _____

16. 7,891 = _____   67,807 = _____

| Problem Solving |
| Reasoning |

Solve.

17. What number in standard form represents one thousand millions?

_____

18. What number in standard form represents one million thousands?

_____

Test Prep ★ Mixed Review

19 What number sentence is in the same family of facts as 8 + 4 = ☐?

A 8 × 4 = ☐

B 8 − 4 = ☐

C ☐ ÷ 4 = 8

D ☐ − 4 = 8

20 What number comes next in this pattern? 40, 38, 36, 34, _____

F 33   H 31

G 32   J 30

Name _____

Round **32** to the nearest ten.

The number line shows that **32** is between **30** and **40**.
It is nearer to **30** than to **40**. Round **32** *down* to **30**.

$$32 \longrightarrow 30$$

Round **250** to the nearest hundred.

The number line shows that **250** is halfway between **200** and **300**.
A number halfway is rounded up. Round **250** *up* to **300**.

$$250 \longrightarrow 300$$

Round **2,843** to the nearest thousand.

The number line shows that **2,843** is between **2,000** and **3,000**.
It is nearer to **3,000** than to **2,000**. Round **2,843** *up* to **3,000**.

$$2,843 \longrightarrow 3,000$$

Round each number to the nearest ten.

1. 13 _____   23 _____   55 _____   49 _____   77 _____

Round each number to the nearest hundred.

2. 267 _____   850 _____   640 _____   99 _____   734 _____

Round each number to the nearest thousand.

3. 967 _____   8,500 _____   3,499 _____   1,300 _____

4. 3,290 _____   2,821 _____   3,500 _____   3,700 _____

You can round numbers without using a number line.

Round **1,238** to the nearest hundred.

Round to this place.

1 2 **3** 8 → **1,200**

less than 5, round *down*

Round **1,278** to the nearest hundred.

Round to this place.

1 2 **7** 8 → **1,300**

greater than 5, round *up*

A rounded number is not exact — it is an **estimate**. Use estimates when:

- an estimate is just as valuable as an exact answer. For example:

  About how many people live in a city?

- an exact answer is not possible. For example:

  How many stars are in the sky?

- an exact answer is possible, but it may be difficult to obtain. For example:

  How many students were absent last year?

Round to the

	nearest ten thousand	nearest hundred thousand	nearest million
5.	4,761,742 _____	4,761,742 _____	4,761,742 _____
6.	6,757,963 _____	6,757,963 _____	6,757,963 _____
7.	1,080,555 _____	1,080,555 _____	1,080,555 _____
8.	5,555,555 _____	5,555,555 _____	5,555,555 _____

Problem Solving
Reasoning

Which of the following represent an exact number? Which represent an estimate? Explain your reasoning.

9. The circumference of the earth at its equator is **24,910** miles.

_____

10. I am almost **12** years old.

_____

11. The speed limit on some highways is **65** miles per hour.

_____

12. My telephone number is **555–1094**.

_____

Test Prep ★ Mixed Review

13 What is the value of the 9 in 1,395,273?

A 9 millions

B 9 hundred thousands

C 9 ten thousands

D 9 thousands

14 $4000.00 + $300.00 + $0.80 + $0.09 =

F $4,389.00

G $4,380.09

H $4,308.09

J $4,300.89

Compare. Tell which is greater.   3,749 ( ) 3,758.

1. Line up the digits.   same ⟶

3	7	4	9
3	7	5	8

2. Compare digits in each place until they are different.

⬆
The digits are different: 4 is less than 5

So, 3,749 is less than 3,758.   **3,749 < 3,758**

> < is less than
> \> is greater than
> = is equal to

Complete. Write <, >, or =.

1. 63 ( ) 65   78 ( ) 87   200 ( ) 212

2. 437 ( ) 428   919 ( ) 922   1,014 ( ) 1,041

3. 5,021 ( ) 5,021   10,155 ( ) 10,135   212,697 ( ) 212,687

Write the numbers in order from least to greatest.

4. 150; 138; 156; 131; 146; 135 _____

5. 6,017; 6,907; 6,871; 6,107; 6,697; 6,077 _____

6. 5,683; 5,428; 8,548; 5,863; 8,508; 8,458 _____

Complete.

7. Arrange the seating capacities in order from least to greatest.

_____

8. Which stadium has a seating capacity closest to **90,000?**

_____

College Football Stadium	Seating Capacity
Ohio State	89,841
Michigan	102,501
Oklahoma State	50,614
Penn State	93,967
Auburn	85,214

9. Which stadium holds **10,000** fewer fans than **95,214?**

_____

10. Suppose a game was played last Saturday and **97,541** spectators attended. In which stadium was the game played? Explain.

_____

Problem Solving / Reasoning — Use this table to solve each problem below.

11. Arrange the six continents in order according to population. Begin with the continent that has the greatest population.

_____

_____

12. Do you think the population data are exact or estimated? Explain.

_____

Population of Six Continents	
Africa	731,500,000
Asia	3,428,300,000
Australia	28,900,000
Europe	799,600,000
North America	295,400,000
South America	488,600,000

13. Which continent now has a population nearest a half billion people? Explain.

_____

14. For every person who lives in Australia, about how many people live in North America?

_____

✓ Quick Check

15. Write 6 billion 472 million in standard form.

_____

Work Space

16. What is the value of the 6 in the number 2,869,472,508?

_____

17. Write the number 4,520,000,017 in short word form.

_____

Round each number to the nearest thousand, then to the nearest million.

18. 5,294,376 _____ _____

19. 23,459,622 _____ _____

Complete. Write <, >, or =.

20. 387 ◯ 372 **21.** 7,437 ◯ 8,200 **22.** 14,462 ◯ 14,398

Copyright © Houghton Mifflin Company. All rights reserved.

Name _____

Exponents and Place Value

An exponent tells how many times a base is used as a factor.

In the expression 6^4, the number **6** represents the **base** and the number **4** represents the **exponent**. The expression 6^4 is read *six to the fourth power*.

$$6^4 \leftarrow \text{Exponent} \\ 6 \leftarrow \text{Base}$$

The exponent tells how many times the base, **6**, is used as a factor.

$$6^4 = 6 \times 6 \times 6 \times 6$$

Read 7^2 as *seven squared*.   Read 7^3 as *seven cubed*.

Which number is the base?

1. 7^2 _____ 3^5 _____ 8^3 _____ 6^1 _____ 4^6 _____ 9^4 _____

Which number is the exponent?

2. 5^3 _____ 1^8 _____ 3^0 _____ 9^2 _____ 7^4 _____ 0^1 _____

Write the exponent for each base.

3. $2 \times 2 \times 2 = 2^?$ _____ $8 \times 8 \times 8 \times 8 \times 8 = 8^?$ _____

4. $5 \times 5 \times 5 \times 5 = 5^?$ _____ $4 \times 4 \times 4 \times 4 \times 4 \times 4 = 4^?$ _____

5. $10 \times 10 \times 10 = 10^?$ _____ $1 \times 1 \times 1 \times 1 = 1^?$ _____

6. $3 \times 3 = 3^?$ _____ $6 \times 6 \times 6 = 6^?$ _____

Write the base and exponent.

7. $3 \times 3 \times 3 \times 3 =$ _____ $8 \times 8 \times 8 =$ _____

8. $4 \times 4 \times 4 \times 4 \times 4 =$ _____ $1 \times 1 \times 1 =$ _____

9. $2 \times 2 \times 2 \times 2 \times 2 \times 2 =$ _____ $7 \times 7 \times 7 \times 7 =$ _____

10. $5 \times 5 =$ _____ $10 \times 10 \times 10 =$ _____

Write each number in standard form.

11. 2^3 _____ 2^2 _____ 2^4 _____ 3^2 _____ 1^5 _____ 5^2 _____

Millions Period			Thousands Period			Ones Period		
Hundred Millions	Ten Millions	Millions	Hundred Thousands	Ten Thousands	Thousands	Hundreds	Tens	Ones
100,000,000 $10 \times 10 \times 10 \times 10 \times 10 \times 10 \times 10 \times 10$	10,000,000 $10 \times 10 \times 10 \times 10 \times 10 \times 10 \times 10$	1,000,000 $10 \times 10 \times 10 \times 10 \times 10 \times 10$	100,000 $10 \times 10 \times 10 \times 10 \times 10$	10,000 $10 \times 10 \times 10 \times 10$	1,000 $10 \times 10 \times 10$	100 10×10	10	1
10^8	10^7	10^6	10^5	10^4	10^3	10^2	10^1	10^0

You can write powers of ten this way:

$700 = 7 \times 10^2$ $\qquad$ $60,000,000 = 6 \times 10^7$ $\qquad$ $200,000 = 2 \times 10^5$

Write in exponent form.

12. 40,000 _____ $\qquad$ 4,000 _____ $\qquad$ 30 _____

13. 9,000,000 _____ $\qquad$ 300,000,000 _____ $\qquad$ 10,000 _____

14. 80,000 _____ $\qquad$ 10 _____ $\qquad$ 2 _____

Write in standard form.

15. $7 \times 10^6 =$ _____ $\qquad$ $5 \times 10^2 =$ _____ $\qquad$ $2 \times 10^3 =$ _____

16. $3 \times 10^5 =$ _____ $\qquad$ $9 \times 10^4 =$ _____ $\qquad$ $8 \times 10^7 =$ _____

Test Prep ★ Mixed Review

17 What is the standard form for three million, one hundred fifty thousand, seventeen?

A 3,150,017

B 3,150,170

C 3,000,150,017

D 3,000,150,170

18 What number is 1,000 more than 86,002?

F 85,002

G 86,102

H 87,002

J 87,102

Name _____

This bar graph shows the results of a survey of the number of each type of pet some people have.

In this lesson, you will need to use the graph to draw conclusions about the data.

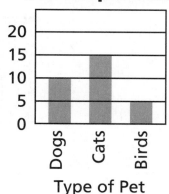

Pets People Own

Tips to Remember

| 1. Understand 2. Decide 3. Solve 4. Look back |

- Ask yourself: Have I solved a problem like this before? If so, how did I solve it?

- Compare the labels on the graph with the words and numbers in the problem. Find the facts you need from the graph.

- When you can, make a prediction about the answer. Then compare your answer with your prediction.

Solve. Use the bar graph above.

1. What is the total number of pets that the people who were surveyed own?

   Think: How can the bars in the graph help you find the number?

   _____

   _____

   Answer_____

2. The number of people surveyed was 15. Is it true that each person surveyed has 2 pets? Explain.

   Think: Does each person surveyed own a pet?

   _____

   Answer_____

   _____

   _____

3. The people surveyed own the least number of which pet?

   _____

   _____

4. The number of cats people own is double the number of birds. Is this statement true or false? Explain.

   _____

   _____

Pets People Own

Solve. Use the bar graph above.

5. The bar graph shows the results of a survey in which people were asked what pets they own and how many. Do people own more dogs than fish? Explain your answer.

_____

_____

6. The people surveyed own the greatest number of which pet? Explain.

_____

_____

7. The number of fish the people own is three times the number of birds. Is this statement true or false? Explain.

_____

_____

8. Of the people surveyed, one person owned 3 pets: a goat, a sheep, and a horse. Which bar above shows the pets that this person owned? Explain.

_____

_____

Extend Your Thinking

9. Suppose one person in the survey bought 4 more dogs. How would this change the data? How would you change the graph to reflect this data? Explain.

_____

_____

Adding and Subtracting Whole Numbers

Use what you learned last year to review addition.
Find **437 + 186.**

Estimate first: **437** rounds to **400**   **186** rounds to **200**   **400 + 200 = 600**

1. Add the ones
and regroup **10** ones
as **1** ten.

$$\begin{array}{r} \overset{1}{4}3\,7 \\ +\ 186 \\ \hline 3 \end{array}$$

2. Add the tens
and regroup **10** tens
as **1** hundred.

$$\begin{array}{r} \overset{1\ 1}{4}3\,7 \\ +\ 186 \\ \hline 23 \end{array}$$

3. Add the hundreds.

$$\begin{array}{r} \overset{1}{4}37 \\ +186 \\ \hline 623 \end{array}$$

The sum, **623**, is close to the estimate, **600**. The answer is reasonable.

**Add. Estimate first. Then use your estimate to check
whether your answer is reasonable.**

1.

783	585	148	736	959
+ 149	+ 258	+ 664	+ 177	+ 172

2.

5,728	3,914	6,051	3,798	7,140
+ 3,307	+ 2,843	+ 3,572	+ 2,473	+ 3,695

3.

29,132	75,213	59,604	72,092	60,380
+ 30,567	+ 75,213	+ 31,572	+ 45,358	+ 27,294

4.

63	45	258	7,425	24,752
42	45	346	6,813	76,874
78	45	91	4,259	80,257
+ 91	+ 45	+ 759	+ 647	+ 323

5.

51	59	272	3,456	76,325
38	61	353	2,851	81,804
29	58	438	1,234	97,325
74	62	686	659	936
+ 51	+ 60	+ 147	+ 154	+ 5,563

Now review subtraction: find **703 − 329**.
Estimate first: **700 − 300 = 400**.

1. Regroup **1** hundred for **10** tens.

$$\begin{array}{r} {\scriptstyle 6\ \ 10} \\ 7\,\cancel{0}\,3 \\ -\ 3\ 2\ 9 \\ \hline \end{array}$$

2. Regroup **1** ten for **10** ones.

$$\begin{array}{r} {\scriptstyle 6\ \ \cancel{10}\ \ 13} \\ 7\,\cancel{\cancel{0}}\,\cancel{3} \\ -\ 3\ 2\ 9 \\ \hline \end{array}$$

3. Subtract.

$$\begin{array}{r} {\scriptstyle 6\ \ \cancel{10}\ \ 13} \\ 7\,\cancel{\cancel{0}}\,\cancel{3} \\ -\ 3\ 2\ 9 \\ \hline 3\ 7\ 4 \end{array}$$

The difference, **374**, is close to **400**. The answer is reasonable.

Subtract. Estimate first. Then use your estimate to check if your answer is reasonable.

6.

407	500	592	904	300
− 348	− 329	− 327	− 457	− 258

7.

6,000	4,780	6,051	5,210	6,400
− 5,532	− 2,219	− 1,883	− 3,782	− 2,588

8.

9,717	9,512	7,115	8,433	9,246
− 7,138	− 2,638	− 2,968	− 5,851	− 1,056

✔ **Quick Check**

Write the standard numeral.

9. 2^3 _____

10. 6×10^5 _____

11. $(9 \times 10^6) + (5 \times 10^0)$ _____

Work Space

Find the sum.

12.

46,802
+ 51,732

13.

50,709
+ 64,757

14.

94,466
18,833
2,346
+ 35,276

Find the difference.

15.

14,080
− 13,783

16.

6,090
− 2,987

17.

498,541
− 372,639

A **variable** is a letter or a symbol that is used to represent an unknown quantity.

Although the letters *x* and *n* are often used as variables, you can use any letter of the alphabet.

When you write an **algebraic expression** for a word phrase, you use numbers, operation signs, and variables.

word phrase	algebraic expression
the sum of a number and **4**	$n + 4$
a number decreased by **10**	$x - 10$
8 more than a number	$h + 8$
25 less than a number	$w - 25$

Write an algebraic expression for the word phrase. Use *n* to represent a variable.

1. twelve more than a number _____

2. a number decreased by **100** _____

3. thirty-four less than a number _____

4. a number increased by **75** _____

Write an algebraic expression for the word phrase.

5. forty decreased by a number *x* _____

6. the sum of a number *b* and **1** _____

7. a number *z* decreased by itself _____

8. a number *p* plus $\frac{1}{2}$ _____

9. a number *r* less **1** _____

10. fourteen increased by a number *q* _____

11. a number *g* increased by itself _____

12. a number *m* decreased by **2** _____

13. three more than a number *y* _____

14. sixty decreased by a number *u* _____

It is possible to evaluate an algebraic expression if the value of a variable is known. To **evaluate** an expression you substitute numbers for variables.

Example: Evaluate the algebraic expression $n - 11$ for $n = 30$.

1. Write the expression. $n - 11$
2. Substitute **30** for n. $30 - 11$
3. Simplify. 19

Evaluate each algebraic expression for $x = 25$.

15. $x + 9$ _____ $x - 13$ _____ $250 + x$ _____

16. $x + 29$ _____ $x + x$ _____ $x - x$ _____

Complete each table.

17.

n	$n - 1$
20	
15	
10	
5	

18.

k	$k + 17$
0	
1	
2	
3	

19.

x	$x - 6$
12	
11	
10	
9	

Problem Solving Reasoning

Write an algebraic expression to represent each situation. For each expression you write, explain what the variable you chose represents.

20. Jamie's brother is two years younger than Jamie.

What is her brother's age?_____

21. The sum of two different numbers is **14**.

_____

22. The difference between two different numbers is **1**.

_____

Test Prep ★ Mixed Review

23 Mr. Gomez read 128 pages in his book on Friday and 273 pages on Saturday. About how many more pages did he read on Saturday?

A 50   C 250
B 150   D 350

24 What is this number in standard form? 7×10^5

F 7,000
G 70,000
H 700,000
J 7,000,000

16 Unit 1 Lesson 7

Copyright © Houghton Mifflin Company. All rights reserved.

Name _____   **Equations**

A mathematical sentence with an equals sign (=) is an
equation. There are three kinds of equations: true, false, and open.

True equation	False Equation	Open equation
$15 - 15 = 0$	$1 + 1 = 9$	$n - 2 = 6$

When you find a number for **n** that makes an open equation
true, you **solve** the equation.

To solve an addition equation,
think of a related subtraction equation.

Think:
$$n + 1 = 4$$
$$n = 4 - 1$$
$$n = 3$$

> Subtraction is the opposite of addition.
> Think: **4** minus **1** is what number?

To solve a subtraction equation,
think of a related addition equation.

Think:
$$n - 5 = 2$$
$$n = 2 + 5$$
$$n = 7$$

> Addition is the opposite of subtraction.
> Think: **2** plus **5** is what number?

Identify each equation. Write *True*, *False*, or *Open*.

1. $10 - 2 = 4$ _____ $n + 3 = 5$ _____

2. $12 - 3 = 9$ _____ $7 + 6 = 13$ _____

3. $5 + a = 20$ _____ $8 - 4 = 1$ _____

Complete.

4. $n + 2 = 6$ $n - 4 = 5$ $n - 3 = 3$

Think: $n = 6 - $ _____   Think: $n = 5 + 4$ Think: $n = 3 + $ _____

$n = 4$ $n = $ _____ $n = 6$

5. $n - 2 = 7$ $7 + n = 15$ $n + 8 = 13$

Think: $n = 7 + 2$ Think: $n = 15 - $ _____   Think: $n = 13 - 8$

$n = $ _____ $n = 8$ $n = $ _____

6. $n - 6 = 2$ $n - 15 = 21$ $10 + n = 20$

Think: $n = 2 + $ _____   Think: $n = 21 + 15$ Think: $n = 20 - $ _____

$n = 8$ $n = $ _____ $n = 10$

Sometimes the properties of addition can help you solve equations.

Commutative Property of Addition		Identity Property of Addition	
Arithmetic	Algebra	Arithmetic	Algebra
$3 + 2 = 2 + 3$	$a + b = b + a$	$7 + 0 = 7$	$n + 0 = n$

The rules for subtraction can help, too.

Rules for Subtraction	
Arithmetic	Algebra
$8 - 8 = 0$	$n - n = 0$
$6 - 0 = 6$	$n - 0 = n$

Find the value of n.

7. $n + 7 = 7 + 3$ _____ $19 + n = 54$ _____ $n - 18 = 40$ _____

8. $n - 9 = 0$ _____ $5 + n = 25$ _____ $100 + n = 500$ _____

9. $n - 0 = 8$ _____ $n - 7 = 11$ _____ $n - 15 = 135$ _____

10. $21 + n = 31$ _____ $n + 12 = 39$ _____ $n + 14 = 33$ _____

| Problem Solving |
| Reasoning |

Solve.

11. At rest, Mark's heart beats **72** times per minute. When he jogs, his heartbeat increases to **95** beats per minute. How can you show this using a variable?

_____

12. Write a problem involving addition or subtraction. Then write an equation to represent the problem.

_____

Test Prep ★ Mixed Review

13 A large cement block weighed 1,548 pounds. What is that number rounded to the nearest thousand pounds?

A 2,000

B 1,150

C 1,140

D 1,000

14 Sarita bought a sandwich for $4.95, a drink for $.75, and an apple for $.35. She gave the clerk a $10 bill. What was her change?

F $3.95

G $4.05

H $4.95

J $6.05

Name _____

**Problem Solving Strategy:
Write an Equation**

Sometimes it is helpful to write an
equation to solve a problem.

Problem
Matt had 12 marbles. Mindy gave him some of her marbles. Now he has 20 marbles. How many marbles did Mindy give him?

1 Understand   As you reread, ask yourself questions.

- What do you know about the number of marbles?

    Matt had 12 marbles.
    Now he has 20 marbles.

    What do you need to find?

    _____

2 Decide   Choose a method for solving.

- Try the strategy Write an Equation.

    Pick a variable to represent what you need to find.

    What variable did you select?

    _____

3 Solve   Try to write a word equation first.

- What equation can you use to help you solve the problem?

    _____

    What is the solution to the equation?

    _____

4 Look back   Check your answer. Replace the variable with its value.

    Write your answer below.

    Answer: _____

    Does your answer make sense? Explain.

    _____

Use the **Write an Equation** strategy or any other strategy you have learned.

1. Lorna had **$58.73** in her savings account. She made a deposit. Her new balance was **$92.09**. How much was the deposit?

Think: What does it mean to make a deposit?

_____

Answer:_____

2. Jamel collects baseball cards. He sold **17** to his friend Mia. Now he has **83** cards left. How many cards did Jamel start with?

Think: Did Jamel start with more cards or fewer cards?

_____

Answer:_____

3. Together Timothy and Lili have **$117**. If Timothy has **$59**, how much does Lili have?

_____

4. Miguel has three times as many CDs as Chen. If Chen has **19** CDs, how many CDs does Miguel have?

_____

5. Gloria has half as many seashells as George. If George has **54** shells, how many shells does Gloria have?

_____

6. A square has a perimeter of **24** inches. What is the length of each side of the square?

_____

7. Taniqua baked **76** cookies. If there were **19** cookies in each batch, how many batches did she bake?

_____

8. One year a fire department responded to fires on **289** days. On how many days were there no fires to put out?

_____

9. I'm thinking of a number. If I subtract **65** from it, the result is **56**. What number am I thinking of?

_____

10. I'm thinking of a number. If I multiply it by **13**, the result is **117**. What number am I thinking of?

_____

Name _____

You can use parentheses to group numbers. In addition, the way you group the numbers does not change the sum. This is called the **associative property of addition**.

$$2 + (3 + 4) = (2 + 3) + 4$$
$$2 + 7 = 5 + 4$$
$$9 = 9$$

In mathematics, parentheses are **grouping symbols**. When parentheses are used in an expression or an equation, you must do the operations inside parentheses first.

grouping symbols
↓ ↓
$(9 - 4) + 3 = ?$
↓
$5 + 3 = 8$

grouping symbols
↓ ↓
$9 - (4 + 3) = ?$
↓
$9 - 7 = 2$

Solve. Remember to work inside the parentheses ( ) first.

1. $(95 - 23) + 47 =$ _____ $95 - (23 + 47) =$ _____

2. $90 - (56 - 29) =$ _____ $(90 - 56) - 29 =$ _____

3. $(349 + 526) - 235 =$ _____ $349 + (526 - 235) =$ _____

4. $290 + (63 + 159) =$ _____ $(290 + 63) + 159 =$ _____

Solve. Let $n = 8$.

5. $n - (4 + 1) =$ _____ $(n + 12) - 3 =$ _____

6. $(16 - n) + 3 =$ _____ $25 - (n + 2) =$ _____

7. $(n + 1) - 5 =$ _____ $(n - 7) - 1 =$ _____

8. $(n + n) - 10 =$ _____ $n + (n - n) =$ _____

9. $(n + 7) - n =$ _____ $(n - 1) + 9 =$ _____

10. $(3 + n) + (10 - n) =$ _____ $(n + 5) - (n - n) =$ _____

Solve. Let $x = 2$.

11. $x - (0 + 1) =$ _____ $(9 - x) - 5 =$ _____

12. $(x + x) - 3 =$ _____ $14 - (x + 7) =$ _____

13. $17 - (8 + x) =$ _____ $(x + 3) - x =$ _____

14. $(x + 5) - (x + 3) =$ _____ $10 - (x - x) - 10 =$ _____

Problem Solving
Reasoning

Insert parentheses ( ) to make each equation true.

15. $10 - 4 + 1 = 7$ $8 - 5 + 2 = 1$

16. $2 + 9 - 3 + 4 = 4$ $14 - 6 + 1 - 5 = 2$

17. Explain why these expressions have different values.

$5 + (3 - 2) + 1$ and $5 + 3 - (2 + 1)$

_____

_____

18. Is this a true equation? Explain.

$6 - 4 + 9 = 15 - 9 + (3 + 2)$

_____

_____

✓ Quick Check

Evaluate for $r = 5$.   **Work Space**

19. $r + 3$ _____   **20.** $16 - r$ _____

21. $r + r$ _____

Find the value of the variable.

22. $77 - v = 0$ _____   **23.** $29 + h = 40$ _____

24. $49 + 27 = c + 49$ _____

Evaluate.

25. $509 + (127 - 23)$ _____   **26.** $(250 + 988) + 750$ _____

27. $500 - (819 - 342)$ _____

Name _____

Write each number in standard form.

1. 3^3 _____   **2.** two million, sixteen thousand, five _____

3. Write **6,450** in word form. _____

Compare. Write <, >, or =.

4. 4,000 ◯ 4,100   **5.** 1,745 ◯ 1,745   **6.** 798,555 ◯ 789,555

Round to the nearest million.

7. 2,354,768 _____   **8.** 5,664,890,722 _____

Add or subtract.

9. 467
    + 398

10. 709
    − 271

11. 6,020
    − 2,354

12. 5,001
    − 687

13. 65,000
    32,000
    + 6,451

Evaluate each expression for $x = 15$.

14. $x + 30$ _____   **15.** $x - 12$ _____   **16.** $75 + x$ _____   **17.** $x - x$ _____

Solve each equation for n.

18. $20 - n = 14$ **19.** $n - 6 = 0$ **20.** $8 + n = 4 + 8$ **21.** $12 - n = 12$

_____   _____   _____   _____

Use the graph to solve each problem.

22. How many more baseball cards does Joe have than Rita? _____

23. How many baseball cards do Joe and his friends have in all? _____

Write an equation to solve the problem. Then solve the equation.

24. Melissa had **9** stamps after she sold **4** stamps at the stamp show. How many stamps did she have before the show? _____

Total Acreage in California

Year	Grapes	Almonds
1996	744,786	466,777
1997	772,973	472,053

1 Which is the almond acreage for 1997 rounded to the nearest ten thousand?

A 770,000   C 472,000

B 700,000   D 470,000

2 What is the difference in total grape acreage between 1996 and 1997?

F 5,276 acres

G 28,187 acres

H 30,000 acres

J 744,786 acres

K 772,973 acres

3 Which value for x makes this equation true? $15,692 - x = 4,000 + 10,692$

A 11,000   C 1,000

B 10,000   D 100

4 What is the value of the 4 in 246,791,539?

A 4×10^6

B 4×10^7

C 4×10^8

D 4×10^9

5 This graph shows the number of miles Anne rode her bike each day for four days.

Anne's Daily Mileage

On which day did Anne ride the greatest number of miles?

F Day 1

G Day 2

H Day 3

J Day 4

6 Dylan lost one piece of his design. Which piece could be used to complete the pattern?

F   H

G   J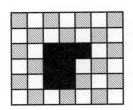

UNIT 2 • TABLE OF CONTENTS

Multiplication of Whole Numbers

We will be using this vocabulary:

factors numbers that are multiplied

product the answer in a multiplication problem

equation a number sentence with an equals (=) sign

multiple a number that is a product of itself and a counting number

distributive property the answer will be the same whether you add first and then multiply or multiply first and then add

Dear Family,

During the next few weeks, our math class will be learning and practicing multiplication of whole numbers.

You can expect to see homework that provides practice with multiplying whole numbers. Here is a sample you may want to keep handy to give help if needed.

Multiplying By Tens and Hundreds

These patterns can help a student understand how to multiply by tens and hundreds.

$$
\begin{array}{cc}
48 & \\
\times 1 & \\
\hline
48 &
\end{array}
\qquad
\begin{array}{cc}
48 & \\
\times 10 & \text{"one zero"}\\
\hline
480 & \text{"one zero"}
\end{array}
\qquad
\begin{array}{cc}
48 & \\
\times 100 & \text{"two zeros"}\\
\hline
4{,}800 & \text{"two zeros"}
\end{array}
$$

The number of zeros in the factors is equal to the number of zeros in the answer, or product.

So, to multiply 800×200, first think $8 \times 2 = 16$, then add **4** zeros to the product because the factors 800×200 contain **4** zeros.

$$
\begin{array}{c}
800 \\
\times 200 \\
\hline
16
\end{array}
\qquad\qquad
\begin{array}{c}
800 \\
\times 200 \\
\hline
160{,}000
\end{array}
$$

During this unit, students will need to continue practicing multiplying by tens and hundreds.

Sincerely,

Name _____

Some word phrases involve multiplication. These word phrases can be written as algebraic expressions.

Word Phrase	Algebraic Expression
the product of **4** and a number *b*	**4** × *b*
seven times a number *r*	**7** × *r*
10 multiplied by a number *c*	*c* × **10**

There are different ways to simplify an algebraic expression that contains multiplication.

Algebraic Expression		Rewritten Algebraic Expression
4 × *b*	Eliminate the multiplication sign.	**4***b*
7 × *r*	Use parentheses.	**7**(*r*) or (**7**)*r* or (**7***r*)
c × **10**	Multiplication is commutative, so write the variable after the numeral.	**10***c*

Write another algebraic expression for the word expression. Let *n* represent the number.

1. 25 multiplied by a number _____

2. a number multiplied by 2 _____

3. the product of **100** and a number _____

4. **12,400** times a number _____

5. the product of a number and **19** _____

6. Multiply the value of *n* by **9** _____

Write a word phrase for each algebraic expression.

7. 34 × *h* _____

8. 480*u* _____

9. 16*x* _____

Look at the table. Decide what is done to *x* each time to find *y*. Write a rule. Then write your rule as an algebraic expression.

10.

x	y
2	10
6	30
4	20
5	25

What's my rule?

_____

_____

_____

Expression:

_____

11.

x	y
0	3
1	4
2	5
3	6

What's my rule?

_____

_____

_____

Expression:

_____

12.

x	y
15	30
25	50
35	70
45	90

What's my rule?

_____

_____

_____

Expression:

_____

Problem Solving Reasoning Write an algebraic expression for the situation.

13. Let *n* represent the average number of hours you study each day.

How many hours do you spend studying in **5** days? _____

14. Let *b* represent the average number of times you blink your eyes

each hour. How many times do you blink your eyes in **8** hours? _____

Test Prep ★ Mixed Review

15 Which expression is equivalent to (*n* + 3) + 8?

A *n* + 3 + 8

B 11*n*

C 3*n* + 8

D 24 × *n*

16 What value for n makes the equation true? *n* + 56 = 83

F 149

G 139

H 33

J 27

Copyright © Houghton Mifflin Company. All rights reserved.

Name _____

The properties of multiplication can help you solve equations.

Commutative Property of Multiplication	
Arithmetic	**Algebra**
$3 \times 2 = 2 \times 3$	$ab = ba$

The order of the factors does not change the product.

Associative Property of Multiplication	
Arithmetic	**Algebra**
$3(2 \times 5) = (3 \times 2) \times 5$	$a(bc) = (ab) \times c$

The grouping of the factors does not change the product.

Property of One for Multiplication	
Arithmetic	**Algebra**
$1 \times 7 = 7$	$1 \times n = n$

Any number multiplied by one equals that number.

Zero Property of Multiplication	
Arithmetic	**Algebra**
$0 \times 5 = 0$	$0 \times n = 0$

Any number multiplied by zero equals zero.

Complete.

1. $7 \times 28 =$ _____ $\times 7$ $(ab) \times c =$ _____ (bc)

2. $5 \times 1 =$ _____ $d \times 1 =$ _____

3. $4 \times$ _____ $= 5 \times 4$ $(5a) \times$ _____ $= 1 \times 5a$

4. $9 \times 0 =$ _____ $ab \times 0 = 0 \times$ _____

5. $3(4 \times 5) = (3 \times$ _____ $) \times 5$ $bdn = n$ _____ b

Complete. Let $n = 6$.

6. $6n =$ _____ $19 + n =$ _____ $n - 2 =$ _____ $5n =$ _____

7. $n \times 0 =$ _____ $52 - n =$ _____ $21n =$ _____ $n(10n) =$ _____

Complete. Let $x = 5$.

8. $x^2 =$ _____ $10x =$ _____

9. $x - (1 - 0) =$ _____ $(9x) - 5 =$ _____

10. $(x^2) - 5 =$ _____ $36 - (x + 7) =$ _____

11. $(15 + x) + 20 =$ _____ $(x + 3) - x =$ _____

12. $(2x) - (x + 3) =$ _____ $100 - (x^2) - 10 =$ _____

| Problem Solving |
| Reasoning |

Write an equation.

13. The Moreles family plans to mail order a scanner for their computer. It costs **$250**. The tax will be **$12.50**. They don't know what the shipping and handling will cost. Write an equation to show the total cost. _____

14. Jamal wants to buy **$70** speakers for his computer. He plans to save **$5** a week for **10** weeks. His father said he would give Jamal **$25**. Write an equation to show how much Jamal will have after **10** weeks. _____

15. Marcia is saving money to buy a computer. She has saved **$120** each month for **10** months. Write an equation to show how much more she needs to buy a **$2,400** computer. _____

16. Jan ran **6** miles each day, Monday through Friday. Write an equation to show how many miles she ran this week. _____

Test Prep ★ Mixed Review

17 In air miles, Los Angeles is 6,296 miles from Rio de Janeiro. What is that number rounded to the nearest 100 miles?

   A 7,000 mi

   B 6,400 mi

   C 6,300 mi

   D 6,000 mi

18 Which symbol makes the statement true?
2,600,000 ? 2 million, 6 hundred thousand

   F +

   G =

   H <

   J >

Name _____

You can use the **Distributive Property** to "break apart" multiplication expressions. Here are two ways to write 2 × 9.

| Multiply. Then add. |

2 × 4   +   2 × 5

(2 × 4) + (2 × 5)
8 + 10
18

There are 18 stars in all.

| Add. Then multiply. |

2 × (4 + 5)

2 × (4 + 5)
2 × 9
18

Distributive Property	
Arithmetic	**Algebra**
6 × (5 + 4) = (6 × 5) + (6 × 4)	a × (b + c) = (a × b) + (a × c)
6(5 + 4) = (6)(5) + (6)(4)	a(b + c) = (ab) + (ac)

Use the distributive property to "break apart" the multiplication expression.

1. 7 × 9 = 7 × (3 + 6) and (7 × 3) + (7 × _____)

2. 8 × 13 = _____ × (10 + 3) and (8 × 10) + (8 × 3)

3. 5 × 14 = 5 × (10 + 4) and (5 × _____) + (5 × 4)

4. 4 × 16 = 4 × (10 + _____) and (4 × 10) + (4 × _____)

5. 2 × 42 = _____ × (40 + 2) and (_____ × 40) + (_____ × 2)

6. 3 × 34 = 3 × (_____ + 4) and (3 × _____) + (_____ × 4)

7. 3 × 21 = 3 × (20 + 1) and (3 × _____) + (3 × 1)

8. 18 × 2 = 2 × (_____ + 8) and (2 × 10) + (2 × _____)

9. 51 × 2 = 2(50 + 1) and (_____ × 50) + (2 × _____)

When you multiply using the short form, you are also using the distributive property.

Expanded form	Short form
$\begin{array}{r} 10 + 5 \\ \times \quad 6 \\ \hline 60 + 30 = 90 \end{array}$	$\begin{array}{r} \overset{3}{1}5 \\ \times \ 6 \\ \hline 90 \end{array}$

Multiply.

10.
$\begin{array}{r} 29 \\ \times\ 9 \\ \hline \end{array}$
$\begin{array}{r} 83 \\ \times\ 4 \\ \hline \end{array}$
$\begin{array}{r} 65 \\ \times\ 5 \\ \hline \end{array}$
$\begin{array}{r} 664 \\ \times\ 7 \\ \hline \end{array}$
$\begin{array}{r} 559 \\ \times\ 3 \\ \hline \end{array}$
$\begin{array}{r} 859 \\ \times\ 4 \\ \hline \end{array}$

11.
$\begin{array}{r} 4{,}126 \\ \times\ 6 \\ \hline \end{array}$
$\begin{array}{r} 4{,}562 \\ \times\ 7 \\ \hline \end{array}$
$\begin{array}{r} 8{,}395 \\ \times\ 2 \\ \hline \end{array}$
$\begin{array}{r} 9{,}517 \\ \times\ 8 \\ \hline \end{array}$
$\begin{array}{r} 3{,}084 \\ \times\ 3 \\ \hline \end{array}$
$\begin{array}{r} 7{,}652 \\ \times\ 5 \\ \hline \end{array}$

Problem Solving
Reasoning
Use the distributive property and mental math to solve.

12. Each car of a train holds **158** people. About how many people can ride on a **6**-car train? _____

 Quick Check

Find the value of the expression when $n = 5$.   **Work Space**

13. $n \times 3$ _____   **14.** $n + n$ _____   **15.** $n \times n$ _____

Solve.

16. $3n = 24$ **17.** $15 = 3 \times p$ **18.** $8 \times y = 4 \times 8$

_____   _____   _____

Multiply. Use the distributive property.

19. 602×3 _____   **20.** $\begin{array}{r} 527 \\ \times\ 8 \\ \hline \end{array}$ **21.** $\begin{array}{r} 432 \\ \times\ 6 \\ \hline \end{array}$

Multiples of 10, 100, and 1,000

These examples show how to multiply by **10**, **100**, or **1,000**.

```
    28
  × 10   ← 1 zero
   280
```

```
    28
  × 100   ← 2 zeros
  2,800
```

```
     28
  × 1,000   ← 3 zeros
   28,000
```

Multiplying **28 × 10** is the same as multiplying **28 × 1** and writing one **0** in the product.

Multiplying **28 × 100** is the same as multiplying **28 × 1** and writing two **0s** in the product.

Multiplying **28 × 1,000** is the same as multiplying **28 × 1** and writing three **0s** in the product.

To multiply a number by **10**, **100**, or **1,000**, write as many zeros in the product as there are in **10**, **100**, or **1,000**.

Multiply.

1.
```
    45        45          45         77         77          77
  × 10     × 100     × 1,000     × 10     × 100     × 1,000
```

2.
```
   823       823         823        961        961         961
  × 10     × 100     × 1,000     × 10     × 100     × 1,000
```

3.
```
      4         7           2         64        275        3193
 × 1,000      × 10     × 100     × 10     × 1,000     × 100
```

Circle the greater product.

4. 36 × 10 or 4 × 100

73 × 10 or 6 × 100

372 × 10 or 41 × 100

5. 804 × 10 or 79 × 100

57 × 100 or 6 × 1,000

26 × 100 or 2 × 1,000

6. 60 × 10 or 5 × 100

800 × 10 or 90 × 100

70 × 100 or 6 × 1,000

7. 47 × 10 or 5 × 100

62 × 100 or 605 × 10

99 × 10 or 10 × 100

8. 702 × 10 or 70 × 100

17 × 1,000 or 105 × 100

76 × 100 or 709 × 10

9. 10 × 1,000 or 100 × 90

906 × 10 or 9 × 1,000

43 × 1,000 or 50 × 100

This pattern shows how to multiply by multiples of 10 and 100.

$$\begin{array}{r} \overset{1\ 2}{258} \\ \times\ 3 \\ \hline 774 \end{array}$$ ↖ Remember to regroup.

$$\begin{array}{r} 258 \\ \times\ 30 \\ \hline 7{,}740 \end{array}$$ ← There is one **0** in the ones place.

$$\begin{array}{r} 258 \\ \times\ 300 \\ \hline 77{,}400 \end{array}$$ ← There are two **0**s.

Multiply.

10.
$$\begin{array}{r} 372 \\ \times\ 4 \end{array}$$
$$\begin{array}{r} 372 \\ \times\ 40 \end{array}$$
$$\begin{array}{r} 703 \\ \times\ 6 \end{array}$$
$$\begin{array}{r} 703 \\ \times\ 60 \end{array}$$
$$\begin{array}{r} 393 \\ \times\ 7 \end{array}$$
$$\begin{array}{r} 393 \\ \times\ 70 \end{array}$$

11.
$$\begin{array}{r} 352 \\ \times\ 50 \end{array}$$
$$\begin{array}{r} 352 \\ \times\ 500 \end{array}$$
$$\begin{array}{r} 720 \\ \times\ 60 \end{array}$$
$$\begin{array}{r} 720 \\ \times\ 600 \end{array}$$
$$\begin{array}{r} 892 \\ \times\ 90 \end{array}$$
$$\begin{array}{r} 892 \\ \times\ 900 \end{array}$$

12.
$$\begin{array}{r} 409 \\ \times\ 70 \end{array}$$
$$\begin{array}{r} 409 \\ \times\ 700 \end{array}$$
$$\begin{array}{r} 390 \\ \times\ 40 \end{array}$$
$$\begin{array}{r} 390 \\ \times\ 400 \end{array}$$
$$\begin{array}{r} 503 \\ \times\ 30 \end{array}$$
$$\begin{array}{r} 503 \\ \times\ 300 \end{array}$$

Multiply.

13. $50 \times 30 = $ _____

$80 \times 700 = $ _____

$800 \times 600 = $ _____

14. $60 \times 70 = $ _____

$90 \times 400 = $ _____

$700 \times 300 = $ _____

15. $80 \times 50 = $ _____

$40 \times 500 = $ _____

$500 \times 600 = $ _____

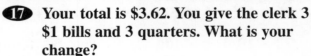

Test Prep ★ Mixed Review

16 What number is the sum closest to?

$$\begin{array}{r} 234{,}629 \\ +\ 492{,}616 \end{array}$$

A 7,000,000

B 700,000

C 70,000

D 7,000

17 Your total is $3.62. You give the clerk 3 $1 bills and 3 quarters. What is your change?

F 3 dimes, 1 nickel, 3 pennies

G 4 nickels

H 1 dime and 3 pennies

J 3 pennies

Multiplying by Two-Digit Numbers

This example shows how to multiply **643** by **35**.

1. Multiply by the ones digit.

```
  2 1
  643
× 35
─────
3215   ← 5 × 643
```

Remember to regroup.

2. Multiply by the tens digit.

```
   1
  643
× 35
─────
3215
19290   ← 30 × 643
  ↑
```

Remember to regroup.

You do not have to write the zero. Start the answer in the tens place.

3. Add the partial products.

```
   643
 × 35
──────
  3215
+ 1929
──────
22,505
```

Multiply.

1.
```
  404        567        390        770        371
× 83       × 42       × 56       × 35       × 50
```

2.
```
  408        573        608        725        937
× 62       × 44       × 55       × 68       × 46
```

3.
```
  685        393        408        380        609
× 24       × 37       × 67       × 54       × 58
```

4.
```
   75         29         47        630        504        480
 × 84       × 36       × 18       × 49       × 35       × 17
```

5.
```
  158        296        342        506        821        142
× 31       × 45       × 62       × 51       × 78       × 46
```

Round each factor to the place indicated. Multiply the rounded numbers to find the estimated product.

Factors	Rounded factors	Estimated product
<u>5</u>6; <u>2</u>3		
<u>3</u>1; <u>3</u>2		
<u>2</u>4; <u>1</u>1		
<u>4</u>2; <u>2</u>2		
<u>4</u>7; <u>8</u>03		

Problem Solving Reasoning

Decide whether you need an exact answer or an estimated answer. Then solve.

6. An egg carton contains **12** eggs. A shipment of eggs contains **310** cartons. How many eggs are in the shipment?

_____

7. A museum is open for **14** hours each day. If an average of **135** people visit the museum per hour, how many people visit the museum each day?

_____

8. A mail carrier estimates she drives **750** miles each month. At that rate, how many miles does she drive in **1** year?

_____

9. Each week, a courier works Monday through Saturday and estimates he drives **225** miles each day. At that rate, how many miles does he drive in **4** weeks?

_____

 Quick Check

Use mental math to multiply.

Work Space

10.   100
    × 97

11.   80
     × 30

12.   200
     × 90

Find the products.

13.   48
     × 57

14.   362
     × 24

15.   89
     × 63

Name _____

Problem Solving Strategy:
Find a Pattern

Sometimes it is helpful to make a table to help you find a pattern.

When you make a table, look for the rule that describes the relationship between the numbers in the pattern.

> **Problem**
>
> Miss Kelly played a game with her class. She asked four students to name a number and then Miss Kelly named another number. When Eva said 2, Miss Kelly said 6. When Joe said 5, Miss Kelly said 15. When Lou said 7, Miss Kelly said 21. When Ryan said 10, what did Miss Kelly say?

1 Understand   As you reread, ask yourself questions.

- Are Miss Kelly's numbers greater than or less than the students' numbers?

_____

2 Decide   Choose a method for solving.

- Try the strategy Find a Pattern.

Students	2	5	7	10
Miss Kelly	6	15	21	

3 Solve   Analyze the numbers in the table.

- Does the pattern appear to be an addition pattern or a multiplication pattern? How can you tell?

_____

- What did Miss Kelly multiply each student's number by?

_____

- What will Miss Kelly's answer be for 10? _____

4 Look back   Check your answer. Write your answer below.

    Answer: _____

left margin
Copyright © Houghton Mifflin Company. All rights reserved.

Unit 2 Lesson 6   **37**

Use the **Find a Pattern** strategy or any other strategy you have learned.

1. If Robert saves **$1** on Sunday, **$2** on Monday, and **$4** on Tuesday, and if the pattern continues, how much will he save on Saturday?

_____

_____

2. Mary bought **2** muffins for **$3**, Jenna bought **4** muffins for **$6**, and Maurice bought **6** muffins for **$9**. How much does a dozen muffins cost?

_____

_____

3. Ray played a number-guessing game with Jay. When Jay said **9**, Ray said **18**. When Jay said **3**, Ray said **12**. When Jay said **1**, Ray said **10**. What was Ray's rule?

_____

4. To make **6** servings of rice, you use **2** cups of water. For **12** servings, you use **4** cups of water. How many cups of water would you need for **24** servings?

_____

5. Emily is **11** years old and her brother is **22**. How old will Emily be when her brother is **44**?

_____

6. A grandfather clock chimes on the hour and then every **15** minutes. How many times does the clock chime in **24** hours?

_____

7. There are **5** children in a family. The oldest gets an allowance of **$20** per week. Each younger child gets **$3** less than the next older brother or sister. How much allowance does the youngest child get?

_____

8. Bath towels are on sale at **2** for **$15**, hand towels are **2** for **$9**, and wash cloths are **2** for **$5**. What is the total cost if you buy **6** of each type of towel?

_____

9. Write a rule for a number pattern. Then fill in the table showing how your pattern works.

Rule _____

First Number						
Second Number						

_____

Name _____

This example shows how to find **187 × 298.**

Estimate first.   **200 × 300 = 60,000**

1. Multiply by the ones digit

```
   298
 × 187
  2086
```

Remember to regroup!

2. Multiply by the tens digit

```
   298
 × 187
  2086
  2384
```

3. Multiply by the hundreds digit

```
   298
 × 187
  2086
  2384
   298
```

4. Add the partial products.

```
   298
 × 187
  2086
  2384
 + 298
 55,726
```

Multiply.

1.

643	142	698	594	328
× 176	× 723	× 293	× 685	× 286

_____ _____ _____ _____ _____

_____ _____ _____ _____ _____

_____ _____ _____ _____ _____

2.

754	976	188	576	739
× 215	× 234	× 368	× 265	× 426

3.

283	543	638	527	293
× 276	× 911	× 419	× 372	× 872

4.

527	831	391	615	302
× 468	× 662	× 125	× 281	× 469

Multiply.

5.
318	651	342	819	489
× 244	× 298	× 723	× 126	× 321

6.
629	721	915	853	276
× 138	× 385	× 211	× 491	× 186

7.
836	125	439	385	721
× 358	× 581	× 682	× 224	× 216

Problem Solving
Reasoning

Solve.

8. A supermarket is open every day of the year. An average of **420** people shops in the supermarket per day. In one year, how many shoppers can the supermarket expect to serve? (Hint: **1** year = **365** days)

_____

9. A non-leap year is **365** days long. A leap year is **366** days long. In a leap year, how many shoppers can the supermarket in exercise 8 expect to serve?

_____

Test Prep ★ Mixed Review

10 Which value of *n* makes the equation true? $75 \times 77 = 75 \times (n + 7)$

A 77

B 75

C 70

D 7

11 Seventy-seven students paid 75¢ for a ticket to a school play. About how much money did they pay for tickets?

F More than $77

G Between $70 and $77

H Between $60 and $70

J Between $50 and $60

Name _____

Sometimes factors contain one or more zeros.

```
     643      Write zero in the
   × 201      partial product to
     643  ↖   show 0 tens. Then
   12860  ←   multiply by hundreds.
  129,243
```

```
     376      Write zero in the
   × 240  ←   partial product to
   15040  ←   show 0 ones. Then
  +  752       multiply by tens.
   90,240
```

Multiply.

1.
```
    729        694        428        376        865
  × 603      × 630      × 702      × 240      × 409
```

2.
```
    421        615        726        843        908
  × 402      × 109      × 305      × 206      × 406
```

3.
```
    662        753        835        444        633
  × 470      × 360      × 290      × 130      × 520
```

4.
```
    842        953        657        570        398
  × 460      × 320      × 590      × 260      × 180
```

5.
```
  3,007      5,600      9,080      4,770      1,919
  × 717      × 906      × 652      × 530      × 381
```

Multiply.

6.
| 385 | 430 | 842 | 609 | 826 |
| × 728 | × 637 | × 160 | × 850 | × 529 |

7.
| 703 | 381 | 834 | 809 | 394 |
| × 806 | × 316 | × 503 | × 845 | × 671 |

Problem Solving
Reasoning
Solve.

8. A book is **320** pages long and has an average of **483** words per page. At that rate, how many words would you expect the book to have?

_____

9. An outdoor theater has **160** rows of seats. Each row has **130** seats. If a person is sitting in each seat, how many people are seated in the theater?

_____

 Quick Check

Multiply.   Work Space

10.   615   **11.** $3.82   **12.** $3.99
         × 114   × 264   × 125

Find the product.

13.   516   **14.**   308   **15.**   860
         × 901   × 604   × 904

Problem Solving Application: Is the Answer Reasonable?

After you solve a problem, check whether the answer makes sense. Is the answer too great? Is the answer too small? Or is it just about right?

In this lesson, use estimation when you can to check whether your answer is reasonable.

Tips to Remember

1. Understand	2. Decide	3. Solve	4. Look back

- Ask yourself questions about the numbers in each statement. Should the answer be an exact answer or an estimate?

- Think about strategies you have learned and use them to help you solve the problem.

- Think about the answer. Is it reasonable?

Solve. Check that your answer is reasonable.

1. A school cafeteria has **15** tables. Each table can seat **12** students. How many students can eat in the cafeteria at one time?

Think: Should you add or multiply? How can you use rounding to estimate?

_____

_____

Answer_____

_____

2. The school is having a book fair. The first book you buy costs **$6** and each additional book is half of this price. What is the cost of **3** books?

Think: How much does each additional book cost?

_____

Answer_____

Solve. Check that your answer is reasonable.

3. There are **375** seats in the school's auditorium. The school play was sold out for each of the **3** performances. How many people saw the play?

_____

4. The students rehearsed **2** hours after school every day for **3** weeks. What was the total number of hours the students rehearsed?

_____

5. The **9** students in the play bought flowers for the play's director. If each student's share was **$4.50**, was the cost of the flowers closer to **$36** or **$40**?

_____

6. The proceeds from a cake and cookie sale at the play were **$33**. Nine cakes sold for **$3** each and cookies sold for **$.50** each. Were there **6** cookies or **12** cookies sold?

_____

7. Tickets for the school play cost **$8** each for adults and **$3** each for students. What was the cost of **2** adult tickets and **1** student ticket?

_____

8. For one performance, **212** adult tickets and **163** student tickets were sold. Was the total amount of money taken in that night closer to **$2,000** or **$3,000**?

_____

Extend Your Thinking

9. There were **225** adult tickets sold for the play one night. What was the total amount of money taken in from ticket sales that night? (Use the information in problem **7** to solve.)

_____

10. Explain your method for solving problem 6. Did you use more than one operation?

_____

_____

_____

**Write an algebraic expression for each word expression.
Let _n_ represent each variable.**

1. 12 multiplied by a number _____

2. the product of a number and 35 _____

Complete each equation.

3. $4 \times 9 =$ _____ $\times 4$ **4.** $(0) x =$ _____   **5.** $2 (6 \times 3) = 2 \times ($_____$)$

6. $1d =$ _____   **7.** $r (st) = (rs)$ _____   **8.** $abc = c$ _____

Solve each equation for _n_ = 3.

9. $n^3 =$ _____   **10.** $6n =$ _____   **11.** $(8n) - 4 =$ _____

**Use the distributive property to break apart each
multiplication.**

12. $5 \times 13 = 5 \times (6 +$ _____$) = (5 \times$ _____$) + ($_____ $\times 7)$

13. $24 \times 3 =$ _____ $\times (20 + 4) = (3 \times$ _____$) + ($_____ $\times 4)$

Multiply.

14. $\begin{array}{r} 34 \\ \times\ 4 \\ \hline \end{array}$ **15.** $\begin{array}{r} 807 \\ \times\ 5 \\ \hline \end{array}$ **16.** $\begin{array}{r} 1{,}044 \\ \times\ 3 \\ \hline \end{array}$ **17.** $\begin{array}{r} 525 \\ \times\ 100 \\ \hline \end{array}$ **18.** $\begin{array}{r} 78 \\ \times\ 10 \\ \hline \end{array}$

19. $\begin{array}{r} 372 \\ \times\ 40 \\ \hline \end{array}$ **20.** $\begin{array}{r} 782 \\ \times\ 45 \\ \hline \end{array}$ **21.** $\begin{array}{r} 470 \\ \times\ 944 \\ \hline \end{array}$ **22.** $\begin{array}{r} 2{,}066 \\ \times\ 649 \\ \hline \end{array}$ **23.** $\begin{array}{r} 1{,}000 \\ \times\ 360 \\ \hline \end{array}$

Solve.

24. Before multiplying **1,999 × 19**, Jim estimated the product
to be **400,000**. Is **400,000** a reasonable estimate? Explain.

_____

25. What amount comes next in this pattern? _____

    $.50 $1.05 $2.15 $4.35 $8.75   _____

Name _____

1 What is another way to express 10^9?

A 1 followed by 6 zeros

B 10 followed by 6 zeros

C 100 followed by 6 zeros

D 1,000 followed by 6 zeros

2 Which number is the product for $n \times 57 = (n \times 50) + (3 \times 7)$?

F 570   H 150

G 171   J 21

3 The product p of each of these three equations will be the same if the places of two circled numbers are switched.

$$12 \times 2 = p$$
$$18 \times 3 = p$$
$$4 \times 9 = p$$

The places of which two numbers should be switched?

A 18 and 4   C 3 and 2

B 9 and 12   D 4 and 12

4 Which value for x makes this equation true? $x + 2,453 = 3,542$

F 5,995   H 1,089

G 1,111   J 144

5 Shaina wants to buy a hat that costs $7.59. If she buys a hat for herself and one hat for each of her two sisters, how much money will she spend?

A $7.59   C $27.59   E Not here

B $22.77   D $30.36

6 This table shows the prices of a 19-inch color television in three different years.

Television Prices

1964	$179.95
1972	$220.00
1987	$209.99

How much more did a 19-inch color television cost in 1972 than in 1987?

F $70.95   H $29.00   K Not here

G $29.05   J $21.00

7 Which number sentence shows the cost of two televisions in 1987?

A $2 \times \$179.95 = \$359.90$

B $2 \times \$209.99 = \$419.98$

C $\$440.00 + 2 = \$442.00$

D $\$359.90 - 2 = \$357.90$

8 Which number shows how many pencils are in 100 boxes?

PENCILS
144 COUNT

F 14,400,000   H 144,000   K 1,440

G 1,440,000   J 14,400

9 Louis walks three miles each day. How many miles does he walk in one year (365 days)?

A 3,650 miles   C 90 miles   E 21 miles

B 1,095 miles   D 30 miles

UNIT 3 • TABLE OF CONTENTS

Division of Whole Numbers

Dear Family,

During the next few weeks, our math class will be learning and practicing the division of whole numbers.

You can expect to see homework that provides practice with dividing and checking whole numbers. Here is a sample you may want to keep handy to give help if needed.

We will be using this vocabulary:

divisor the number by which a number is divided

dividend the number that is divided

quotient the number of groups or the number in each group

remainder the number left over after you find the quotient

Checking Division

To divide **407** by **23**, first think about how many digits will be in the quotient.

$$23\overline{)407}$$

Think about hundreds.
23 > 4
The quotient will not have hundreds.

There will be two digits in the quotient. The first digit will be in the tens.

```
        17 R16
23)407
      - 23
       177
     - 161
        16
```

To check if the answer is correct, multiply the divisor **(23)** by the quotient **(17)**. Then add the remainder **(16)**. The result should be the same as the dividend **(407)**.

```
        17
      × 23
        51
       340
       391
     +  16
       407
```

During this unit, students will need to continue practicing addition, subtraction, multiplication, and division facts.

Sincerely,

Name _____

You know that you can use opposite or **inverse** operations to solve an equation.

To solve a division equation, use multiplication.

$$n \div 4 = 8$$

Think: $n = 8 \times 4$

$$n = 32$$

Multiplication is the inverse of division.

Think: 8 times **4** is what number?

To solve a multiplication equation, use division.

$$y \times 3 = 15$$

Think: $y = 15 \div 3$

$$y = 5$$

Division is the inverse of multiplication.

Think: 15 divided by **3** is what number?

Complete.

1. $n \div 5 = 9$ $y \div 6 = 7$ $a \div 5 = 6$

Think: $n = 9 \times$ _____   **Think:** $y =$ _____ $\times 6$ **Think:** $a = 6 \times 5$

$\qquad n = 45$ $\qquad y = 42$ $\qquad a =$ _____

2. $b \times 4 = 12$ $7 \times n = 21$ $9 \times y = 27$

Think: $b = 12 \div 4$ **Think:** $n = 21 \div$ _____   **Think:** $y = 27$ _____ 9

$\qquad b =$ _____ $\qquad n = 3$ $\qquad y = 3$

3. $n \div 9 = 7$ $8 \times a = 40$ $h \times 4 = 28$

Think: $n = 7 \times$ _____   **Think:** $a = 40 \div$ _____   **Think:** $h =$ _____ $\div 4$

$\qquad n =$ _____ $\qquad a =$ _____ $\qquad h =$ _____

4. $a \div 5 = 7$ $n \times 4 = 24$ $y \div 8 = 2$

Think: $a = 7$ _____ 5 **Think:** $n = 24$ _____ 4 **Think:** $y =$ ____ $\times$ ____

$\qquad a =$ _____ $\qquad n =$ _____ $\qquad y =$ _____

Find the value of _y_.

5. $y \div 6 = 2$ $y \times 4 = 20$ $y \div 8 = 7$ $4 \times y = 36$

6. $y \times 4 = 16$ $y \div 9 = 2$ $3 \times y = 18$ $y \div 6 = 9$

Find the value of *h*.

7. $h \times 4 = 40$ $h \div 7 = 2$ $5 \times h = 25$ $h \div 7 = 7$

8. $h \div 9 = 9$ $h \times 5 = 10$ $h \div 8 = 10$ $3 \times h = 9$

9. $h \times 4 = 8$ $h \div 3 = 9$ $h \div 9 = 10$ $3 \times h = 6$

Problem Solving
Reasoning

Circle the equation that represents the problem. Then find the value of *t*.

10. Members of a hiking club hiked **54** miles in **6** days. They hiked the same number of miles each day. How many miles did they hike each day?

$t \div 6 = 54$

$t \times 6 = 54$

$t = $ _____

11. Three hikers sleep in each of **6** tents. How many hikers are there?

$h \div 3 = 6$

$h \times 3 = 6$

$h = $ _____

Write a problem that could be represented by the equation $n \div 7 = 3$. Then find the value of *n*.

12. _____

_____

_____

Test Prep ★ Mixed Review

13 What number sentence is in the same family of facts as $6 \times 4 = \square$?

   A $6 + 4 = \square$

   B $\square \times 4 = 6$

   C $\square = 6 \div 4$

   D $\square \div 4 = 6$

14 A pad and pencil costs $7.83. You give the clerk a $10 bill and 3 pennies. What change do you get?

   F 3 $1 bills

   G 2 dimes, 2 $1 bills

   H 2 pennies, 1 nickel, 1 dime, 2 $1 bills

   J 2 pennies, 2 dimes, 2 $1 bills

Order of Operations

To evaluate an expression that has more than one operation, follow the rules for the order of operations.

Evaluate $72 \div x^2 + (4 - 2)$ for $x = 3$.

1. Perform all operations inside parentheses first.

2. Evaluate exponents.

3. Multiply and divide from left to right.

4. Add and subtract from left to right.

$$72 \div x^2 \quad + \quad (4 - 2)$$
$$\downarrow$$
$$72 \div x^2 \quad + \quad 2$$
$$\downarrow$$
$$72 \div 9 \quad + \quad 2$$
$$\downarrow$$
$$8 \quad + \quad 2$$
$$\downarrow$$
$$10$$

Remember: When you **evaluate an expression**, you substitute the value of the variable in the expression.

Write the operation you would perform first to evaluate each expression for $n = 3$.

1. $3 + 9 \times n$ _____

$18 - n^2 \div 3$ _____

$8 \times (9 - n)$ _____

2. $n - 2 \div 2$ _____

$36 \div (n + 1)$ _____

$8 - n \times 2^2$ _____

Complete to evaluate each expression for $a = 2$.

3. $10 - 4 \div a$
$$\downarrow$$
$10 -$ _____
$$\downarrow$$
_____

$6 + 4 \times a$
$$\downarrow$$
$6 +$ _____
$$\downarrow$$
_____

$13 - 6 + a$
$$\downarrow$$
_____ $+ a$
$$\downarrow$$
_____

4. $6 \times (10 - a) \div 8$
$$\downarrow$$
$6 \times$ _____ $\div 8$
$$\downarrow$$
_____ $\div 8$
$$\downarrow$$
_____

$a + 3^2 - 7$
$$\downarrow$$
$a +$ _____ $- 7$
$$\downarrow$$
_____ $- 7$
$$\downarrow$$
_____

$a^3 + (7 - 1) \div a$
$$\swarrow \qquad \downarrow$$
_____ $+$ _____ $\div a$
$$\downarrow \qquad \swarrow$$
_____ $+$ _____
$$\downarrow$$
_____

You can use the division rules for **0** and **1** when you evaluate expressions.

- When you divide a number by **1**, $9 \div 1 = 9$ the quotient is that number.
- When you divide any number except **0** by itself, $12 \div 12 = 1$ the quotient is **1**.
- When you divide **0** by any number except **0**, $0 \div 4 = 0$ the quotient is **0**.
  But remember, you cannot divide a number by **0**.

Evaluate each expression. Replace the variable with the given value.

5. $3^2 \div (3 + a)$ for $a = 6$ _____ $(s - 3^2) \div 6$ for $s = 9$ _____

6. $15 \div s + 2$ for $s = 3$ _____ $x - (3 \times 3)$ for $x = 18$ _____

7. $4 - 2 \times 6 \div s$ for $s = 3$ _____ $a \times (3 + 2)^2$ for $a = 1$ _____

8. $5 \times 2 - (2 + x)$ for $x = 3$ _____ $(n \div 2)^2 - 7$ for $n = 8$ _____

9. $n \div 4 + 9 \times 2$ for $n = 0$ _____ $(2 + s - 1) \times 2 \div 8$ for $s = 3$ _____

10. $11 \div (9 - y)$ for $y = 8$ _____ $0 \div y^2$ for $y = 5$ _____

Problem Solving
Reasoning

Write an expression that represents the problem. Use x for the variable. Evaluate the expression for $x = \$25$.

11. Jamie donated her award money to her 5 favorite charities. She gave the same amount to each charity. How much did she give to each charity?

_____

12. Sean put $10 of his award money in a savings account. He gave the rest to 3 charities. He gave the same amount to each charity. How much money did he give to each charity?

_____

Test Prep ★ Mixed Review

13 Which numbers complete the pattern?

Pattern: 20, 19, 17, 14, ___, ____

A 18, 23

B 113, 12

C 10, 5

D 10, 1

14 It is 154 miles to the beach and 196 miles to the mountains. What is the best estimate of how much farther it is to travel to the mountains?

F 50 miles

G 100 miles

H 300 miles

J 350 miles

Name _____

Follow these steps to divide by a one-digit number.

1. Look at the dividend and the divisor. Decide if you can divide.

$$\frac{1}{6)\overline{85}}$$

Think: 6)8
Try **1** in the quotient.

2. Multiply. Then compare the product to the dividend number.

$$\begin{array}{r} 1 \\ 6)\overline{85} \\ -\,6 \end{array}$$

1 × 6 = 6
6 < 8 If the product is greater than the dividend digit, try a lesser digit in the quotient.

3. Subtract. Then compare the difference to the divisor.

$$\begin{array}{r} 1 \\ 6)\overline{85} \\ -\,6 \\ \hline 2 \end{array}$$

Since **2 < 6** you cannot divide until you bring down another digit.

4. Bring down the next digit in the dividend. Subtract. Repeat these steps until there are no numbers left to bring down.

quotient

$$\begin{array}{r} 14 \text{ R1} \\ 6)\overline{85} \\ -\,6 \\ \hline 25 \\ -\,24 \\ \hline 1 \end{array}$$

divisor →   ← remainder
    ← dividend
    ← remainder

- To check the answer:

- Multiply the quotient by the divisor. Then add the remainder.

- The result should be the same as the dividend.

$$\begin{array}{r} 14 \\ \times\,6 \\ \hline 84 \\ +\,1 \\ \hline 85 \end{array}$$

← quotient
← divisor

← remainder

The dividend is **85**.
So the answer is correct.

Divide.

1. 6)59   3)98   4)85   8)70   6)87

2. 5)93   7)43   6)75   3)45   2)51

Divide. Use multiplication to check.

3. $3\overline{)126}$ $6\overline{)504}$ $5\overline{)408}$ $5\overline{)762}$

4. $6\overline{)416}$ $3\overline{)498}$ $7\overline{)628}$ $6\overline{)958}$

Problem Solving Reasoning   Solve. If there is a remainder, explain how you got your answer.

5. One hundred seventy people are going on a bus tour. They will fill **5** buses. How many people will be on each bus?

_____

_____

_____

6. To reach the mountain top, sightseers can ride in cable cars. Each cable car seats **8** people. One hundred people want to reach the mountain top. How many cable cars will they need?

_____

_____

 Quick Check

Find the value of the variable in the equation.

Work Space

7. $5 = s \div 5$ **8.** $x \div 3 = 9$ **9.** $t \times 6 = 54$

_____   _____   _____

Use the order of operations to find the value of the expression.

10. $(7 + 7^2) \div 7$ _____

11. $2 + 11 - (13 - 4)$ _____

12. $5^2 - 7 \times 3$ _____

Divide.

13. $9\overline{)369}$ **14.** $6\overline{)381}$ **15.** $7\overline{)203}$

Name _____

Dividing Money

Here are some examples of dividing money. Remember to place the cent sign, dollar sign, and decimal point in the quotient as necessary.

$$\begin{array}{r} 43\cent \\ 2\overline{)86\cent} \\ -8 \\ \hline 6 \\ -6 \\ \hline 0 \end{array}$$

Divide as you would with whole numbers.

$$\begin{array}{r} \$25 \\ 5\overline{)\$125} \\ -10 \\ \hline 25 \\ -25 \\ \hline 0 \end{array}$$

$$\begin{array}{r} \$.14 \\ 7\overline{)\$.98} \\ -7 \\ \hline 28 \\ -28 \\ \hline 0 \end{array}$$

Write the decimal point in the quotient above the decimal point in the dividend.

$$\begin{array}{r} \$2.45 \\ 3\overline{)\$7.35} \\ -6 \\ \hline 13 \\ -12 \\ \hline 15 \\ -15 \\ \hline 0 \end{array}$$

Divide.

1. $8\overline{)96\cent}$ $4\overline{)\$60}$ $3\overline{)72\cent}$ $4\overline{)\$88}$

2. $4\overline{)\$.96}$ $2\overline{)\$58}$ $2\overline{)\$.76}$ $3\overline{)\$75}$

3. $4\overline{)\$5.64}$ $3\overline{)\$8.10}$ $4\overline{)\$5.00}$ $2\overline{)\$7.06}$

4. $6\overline{)\$4.74}$ $7\overline{)\$5.53}$ $5\overline{)\$2.90}$ $8\overline{)\$7.76}$

Divide.

5. $4\overline{)\$7.64}$ $8\overline{)\$496}$ $3\overline{)\$813}$ $9\overline{)\$6.66}$

6. $9\overline{)\$8.64}$ $7\overline{)\$595}$ $2\overline{)\$918}$ $4\overline{)\$9.00}$

7. $4\overline{)76¢}$ $6\overline{)\$9.96}$ $2\overline{)\$.74}$ $5\overline{)\$110}$

**Problem Solving
Reasoning**

Solve. Explain your answer.

8. A basket of chicken wings costs **$9.99**. If **4** people share **1** basket, what is the cost per person?

_____

_____

_____

9. An order of vegetables costs **$8.50**. If six people share the order, what is the cost per person?

_____

_____

_____

Test Prep ★ Mixed Review

10 Which pair of numbers when rounded will give a sum of about 100 and a product of about 2,100?

A 45 and 42

B 56 and 41

C 65 and 32

D 75 and 29

11 There are 48 cartons on a shelf. Each carton contains 64 books. What is a good estimate of how many books there are?

F 10

G 100

H 2,400

J 3,000

Sometimes when you divide, you must write a zero in the quotient.

Divide **2,013** by **4**.

1. Divide hundreds.   **2.** Divide tens.   **3.** Bring down the next digit. Divide ones.   **4.** Multiply to check.

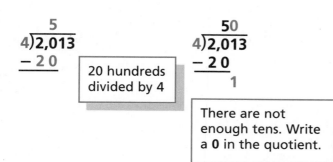

```
      5
  4)2,013
  − 2 0
```
20 hundreds divided by 4

```
     50
  4)2,013
  − 2 0
      1
```
There are not enough tens. Write a **0** in the quotient.

```
    503 R1
  4)2,013
  − 2 0
     13
   − 12
      1
```

```
    503   ← quotient
  ×   4
  2,012
  +   1   ← remainder
  2,013   ← dividend
```

It checks. The answer, **503 R1**, is correct.

Divide. Use multiplication to check.

1. 4)836   5)$5.20   3)962

2. 2)$6.10   7)743   8)645

3. 6)542   4)428   8)$8.72

4. 5)1,520   6)1,255   8)4,856

Divide. Use multiplication to check.

5. $3\overline{)1{,}521}$ $4\overline{)1{,}234}$ $2\overline{)\$14.18}$

6. $6\overline{)2{,}448}$ $9\overline{)\$27.54}$ $7\overline{)3{,}539}$

Problem Solving
Reasoning

Solve.

7. There are **3,654** people seated in **6** sections of a stadium. An equal number is in each section. How many people are in each section?

_____

8. Three season passes to football games cost **$306**. How much does **1** season pass cost?

_____

9. Each team van can seat **6** people. How many vans are needed for **125** people? Explain what you did with the remainder.

_____

_____

Test Prep ★ Mixed Review

10 What is the value of the expression $4 \times (15 - 2) \div 13$?

A 30

B 26

C 17

D 4

11 A Thanksgiving turkey weighs 18 pounds. If 1 pound = 16 ounces, what is the weight of the turkey in ounces?

F 288

G 34

H 22

J 2

Name _____

This **line plot** shows the number of pennies **8** students have in their pockets. What is the average number of pennies the students have?

To find the **average** or **mean** of a set of numbers:

1. Add the numbers.

2. Divide the sum by the number of addends.

0 + 0 + 1 + 4 + 4 + 6 + 7 + 10 = 32

8 addends   sum

32 ÷ 8 = 4

The average number of pennies is **4.**

Find the average of each group of numbers.

1. 3, 6, 9 _____   0, 2, 4 _____   1, 5, 9 _____

2. 7, 11, 30 _____ $11, $13 _____   100, 200 _____

3. 42, 76, 83 _____   1, 2, 3, 4, 5 _____   5, 12, 15, 8 _____

4. 6, 8, 19, 15 _____   59¢, 42¢, 58¢ _____   19, 42, 31, 8 _____

5. 183, 157, 170 _____   562, 571, 538, 573 _____

6. 110, 108, 98, 60, 139 _____   80, 59, 43, 46 _____

7. 79, 95, 80, 66, 77, 77 _____   72, 65, 36, 57, 87, 97, 57, 65 _____

8. 86, 95, 59, 74, 58, 83, 70 _____   125, 240, 360, 255, 190 _____

9. 65, 37, 45, 18, 21, 44 _____   100, 112, 114, 118, 106 _____

10. Susan's test scores in mathematics for the past eight weeks are: **80, 85, 90, 75, 75, 100, 85,** and **90.**

What is Susan's average test score? _____

11. During the four periods of a basketball game, the Jets scored **24, 17, 29,** and **26** points. What is the average number of points the Jets scored in a period?

_____

12. Ben's bowling scores for the past seven weeks are: **150, 124, 115, 160, 130, 140, 140.** What is Ben's average bowling score?

_____

13. The average temperature during one week in January was **17°F.** Write **7** different temperatures that could have an average of **17°F.**

_____

 Quick Check

Divide.

Work Space

14. 2)$4.70   **15.** 7)$1.40   **16.** 3)$0.18

17. 5)815   **18.** 6)6,581   **19.** 7)915

Find the average.

20. 26, 35, 60, 31, 26, 50 _____

21. $8, $0, $6, $14, $7, $10, $4 _____

22. 236, 473, 286, 505 _____

Name _____

Sometimes a problem may give you more facts than you need. You have to decide which facts you need to answer the question.

Other times you may not have enough facts.

In this lesson you will identify the extra information or name the fact or facts that you need to solve a problem.

Tips to Remember

1. Understand	2. Decide	3. Solve	4. Look back

- Write down the facts in the problem. Decide if there are extra facts. Is any information missing?

- Read each problem more than once. Circle the important words and numbers. Cross out the words and numbers that you don't need.

- Think about each fact in the problem. Ask yourself: Is this an extra fact? Or do I need it to find a solution?

Cross out the extra information. Then solve the problem. If information is missing, name the fact or facts needed on the answer lines.

1. The fifth grade at the Lakewood School is taking a field trip to the zoo. If there are **135** people going on the trip, how many buses are needed?

Think: What two pieces of information do you need to answer the question?

_____

_____

Answer

_____

2. Judy's father bought a living room rug. How much did the rug cost if he paid **$31.50** a month for **24** months?

Think: What two pieces of information do you need to find the total cost of the rug?

_____

_____

Answer

_____

**Cross out the extra information. Then solve the problem.
If information is missing, name the fact or facts that you need.**

3. There are **28** seats in each row of a section of a baseball stadium. There are **336** seats in a section. How many seats are there in the stadium?

_____

_____

4. Carla earns **$84** each day that she works. Last week she worked on Monday, Tuesday, and Friday for **4** hours each day. How much did she earn last week?

_____

5. Mr. Howard cut **15** pieces of silk from a large roll of **1,000** yards. How much was left?

_____

_____

6. Last week, Tom, David, and Jackie earned **$316.98**, **$271.02**, and **$183.45** respectively. How much did Tom and David earn together?

_____

7. Mrs. Balch's class had **1** package of red paper and **2** packages of green paper. How many sheets of red paper were used if there were **45** sheets left in a pack of **500** sheets?

_____

_____

_____

8. The Wallaces bought **3** sandwiches, a salad, and **3** drinks to take to the beach. Each sandwich cost **$2.95** and each drink was **$.85**. How much did they spend on food for the beach?

_____

_____

_____

Extend Your Thinking

9. How can you find the number of square yards in the area of the rug in problem **2**? Find the area of the rug

_____

_____

_____

10. Look back at problem **8**. Explain the method you used to solve the problem.

_____

_____

_____

Divisibility

A number is **divisible** by another number when the quotient is a whole number and the remainder is zero.

Here are ways to test if a number is divisible by another number.

> If a number is divisible by **2**, it is even. If it is not divisible by **2**, the number is odd.

564
4 is divisible by **2**, so
564 is divisible by **2**.

465
5 is not divisible by **2**, so
465 is not divisible by **2**.

> A number is divisible by **3** if the sum of the digits is divisible by **3**.

243
2 + 4 + 3 = 9
9 is divisible by **3**, so
243 is divisible by **3**.

> A number is divisible by **9** if the sum of the digits is divisible by **9**.

891
8 + 9 + 1 = **18**
18 is divisible by **9**, so
891 is divisible by **9**.

> A number is divisible by **4** if the last two digits are divisible by **4**.

132
32 is divisible by **4**, so
132 is divisible by **4**.

218
18 is not divisible by **4**, so
218 is not divisible by **4**.

Place a ✔ by each number that is divisible by 2.

1. 23   54   90   233   127   1,124

2. 12   97   45   234   721   4,112

Put a ✔ in the box to show that the number is divisible by 2, 4, 3, or 9.

		2	4	3	9
3.	164				
4.	45				
5.	503				

		2	4	3	9
6.	71				
7.	252				
8.	116				

A number is divisible by **5** if the digit in the ones' place is **0** or **5**.

365 is divisible by **5**.
563 is not divisible by **5**.

A number is divisible by **10** if the digit in the ones' place is **0**.

470 is divisible by **10**.
407 is not divisible by **10**.

Place a ✔ in the box to show that the number is divisible by 2, 3, 4, 5, 9, or 10.

		2	3	4	5	9	10
9.	108						
10.	130						
11.	246						
12.	333						
13.	782						
14.	880						

Problem Solving Reasoning | Solve.

15. One hundred thirty students will attend a school party. Can they all be seated at tables of **5**? Can they all be seated at tables of **10**? Explain your answers.

_____

_____

16. Can **130** students all be seated at tables of **6**? Explain your answer.

_____

_____

Test Prep ★ Mixed Review

17 In which number does the 6 have the greatest value?

A 99,246,072

B 840,506

C 640,508

D 57,600

18 Maria is 3 years older than her sister. If her sister is s years old, then which expression tells how old Maria is?

F $s + 3$

G $s - 3$

H $s \times 3$

J $s \div 3$

Every counting number (**1, 2, 3, . . .**) has at least one pair of **factors**. A factor of a number is also a **divisor** of that number.

$24 = 3 \times 8$ $24 = 8 \times 3$

3 and **8** are *factors* of **24**.

3 and **8** are *divisors* of **24**.

Write each number as a product of a pair or pairs of factors.

	1	2	3	4	5	6	7
1.							

	8	9	10	11	12	13	14
2.							

	15	16	17	18	19	20	21
3.							

Notice that some of the numbers above have only **2** factors.

- If a counting number has only two factors (itself and **1**), then it is called a **prime number**.

- The numbers above that are prime numbers are: **2, 3, 5, 7, 11, 13, 17**, and **19**.

- The number **1** has only one factor. It is therefore neither prime nor composite.

Notice that the other numbers above have more than **2** factors.

- If a counting number has more than two factors, then it is called a **composite number**.

- The numbers above that are composite numbers are: **4, 6, 8, 9, 10, 12, 14, 15, 16, 18, 20**, and **21**.

Complete by writing the products with as many different pairs of factors as you can. Circle the prime numbers.

	23	25	27	29	31	33	35
4.							

Write *P* for prime or *C* for composite. If the number is composite, then write it as a product of a pair of factors other than itself and 1.

5. 32 _____   17 _____

6. 31 _____   57 _____

7. 97 _____   42 _____

8. 99 _____   29 _____

9. 63 _____   51 _____

Write *E* for even numbers, *O* for odd numbers. Then write *P* for prime or *C* for composite.

10. 14 ___ ___   15 ___ ___   16 ___ ___

11. 18 ___ ___   20 ___ ___   21 ___ ___

12. 22 ___ ___   23 ___ ___   34 ___ ___

13. 40 ___ ___   42 ___ ___   45 ___ ___

14. 1 ___ ___   57 ___ ___   62 ___ ___

15. 64 ___ ___   72 ___ ___   75 ___ ___

Problem Solving Reasoning

Write *True* or *False*. Then explain your answer.

16. All prime numbers are odd. _____

17. All composite numbers are even. _____

Solve.

18. Predict which of the numbers to the right will have the *greatest* number of pairs of factors. Which will have the *least*? Then test your prediction by finding the pairs of factors for each number.

32 33 34

35 36 37

_____

Test Prep ★ Mixed Review

19 A can of cat food costs 33¢ + 1¢ tax. Which expression shows how much 16 cans will cost?

    A 16 × 33¢ + 1¢

    B $16 × 33 + $1

    C $16 × 33 + $16 × 1

    D 16 × (33¢ + 1¢)

20 Edda is 3 times older than her nephew. If Edda is *d* years old, then which expression tells how old her nephew is?

    F *d* ÷ 3

    G *d* − 3

    H *d* × 3

    J *d* + 3

66 Unit 3 Lesson 9

Prime Factorization

When you write a composite number as the product of prime factors, it is called **prime factorization.**

You can make a **factor tree** to find the prime factorization of a composite number.

Follow these steps to make a factor tree for **36**.

1. Write a pair of factors for **36**.	**2.** Write each factor as a pair of factors until all the factors are prime numbers.	**3.** Use exponents, when you can, to write the prime factorization.
36 6 × 6	36 6 × 6 2 × 3 × 2 × 3	$36 = 2 \times 2 \times 3 \times 3$ $36 = 2^2 \times 3^2$ Write the factors in order, from least to greatest.

Complete the factor trees for each number. Notice that the prime factors are the same. Then use exponents to write the prime factorization.

1.

70
7 × 10
_ × _ × _

70
5 × 14
_ × _ × _

70 = _____

2.

45
5 × 9
_ × _ × _

45
3 × 15
_ × _ × _

45 = _____

3.

48
4 × ___

48
6 × ___

_____

_____

48 = _____

4.

84
2 × ___

84
___ × ___

_____

84 = _____

Write each prime factorization. Use exponents when you can.

5. 12 = _____ 15 = _____ 16 = _____

6. 18 = _____ 20 = _____ 21 = _____

7. 22 = _____ 24 = _____ 25 = _____

8. 26 = _____ 27 = _____ 28 = _____

Problem Solving Reasoning

Write *True* or *False*. Explain your answer.

9. The prime factorization of any composite number includes prime and composite numbers.

_____

_____

10. The prime factorization of any composite number includes three or more prime numbers.

_____

_____

✔ Quick Check

Put a ✔ in the box to show that the number is divisible by 2, 3, 4, 5, or 10.

Work Space

		2	3	4	5	10
11.	450					
12.	184					
13.	90					

Write prime or composite. If the number is composite, then write it as a product of factors other than itself and 1.

14. 36   **15.** 57   **16.** 43

_____   _____   _____

Use factor trees to write the prime factorization in exponent form.

17. 72   **18.** 60   **19.** 48

_____   _____   _____

When two or more numbers have some factors that are the same, then those factors are called **common factors**. To find the common factors of two numbers:

1. List all the factors of each number.

2. Identify the factors that are in **both** lists.

Factors of **14**: **1**, **2**, **7**, 14

Factors of **35**: **1**, **5**, **7**, 35

Common factors of **14** and **35**: **1**, **7**

Factors of **27**: **1**, **3**, **9**, 27

Factors of **45**: **1**, **3**, **5**, **9**, 15, 45

Common factors of **27** and **45**: **1**, **3**, **9**

Write all the factors of each number. Then write the common factors of the numbers.

1. Factors of **12**: _____

Factors of **20**: _____

Common factors: _____

Factors of **10**: _____

Factors of **12**: _____

Common factors: _____

2. Factors of **14**: _____

Factors of **56**: _____

Common factors: _____

Factors of **15**: _____

Factors of **16**: _____

Common factors: _____

3. Factors of **7**: _____

Factors of **32**: _____

Common factors: _____

Factors of **21**: _____

Factors of **28**: _____

Common factors: _____

4. Factors of **9**: _____

Factors of **45**: _____

Common factors: _____

Factors of **13**: _____

Factors of **53**: _____

Common factors: _____

5. Factors of **25**: _____

Factors of **40**: _____

Common factors: _____

Factors of **14**: _____

Factors of **18**: _____

Common factors: _____

The **greatest common factor**, or **GCF**, of two numbers is the greatest number in the lists of common factors.

Factors of **12**: **1**, **2**, **3**, **4**, **6**, **12**   Factors of **9**: **1**, **3**, **9**

Factors of **20**: **1**, **2**, **4**, **5**, **10**, **20**   Factors of **16**: **1**, **2**, **4**, **8**, **16**

Common factors: **1**, **2**, **4**   Common factors: **1**

The **GCF** of **12** and **20** is **4**.   The **GCF** of **9** and **16** is **1**.

Find the GCF of each pair of numbers.

6. 10, 12 _____   25, 9 _____   15, 25 _____

7. 20, 38 _____   26, 34 _____   15, 18 _____

8. 32, 48 _____   30, 45 _____   18, 24 _____

9. 14, 21 _____   24, 15 _____   40, 25 _____

10. 21, 51 _____   13, 17 _____   26, 34 _____

| Problem Solving |
| Reasoning |

Solve.

11. Ellen is making corsages of red and white roses. She has **24** red roses and **16** white roses. She wants to put the same number of red roses and the same number of white roses in each corsage. What is the greatest number of corsages she can make and not have any roses left over?

_____

12. Mark is making balloon bouquets for a birthday party. He **20** yellow balloons and **10** green balloons. He wants to put the same number of yellow balloons and the same number of green balloons in each bouquet. What is the greatest number of bouquets he can make and not have any balloons left over?

_____

Test Prep ★ Mixed Review

13 A year has 365 days. A leap year has 366 days. How many days are there in 4 years, that is, 3 years and 1 leap year?

A 2,921   **C** 1,463

B 1,826   **D** 1,461

14 What is the value of the expression $6 + 4^3 \div 8 - 6$?

F 500

G 119

H 8

J 6

Before you divide, think about how many digits will be in the quotient. For example, think about finding 659 ÷ 21.

1. Start with hundreds.

$21\overline{)659}$

Think: **21 > 6**
The quotient will not have hundreds.

Then look at tens.

$21\overline{)659}$

Think: **21 < 65**
The first digit will be in the tens' place.

2. Estimate. Then multiply.

$$\begin{array}{r} 3 \\ 21\overline{)659} \\ 63 \end{array}$$

Think: **65 ÷ 21**
↓   ↓
70 ÷ 20 is about **3**.

3 × 21 = 63

3. Subtract.

$$\begin{array}{r} 3 \\ 21\overline{)659} \\ -63 \\ \hline 2 \end{array}$$

4. Bring down the next digit in the dividend. Repeat the steps until there are no digits left to bring down.

$$\begin{array}{r} 31 \text{ R8} \\ 21\overline{)659} \\ -63\downarrow \\ \hline 29 \\ -21 \\ \hline 8 \end{array}$$ ← remainder

Check the answer.
• **Multiply** the quotient by the divisor. Then **add** the remainder.

659 is the dividend.
So the answer is correct.

$$\begin{array}{r} 31 \\ \times 21 \\ \hline 31 \\ +62 \\ \hline 651 \\ +8 \\ \hline 659 \end{array}$$

31 ← quotient
× 21 ← divisor
+ 8 ← remainder

Divide. Use multiplication to check.

1. $13\overline{)39}$ $24\overline{)49}$ $44\overline{)50}$

2. $32\overline{)99}$ $19\overline{)76}$ $23\overline{)95}$

Divide. Use multiplication to check.

3. $10\overline{)114}$ $20\overline{)346}$ $45\overline{)738}$

4. $44\overline{)469}$ $32\overline{)352}$ $19\overline{)564}$

5. $65\overline{)567}$ $59\overline{)531}$ $74\overline{)917}$

| Problem Solving |
| Reasoning |

Solve. Check to make sure your answer is reasonable.

6. A theater has **418** seats arranged in rows of **19** seats each. How many rows are in the theater?

_____

7. Tickets for a play cost **$12** each. If the box office received **$648** for ticket sales, how many tickets were sold?

_____

8. Mr. Jackson paid **$960** for **15** CD players to sell in his store. How much did each CD player cost?

_____

9. Mr. Jackson has **20** boxes ready to be unpacked. There are **18** radios in each box. How many radios are there altogether?

_____

Test Prep ★ Mixed Review

10 What is $2^3 \times 3^2$ equivalent to?

A 734

B 216

C 144

D 72

11 $8 \times n = 6,400$
What is the missing number n?

F 10

G 80

H 800

J 1000

Copyright © Houghton Mifflin Company. All rights reserved.

Name _____

Sometimes when you divide, your first estimate is too large.

Find 24)829.

1. The first digit in the quotient will be in the tens' place. Try **4**.

```
     4
24)829
  − 96
```

Think: 96 > 82, so 4 is too large.

2. Try **3** in the quotient. Multiply.

```
     3
24)829
  − 72
```

Think: 72 < 82, so 3 is correct.

3. Subtract. Bring down the next digit. Try **5**.

```
    35
24)829
  − 72
   109
 − 120
```

Think: 120 > 109, so 5 is too large.

4. Try **4** in the quotient.

```
    34 R13
24)829
  − 72
   109
  − 96
    13
```

Think: 96 < 109, so 4 is correct. Remember to check the answer.

Is the quotient too large? Write *Yes* or *No*.

1. 9)56 ____   31)91 ____   14)70 ____   18)67 ____
(7)   (3)   (5)   (3)

2. 27)379 ____   61)782 ____   45)742 ____   28)745 ____
(15)   (12)   (17)   (28)

Divide.

3. 35)140   13)117   19)144   79)478   51)275

4. 71)891   14)439   32)767   59)828   32)581

Sometimes when you divide, your first estimate is too small. When you subtract, the result must always be less than the divisor.

1. The first digit in the quotient will be in the tens' place. Try **3**.

$$\begin{array}{r} 3 \\ 17\overline{)821} \\ -51 \\ \hline 31 \end{array}$$

Think: **31 > 17**, so **3** is too small.

2. Try **4**. Multiply and subtract.

$$\begin{array}{r} 4 \\ 17\overline{)821} \\ -68 \\ \hline 14 \end{array}$$

Think: **14 < 17**, so **4** is correct.

3. Bring down the next digit. Try **7**.

$$\begin{array}{r} 47 \\ 17\overline{)821} \\ -68 \\ \hline 141 \\ -119 \\ \hline 22 \end{array}$$

Think: **22 > 17**, so **7** is too small.

4. Try **8** in the quotient.

$$\begin{array}{r} 48 \text{ R5} \\ 17\overline{)821} \\ -68 \\ \hline 141 \\ -136 \\ \hline \end{array}$$
remainder ➝ 5

Think: **5 < 17**, so **8** is correct. Remember to check the answer.

Divide.

5. 45)289   73)611   89)827   91)737

6. 12)568   24)955   22)747   19)496

 Quick Check

Find the greatest common factor of the numbers.

7. 20, 45   **8.** 14, 28, 63   **9.** 16, 56, 64

_____   _____   _____

Work Space

Divide.

10. 33)860   **11.** 64)390   **12.** 43)165

13. 26)1,456   **14.** 57)3,898   **15.** 38)2,940

Dividing Greater Numbers

Follow the same steps to divide greater numbers as you have with 2- and 3-digit numbers. For example, find 19,859 ÷ 32.

1. The first digit in the quotient will be in the ones' place.

$$32\overline{)19{,}859} \quad \overset{6}{}$$

Think **200 ÷ 30 is about 6.**

2. Multiply.

Think:
6 × 32 = 192

$$32\overline{)19{,}859} \quad \overset{6}{} \\ -19\ 2$$

Think: **192 < 198.**

3. Subtract. Then compare the difference to the divisor.

$$32\overline{)19{,}859} \quad \overset{6}{} \\ \underline{-19\ 2} \\ 6$$

Think: **6 < 32.**

4. Bring down the next digit in the dividend. Repeat these steps until there are no digits left to bring down.

$$32\overline{)19{,}859} \quad \overset{6\,20\ R19}{} \\ \underline{-19\ 2} \\ 65 \\ \underline{-64} \\ 19 \\ \underline{-0} \\ 19$$

Remember to check the answer.

Divide.

1. $48\overline{)2{,}496}$ $38\overline{)5{,}375}$ $42\overline{)5{,}420}$ $36\overline{)8{,}319}$

2. $32\overline{)1{,}664}$ $43\overline{)1{,}078}$ $64\overline{)2{,}176}$ $23\overline{)1{,}104}$

Divide.

3. $17\overline{)6{,}021}$ $53\overline{)5{,}726}$ $31\overline{)8{,}063}$ $26\overline{)4{,}655}$

4. $19\overline{)81{,}035}$ $41\overline{)64{,}087}$ $33\overline{)48{,}679}$ $23\overline{)87{,}264}$

5. $43\overline{)31{,}965}$ $25\overline{)10{,}600}$ $53\overline{)14{,}628}$ $89\overline{)72{,}561}$

Problem Solving
Reasoning

Solve.

6. Reggie delivers **1,495** newspapers in **65** days. He delivers the same number of newspapers each day. How many newspapers does he deliver each day?

_____

7. The Bradleys pay a subscription price of **$39.00** for **52** newspapers. What is the cost of each newspaper?

_____

Test Prep ★ Mixed Review

8 Which expression is equivalent to $3 \times (80 + x)$?

  A $3 \times 80 + x$

  B $3 \times 80 + 3 \times x$

  C $(3 \times 80) + x$

  D $(3 + x) \times 80$

9 Sal is going on vacation for 19 days. Which equation shows how many weeks this is?

  F $19 + 7 = w$

  G $19 - 7 = w$

  H $19 \times 7 = w$

  J $19 \div 7 = w$

You can use **compatible numbers** to estimate quotients.

Compatible numbers are numbers that are easy to divide mentally.

You should choose compatible numbers that are close to the actual numbers.

$$7\overline{)418} \rightarrow 7\overset{60}{\overline{)420}} \qquad 78\overline{)317} \rightarrow 80\overset{4}{\overline{)320}} \qquad 62\overline{)1,860} \rightarrow 60\overset{30}{\overline{)1,800}}$$

Rewrite each exercise using compatible numbers that are close to the actual numbers. Then estimate each quotient.

1. $6\overline{)38}$ $7\overline{)50}$ $8\overline{)74}$

2. $3\overline{)272}$ $5\overline{)241}$ $2\overline{)170}$

3. $4\overline{)3,434}$ $8\overline{)6,188}$ $2\overline{)1,196}$

4. $32\overline{)684}$ $21\overline{)181}$ $42\overline{)761}$

5. $35\overline{)2,850}$ $57\overline{)5,623}$ $74\overline{)6,243}$

6. $72\overline{)20,967}$ $48\overline{)19,901}$ $56\overline{)42,332}$

Estimate each quotient.

7. $2\overline{)98}$ $\qquad$ $4\overline{)39}$ $\qquad$ $5\overline{)433}$ $\qquad$ $8\overline{)705}$

8. $6\overline{)238}$ $\qquad$ $4\overline{)3,503}$ $\qquad$ $9\overline{)5,281}$ $\qquad$ $8\overline{)2,290}$

9. $62\overline{)545}$ $\qquad$ $41\overline{)3,774}$ $\qquad$ $59\overline{)3,742}$ $\qquad$ $63\overline{)5,991}$

10. $57\overline{)42,305}$ $\qquad$ $71\overline{)47,101}$ $\qquad$ $82\overline{)41,163}$ $\qquad$ $45\overline{)11,782}$

| Problem Solving |
| Reasoning |

Solve.

11. A garden supply company ships flower bulbs in boxes of **46** bulbs. About how many boxes will they need to fill an order for **490** bulbs?

_____

12. Roger is planting **5,701** seeds in **81** pots. He wants to plant about the same number of seeds in each pot. About how many seeds will he plant in each pot?

_____

 Quick Check

Divide.

13. $24\overline{)7,006}$ $\qquad$ **14.** $15\overline{)11,405}$ $\qquad$ **15.** $49\overline{)9,803}$

Estimate. Then divide.

16. $305\overline{)54,780}$ $\qquad$ **17.** $816\overline{)64,344}$ $\qquad$ **18.** $745\overline{)72,529}$

Work Space

Sometimes it is helpful to make a table in order to solve a problem.

Problem

Mrs. Red, Mrs. Black, and Mrs. White each is wearing a different color dress. One dress is red, one is black, and one is white. Use the clues to match each woman with the color of her dress.

Clues:

No woman's dress is the same color as her last name.

Mrs. White does not own a red dress.

1 Understand As you reread, ask yourself questions.

- What do you know about the given clues?

    No woman's dress is the same color as her last name.
    Mrs. White does not own a red dress.

- What do you need to do?

    _____

2 Decide Choose a method for solving. Try the strategy Make a Table.

	Mrs.Red	Mrs.Black	Mrs.White
Red			
Black			
White			

3 Solve Use the clues to put X's in the table.

- From the clues, we can write the following X's.

	Mrs.Red	Mrs.Black	Mrs.White
Red	X		X
Black		X	
White			X

4 Look back Check your answer. Write the answer below.

_____

Use the **Make a Table** strategy or any other strategy you have learned.

1. Find **2** numbers less than **50** that are divisible by both **2** and **9**.
Think: How do you know a number is divisible by **9**?

_____

Answer _____

2. Find a composite number between **40** and **50** that is divisible by **2, 3,** and **4**.

Think: Which prime numbers can you immediately eliminate?

_____

Answer _____

3. Paul, Arthur, and Jim are each the captain of a team. One is the soccer captain, one is the baseball captain, and one is the basketball captain. Use the clues to match the boys with their sports.

Clues:
Arthur and the baseball captain both like to swim.
The baseball captain and the basketball captain are brothers.
Jim is an only child.

_____

_____

_____

4. Betty, Nina, Carol, and Dot each live in one of these cities: Boston, New York, Chicago, and Denver. Use the clues to match the girls with the cities.
Clues:
No girl lives in a city that begins with the same letter as her first name.
Nina and Carol have never been to Boston.
Betty has never been to New York or Chicago.

_____

_____

_____

_____

5. A school bus can hold **45** children. How many school buses will be needed to take **354** children to school?

_____

6. How much change would you get from a **$20** bill if you bought some ground beef for **$3.75** and a package of buns for **$1.69**?

_____

7. Find all the numbers less than **60** that are prime and have a remainder of **3** when they are divided by **7**.

_____

8. Jeremy read **43** library books. Jill read **29** more books than Jeremy. How many books did they read altogether?

_____

Name _____

Complete.

1. $4 \times n = 36$

$n =$ ___ $\div$ ___

$n =$ ___

2. $a \div 4 = 8$

$a =$ ___ $\times$ ___

$a =$ ___

Evaluate using the order of operations.

3. $42 + n \div 4$ for $n = 8$ _____

4. $a - 3 \times 2 + 1$ for $a = 10$ _____

Divide.

5. $7\overline{)459}$

6. $5\overline{)5,216}$

7. $68\overline{)479}$

8. $35\overline{)7,084}$

Find the average of each group of numbers.

9. 18, 56, 34 _____

10. 465, 89, 123, 557, 77, 117 _____

Write all the factors of each number. Then write the common factors of each pair of numbers.

11. Factors of **32**: _____

Factors of **40**: _____

Common factors: _____

12. Factors of **25**: _____

Factors of **35**: _____

Common factors: _____

Use exponents to write each prime factorization.

13. $63 =$ _____

14. $40 =$ _____

Is enough information given to solve the problem? Write *Yes* or *No*.

15. Juanita has **$70** to buy certificates for the contestants in the math contest. How much will each certificate cost? _____

16. Suppose each certificate for participants in the Science Fair costs $1.50. On another sheet of paper, make a table that shows the different numbers of certificates you could buy if you spent **$10.00** or less. _____

Name _____

Cumulative Review
★ Test Prep

The chart shows the number of letters in the first names of a fifth-grade class.

Number of Letters in First Name

Number of Letters	Tally
2	/
3	//
4	##1
5	////
6	##1 /
7	
8	//

Use the tally chart to answer questions 1 and 2.

1 How many students are in the class?

A 7   C 100

B 20   D 107

2 What is the average, or mean, number of letters?

F between 2 and 3   H exactly 5

G exactly 3   J more than 5

3 A number machine used a rule to change an input number into an output number.

Input number	1	2	3	5	6
Output number	3	5	7	11	?

What would the number machine change 6 into?

A 13   C 15

B 14   D 20

4 Jordan bought a cheese sandwich for $2.49 and a fruit drink for $0.75. What information do you need to know in order to find out how much change he got?

F The price of a tuna sandwich

G The price of fruit

H The amount of money Jordan has in his wallet

J The amount of money Jordan gave to the clerk

5 A trail is 1,344 meters long. If you walked an average of 16 meters a minute, how long would it take you to walk the entire trail?

A 94 minutes

B 94 meters

C 1,328 minutes

D 1,328 meters

E Not here

6 In 1980, the state of California had a population of 23,668,562. What is that number rounded to the nearest million?

F 24,000,000

G 23,000,000

H 23,700,000

J 23,670,000

K 23,660,000

7 There are 24 classes in the school. Ten of the classes have an average of 25 students in each class. The rest have an average of 22 students. How many students are enrolled in the school?

A 71   C 558

B 81   D 1,340   E Not here

8 A student spent $2.75 and bought 3 pads of paper and 2 erasers. The pads of paper are 75¢ each. How much does each eraser cost?

F $2.25   H 55¢

G $2.00   J 50¢   K 25¢

Copyright © Houghton Mifflin Company. All rights reserved.

82   Unit 3 Cumulative Review

UNIT 4 • TABLE OF CONTENTS

Addition and Subtraction of Fractions and Mixed Numbers

Dear Family,

During the next few weeks, our math class will be learning and practicing the addition and subtraction of fractions and mixed numbers.

You can expect to see homework that provides practice with writing fractions in simplest form. Here is a sample you may want to keep handy to give help if needed.

Simplest Form

Example   Write $\frac{2}{8}$ in simplest form.

To write *some* fractions in simplest form, divide the numerator (top number) and the denominator (bottom number) by the numerator.

    $\frac{2}{8} = \frac{2 \div 2}{8 \div 2} \rightarrow \frac{1}{4}$

For other fractions, dividing by the numerator is not possible. For these fractions, choose a number that is a common factor of the numerator and the denominator and divide the numerator and denominator by that number.

Example   Write $\frac{6}{9}$ in simplest form.

    $\frac{6}{9} = \frac{6 \div 3}{9 \div 3} \rightarrow \frac{2}{3}$

A fraction is in simplest form when the only number that divides the numerator and the denominator is **1**.

During this unit, students will need to continue practicing division, addition, and subtraction facts.

Sincerely,

Name _____

Operations with fractions often involve finding **equivalent fractions** first. Fractions that are equivalent name the same number. You can use *fraction model*s to find equivalent fractions.

Example Write three fractions that are equivalent to $\frac{1}{2}$.

$$\frac{1}{2} \quad \rightarrow \quad \frac{2}{4} \quad \rightarrow \quad \frac{3}{6} \quad \rightarrow \quad \frac{4}{8}$$

The fractions $\frac{1}{2}$, $\frac{2}{4}$, $\frac{3}{6}$, and $\frac{4}{8}$ are equivalent fractions.

You can also use *multiplication* to find equivalent fractions. To use multiplication, choose a number and multiply the numerator and the denominator by that number.

Example Write three fractions that are equivalent to $\frac{2}{5}$.

$$\frac{2 \times 2}{5 \times 2} = \frac{4}{10} \qquad\qquad \frac{2 \times 3}{5 \times 3} = \frac{6}{15} \qquad\qquad \frac{2 \times 10}{5 \times 10} = \frac{20}{50}$$

The fractions $\frac{4}{10}$, $\frac{6}{15}$, and $\frac{20}{50}$ are all equivalent to $\frac{2}{5}$.

What equivalent fractions are shown by these models?

1.

_____

2.

_____

Complete.

3. $\frac{1 \times 3}{2 \times 3} = \frac{3}{}$ $\qquad$ $\frac{3 \times 5}{4 \times 5} = \frac{15}{}$ $\qquad$ $\frac{5 \times 4}{8 \times 4} = \frac{}{32}$ $\qquad$ $\frac{1 \times 6}{4 \times 6} = \frac{6}{}$

Write five equivalent fractions.

4. $\frac{1}{3}$ _____ _____ _____ _____ _____ $\qquad$ $\frac{3}{5}$ _____ _____ _____ _____ _____

5. $\frac{1}{8}$ _____ _____ _____ _____ _____ $\qquad$ $\frac{1}{10}$ _____ _____ _____ _____ _____

You can also use *division* to find one or more equivalent fractions.

To write three fractions that are equivalent to $\frac{12}{18}$, choose

a number that is a **common factor** of the numerator and denominator,

and divide the numerator and the denominator by that number.

> Remember: A common factor of two numbers divides each number without having a remainder.

Choose 2: $\frac{12 \div 2}{18 \div 2} = \frac{6}{9}$ Choose 3: $\frac{12 \div 3}{18 \div 3} = \frac{4}{6}$ Choose 6: $\frac{12 \div 6}{18 \div 6} = \frac{2}{3}$

The fractions $\frac{6}{9}$, $\frac{4}{6}$, and $\frac{2}{3}$ are equivalent to $\frac{12}{18}$.

Use division to write three equivalent fractions.

6. $\frac{24}{30}$ _____ _____ _____ $\frac{20}{40}$ _____ _____ _____

7. $\frac{36}{48}$ _____ _____ _____ $\frac{60}{100}$ _____ _____ _____

8. $\frac{50}{80}$ _____ _____ _____ $\frac{64}{96}$ _____ _____ _____

Problem Solving Reasoning

Complete the table. Describe the rule.

9.

Input	$\frac{1}{6}$	$\frac{2}{6}$	$\frac{3}{6}$	$\frac{4}{6}$	$\frac{5}{6}$
Output	$\frac{3}{18}$	$\frac{6}{18}$			

10.

Input	$\frac{1}{8}$	$\frac{2}{4}$			
Output	$\frac{2}{16}$	$\frac{4}{8}$	$\frac{6}{12}$		

Rule: _____   Rule: _____

Test Prep ★ Mixed Review

11. Lincoln school has 256 students. On Monday, 78 students were absent. Which equation can be used to find the number of students who were present on Monday?

A $m - 78 = 256$ C $256 = m - 78$

B $256 + m = 78$ D $256 = m + 78$

12. What is the value of the expression $20 \times a$ when $a = 14$?

F 28

G 34

H 280

J 300

Name _____

Some fractions name whole numbers.

This number line shows that $\frac{3}{3} = 1$, $\frac{6}{3} = 2$, and $\frac{9}{3} = 3$.

On the number line, the fractions $\frac{0}{3}$, $\frac{1}{3}$, and $\frac{2}{3}$ *are less than* 1.

All of the other fractions on the number line *are equal to or greater than* 1.

You can use division to rewrite a fraction as a whole number.

Example: $\frac{12}{4} = 12 \div 4 \rightarrow 3$

Read $\frac{12}{4}$ as "twelve divided by four" or "twelve fourths."

Example: $\frac{35}{7} = 35 \div 7 \rightarrow 5$

Read $\frac{35}{7}$ as "thirty-five divided by seven" or "thirty-five sevenths."

Write each missing fraction for the whole numbers.

1.

Write each whole number.

2.

Write each missing numerator.

3. $1 = \dfrac{}{2}$ $2 = \dfrac{}{2}$ $3 = \dfrac{}{2}$ $1 = \dfrac{}{3}$ $2 = \dfrac{}{3}$

4. $5 = \dfrac{}{3}$ $4 = \dfrac{}{4}$ $6 = \dfrac{}{2}$ $8 = \dfrac{}{3}$ $8 = \dfrac{}{4}$

A **mixed number** is made up of a
whole number and a fraction.

$1\frac{3}{4}$

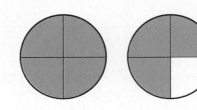

.

To write a mixed number as a fraction, follow these steps.	Write $4\frac{1}{2}$ as a fraction.
1. Multiply the whole number by the denominator.	2×4
2. Add the numerator to the product.	$8 + 1$
3. Write the sum over the denominator.	$\frac{9}{2}$ So, $4\frac{1}{2} = \frac{9}{2}$.

To write a fraction as a mixed number, divide. Write the remainder over the denominator.	Write $\frac{14}{5}$ as a mixed number
	$14 \div 5 = 2\frac{4}{5}$

**Write each mixed number as a fraction and write
each fraction as a mixed number.**

5. $2\frac{1}{4}$ _____ $\frac{7}{2}$ _____ $1\frac{3}{8}$ _____ $\frac{10}{3}$ _____

6. $\frac{12}{5}$ _____ $3\frac{1}{16}$ _____ $\frac{17}{9}$ _____ $4\frac{9}{10}$ _____

Problem Solving
Reasoning

Solve.

7. After every $\frac{1}{3}$ mile of a nature trail, there is a place to
rest. How many places to rest are there on a trail that is
$1\frac{2}{3}$ mile long?

_____

_____

Test Prep ★ Mixed Review

8 What is the best estimate of the quotient
2,483 ÷ 25?

     A 1

     B 10

     C 100

     D 1,000

9 $90 = 2 \times 3^2 \times 5$. Which statement is also
true?

     F 90 is a multiple of 20

     G 90 is divisible by 12

     H 10 is a factor of 90

     J 4×10 is a factor of 90

When the only common factor of the numerator and the denominator of a fraction is 1, the fraction is in **simplest form.**

If a fraction such as $\frac{12}{18}$ is not in simplest form, divide the numerator and the denominator by the **greatest common factor (GCF)** to simplify it.

> Remember: To find an equivalent fraction, you can divide the numerator and denominator by a common factor.
>
> $$\frac{10}{12} \rightarrow \frac{10 \div 2}{12 \div 2} = \frac{5}{6}$$

1. Find the factors of **12** and **18**.

   Factors of **12: 1, 2, 3, 4, 6, 12**

   Factors of **18: 1, 2, 3, 6, 18**

   The **GCF** of **12** and **18** is **6**.

> Circle the greatest factor that is in both lists.

2. Divide **12** and **18** by **6**, the **GCF**.

   $$\frac{12 \div 6}{18 \div 6} = \frac{2}{3}$$ In simplest form, $\frac{12}{18}$ is $\frac{2}{3}$.

You can write a fraction such as $\frac{14}{10}$ in simplest form by following these steps.

   1. Write $\frac{14}{10}$ as a mixed number. $\frac{14}{10} = 1\frac{4}{10}$

   2. Simplify $1\frac{4}{10}$. $= 1\frac{4}{10} \rightarrow 1\frac{4 \div 2}{10 \div 2} \rightarrow 1\frac{2}{5}$

Write the fraction in simplest form.

1. $\frac{6}{18} =$ _____ $\frac{9}{21} =$ _____ $\frac{6}{9} =$ _____ $\frac{12}{16} =$ _____

2. $\frac{4}{6} =$ _____ $\frac{2}{4} =$ _____ $\frac{8}{14} =$ _____ $\frac{2}{6} =$ _____

3. $\frac{6}{12} =$ _____ $\frac{8}{12} =$ _____ $\frac{10}{15} =$ _____ $\frac{7}{28} =$ _____

4. $\frac{2}{8} =$ _____ $\frac{3}{6} =$ _____ $\frac{6}{8} =$ _____ $\frac{10}{16} =$ _____

5. $\frac{7}{21} =$ _____ $\frac{8}{10} =$ _____ $\frac{3}{12} =$ _____ $\frac{15}{20} =$ _____

6. $\frac{9}{12} =$ _____ $\frac{12}{20} =$ _____ $\frac{10}{18} =$ _____ $\frac{6}{10} =$ _____

7. $\frac{8}{16} =$ _____ $\frac{10}{25} =$ _____ $\frac{15}{24} =$ _____ $\frac{16}{48} =$ _____

You can write a mixed number such as $2\frac{9}{15}$ in simplest form.

1. Divide **9** and **15** by **3**, the **GCF**. $\frac{9 \div 3}{15 \div 3} = \frac{3}{5}$

2. Write the mixed number in simplest form. $2\frac{9}{15} = 2\frac{3}{5}$

Write the mixed number in simplest form.

8. $1\frac{4}{12}$ _____ $3\frac{6}{8}$ _____ $4\frac{6}{16}$ _____ $7\frac{2}{4}$ _____

9. $2\frac{12}{18}$ _____ $5\frac{5}{20}$ _____ $1\frac{8}{10}$ _____ $2\frac{10}{12}$ _____

Problem Solving
Reasoning

Solve.

10. A paper clip is $\frac{12}{16}$ inch long. If you measured it with a ruler marked in $\frac{1}{4}$ inches, what would the measurement be? Is your answer in simplest form?

Explain. _____

_____

11. A pencil eraser is $\frac{16}{32}$ inch long. If you measured it with a ruler marked in $\frac{1}{8}$ inches, what would the measurement be? Is your answer in simplest form?

Explain. _____

_____

 Quick Check

Find the missing numerator or denominator.

12. $\frac{?}{4} = \frac{4}{16}$ **13.** $\frac{2}{?} = \frac{8}{12}$ **14.** $\frac{?}{5} = \frac{12}{30}$

_____   _____   _____

Work Space

Rename the fraction as a whole number or mixed number.

15. $\frac{28}{7}$ **16.** $\frac{14}{3}$ **17.** $\frac{39}{5}$

_____   _____   _____

Write the fraction in simplest form.

18. $\frac{18}{36}$ **19.** $\frac{8}{6}$ **20.** $\frac{18}{9}$

_____   _____   _____

Name _____

The region is divided into **9** equal parts.

Each part is $\frac{1}{9}$ of the whole.

How much of the whole region is shaded?

$\frac{5}{9}$ shaded red $\qquad$ $\frac{2}{9}$ shaded gray

To solve this problem, you can add fractions that have **like denominators**:

1. Add the numerators.

2. Write the sum over the denominator.

$\frac{5}{9} + \frac{2}{9} = \frac{7}{9}$

$\frac{7}{9}$ of the whole is shaded.

Think:
5 ninths
+ 2 ninths
7 ninths

Add. Use the shaded region. Simplify your answers if possible.

1. $\frac{1}{4} + \frac{2}{4} =$ _____ $\frac{2}{8} + \frac{5}{8} =$ _____ $\frac{3}{10} + \frac{4}{10} =$ _____

2. $\frac{3}{9} + \frac{4}{9} =$ _____ $\frac{1}{7} + \frac{3}{7} =$ _____ $\frac{2}{6} + \frac{4}{6} =$ _____

Add. Simplify your answers if possible.

3. $\frac{1}{3} + \frac{1}{3} =$ _____ $\frac{4}{6} + \frac{1}{6} =$ _____ $\frac{2}{5} + \frac{2}{5} =$ _____ $\frac{3}{8} + \frac{4}{8} =$ _____

4. $\frac{4}{9} + \frac{1}{9} =$ _____ $\frac{3}{10} + \frac{6}{10} =$ _____ $\frac{3}{7} + \frac{2}{7} =$ _____ $\frac{1}{10} + \frac{3}{10} =$ _____

5.
$\begin{array}{r} \frac{5}{12} \\ + \frac{3}{12} \\ \hline \end{array}$
$\qquad$
$\begin{array}{r} \frac{2}{7} \\ + \frac{1}{7} \\ \hline \end{array}$
$\qquad$
$\begin{array}{r} \frac{1}{5} \\ + \frac{1}{5} \\ \hline \end{array}$
$\qquad$
$\begin{array}{r} \frac{7}{8} \\ + \frac{1}{8} \\ \hline \end{array}$
$\qquad$
$\begin{array}{r} \frac{1}{2} \\ + \frac{1}{2} \\ \hline \end{array}$

To add two mixed numbers, follow these steps: $3\frac{5}{8} + 4\frac{1}{8}$

Add the fractions.   Add the whole numbers.   Simplify if possible.

$$3\frac{5}{8}$$
$$\underline{+\ 4\frac{1}{8}}$$
$$\frac{6}{8}$$

$$3\frac{5}{8}$$
$$\underline{+\ 4\frac{1}{8}}$$
$$7\frac{6}{8}$$

$$3\frac{5}{8}$$
$$\underline{+\ 4\frac{1}{8}}$$
$$7\frac{6}{8} = 7\frac{3}{4}\ \leftarrow\ \text{simplest form}$$

Add. Write the sum in simplest form.

6.
$$5\frac{4}{9}$$
$$\underline{+\ 1\frac{1}{9}}$$

$$1\frac{3}{8}$$
$$\underline{+\ 4\frac{1}{8}}$$

$$5\frac{1}{7}$$
$$\underline{+\ \ \frac{3}{7}}$$

$$4\frac{1}{3}$$
$$\underline{+\ 1\frac{1}{3}}$$

$$3\frac{1}{4}$$
$$\underline{+\ \ \frac{2}{4}}$$

$$1\frac{7}{8}$$
$$\underline{+\ 3}$$

7.
$$7\frac{1}{5}$$
$$\underline{+\ \ \frac{3}{5}}$$

$$6\frac{1}{9}$$
$$\underline{+\ 1\frac{2}{9}}$$

$$3\frac{1}{7}$$
$$\underline{+\ 1\frac{1}{7}}$$

$$\frac{5}{8}$$
$$\underline{+\ \ \frac{2}{8}}$$

$$3\frac{1}{3}$$
$$\underline{+\ \ \frac{1}{3}}$$

$$2\frac{3}{5}$$
$$\underline{+\ 4\frac{0}{5}}$$

| Problem Solving |
| Reasoning |

Solve.

8. Bike Trail A is $4\frac{9}{10}$ miles long, Trail B is $3\frac{3}{4}$ miles long, and Trail C is $5\frac{5}{8}$ miles long. Which two trails should Derrick ride if he wants to ride between **9** and **10** miles?

_____

Test Prep ★ Mixed Review

9 Which fractions are in order from least to greatest?

A $\frac{2}{3}, \frac{9}{12}, \frac{1}{2}, \frac{5}{6}$ **C** $\frac{1}{2}, \frac{9}{12}, \frac{2}{3}, \frac{5}{6}$

B $\frac{1}{2}, \frac{2}{3}, \frac{9}{12}, \frac{5}{6}$ **D** $\frac{9}{12}, \frac{2}{3}, \frac{1}{2}, \frac{5}{6}$

10 12 is the GCF of which numbers?

F 24 and 36

G 12 and 30

H 24 and 48

J 30 and 48

Name _____

You can see that $\frac{7}{9}$ of the whole is shaded. What part of the whole is shaded red?

$\frac{7}{9}$ shaded $\frac{2}{9}$ shaded gray

Think:
$$\begin{array}{r} 7 \text{ ninths} \\ -\ 2 \text{ ninths} \\ \hline 5 \text{ ninths} \end{array}$$

To solve this problem, you can subtract fractions with **like denominators**:

1. Subtract the numerators.

$$\frac{7}{9} - \frac{2}{9} = \frac{5}{9}$$

2. Write the difference over the denominator.

$\frac{5}{9}$ are shaded red.

Subtract. Use the shaded regions.

1. $\frac{4}{6} - \frac{3}{6} =$ _____ $\frac{5}{8} - \frac{2}{8} =$ _____ $\frac{7}{8} - \frac{6}{8} =$ _____

Subtract. Simplify your answer if possible.

2. $\frac{5}{6} - \frac{4}{6} =$ _____ $\frac{3}{5} - \frac{2}{5} =$ _____ $\frac{4}{8} - \frac{1}{8} =$ _____ $\frac{5}{9} - \frac{4}{9} =$ _____

3. $\frac{3}{8} - \frac{1}{8} =$ _____ $\frac{3}{4} - \frac{1}{4} =$ _____ $\frac{5}{8} - \frac{3}{8} =$ _____ $\frac{11}{16} - \frac{7}{16} =$ _____

4. $\frac{6}{7} - \frac{1}{7} =$ _____ $\frac{2}{3} - \frac{1}{3} =$ _____ $\frac{9}{10} - \frac{6}{10} =$ _____ $\frac{1}{4} - \frac{1}{4} =$ _____

5.
$\begin{array}{r} \frac{5}{6} \\ -\frac{4}{6} \\ \hline \end{array}$
$\begin{array}{r} \frac{11}{12} \\ -\frac{1}{12} \\ \hline \end{array}$
$\begin{array}{r} \frac{3}{5} \\ -\frac{1}{5} \\ \hline \end{array}$
$\begin{array}{r} \frac{4}{4} \\ -\frac{1}{4} \\ \hline \end{array}$
$\begin{array}{r} \frac{7}{8} \\ -\frac{4}{8} \\ \hline \end{array}$
$\begin{array}{r} \frac{6}{9} \\ -\frac{2}{9} \\ \hline \end{array}$

6.
$\begin{array}{r} \frac{7}{8} \\ -\frac{1}{8} \\ \hline \end{array}$
$\begin{array}{r} \frac{9}{10} \\ -\frac{1}{10} \\ \hline \end{array}$
$\begin{array}{r} \frac{2}{3} \\ -\frac{2}{3} \\ \hline \end{array}$
$\begin{array}{r} \frac{5}{7} \\ -\frac{2}{7} \\ \hline \end{array}$
$\begin{array}{r} \frac{8}{9} \\ -\frac{4}{9} \\ \hline \end{array}$
$\begin{array}{r} \frac{7}{12} \\ -\frac{1}{12} \\ \hline \end{array}$

To find the difference between two mixed numbers, such as $8\frac{5}{6} - 7\frac{1}{6}$, follow these steps:

Subtract the fractions.	Subtract the whole numbers.	Write the difference in simplest form.
$\begin{array}{r} 8\frac{5}{6} \\ -\ 7\frac{1}{6} \\ \hline \frac{4}{6} \end{array}$	$\begin{array}{r} 8\frac{5}{6} \\ -\ 7\frac{1}{6} \\ \hline 1\frac{4}{6} \end{array}$	$\begin{array}{r} 8\frac{5}{6} \\ -\ 7\frac{1}{6} \\ \hline 1\frac{4}{6} = 1\frac{2}{3} \end{array}$ ← simplest form

Subtract. Write the difference in simplest form.

7.
$\begin{array}{r} 3\frac{7}{8} \\ -\ 2\frac{1}{8} \\ \hline \end{array}$
$\begin{array}{r} 9\frac{7}{10} \\ -\ 6\frac{3}{10} \\ \hline \end{array}$
$\begin{array}{r} 8\frac{4}{5} \\ -\ 7\frac{2}{5} \\ \hline \end{array}$
$\begin{array}{r} 7\frac{11}{12} \\ -\ 4\frac{5}{12} \\ \hline \end{array}$
$\begin{array}{r} 5\frac{6}{7} \\ -\ 3\frac{1}{7} \\ \hline \end{array}$
$\begin{array}{r} 6\frac{1}{2} \\ -\ 2\frac{1}{2} \\ \hline \end{array}$

8. $7\frac{9}{10} - 2\frac{7}{10} = $ _____

$8\frac{4}{5} - 6\frac{4}{5} = $ _____

$2\frac{13}{16} - 1\frac{7}{16} = $ _____

Problem Solving Reasoning Solve.

9. Sam has a board $4\frac{3}{4}$ feet long. He cuts $2\frac{1}{4}$ feet from the board to make a shelf. Will he have enough wood left to make another shelf the same length? Explain. _____

_____

Test Prep ★ Mixed Review

10 Which number is composite?

A 17

B 27

C 37

D 47

11 A whale weighs about 62,400 pounds. A seal weighs about 197 pounds. *About* how many times heavier is the whale?

F 3,000

G 300

H 30

J 3

94   Unit 4 Lesson 5

Copyright © Houghton Mifflin Company. All rights reserved.

Problem Solving Strategy: Draw a Diagram

Sometimes drawing a diagram can help you solve a problem.

When you draw a diagram, you can label it with the information given in the problem.

Problem

A scout group went on a hike. First they walked $\frac{1}{2}$ mile east, then $\frac{3}{4}$ mile south, then 1 mile west, then $\frac{1}{4}$ mile north, then $\frac{1}{2}$ mile east. How far is the scout group from their starting point?

---

❶ Understand   As you reread, ask yourself questions.

- What do you know about the distances walked?

    The scout group walked $\frac{1}{2}$ mile east, $\frac{3}{4}$ mile south, 1 mile west, $\frac{1}{4}$ mile north, $\frac{1}{2}$ mile east.

- What information do you need to find?

    _____

---

❷ Decide   Choose a method for solving. Try the strategy Draw a Diagram.

- Make a diagram, or map, of the distances and directions walked.

---

❸ Solve   Choose the operation for solving.

- What numbers will you use to find the distance between the starting point and where the group stopped hiking? What operation will you use?

    _____

---

❹ Look back   Check your answer. Write your answer below.

Answer: _____

Use the **Draw a Diagram** strategy or any other strategy you have learned.

1. A picture frame containing a photograph is **11** inches wide and **14** inches high. A mat around the photograph is $1\frac{1}{2}$ inches wide on all sides. What are the dimensions of the photograph?

Think: Do you want to add to or subtract from each side?

_____

Answer _____

2. A carpenter used **3** pieces of wood, each $\frac{3}{4}$ inch thick, to make a **2**-shelf bookcase. He spaced the shelves **14** inches apart. What was the height of the bookcase?

Think: How many times do you need to add $\frac{3}{4}$ inch to find the total height?

_____

Answer _____

3. The Jansons, the Klines, the Littles, the Meegans, and the Nelsons all live on the same straight road. The Littles live in the middle house. The Meegans live in the last house. The Jansons live between the Nelsons and the Littles. Who are the Meegans' next-door neighbors?

_____

4. Lisa ordered **3** pizzas for a party. Each had a different topping. There were **8** slices in each pizza. After the party, **2** slices were left in one pie, **3** left in another pie, and none left in the third pie. What fractional part of the pizzas was eaten?

_____

5. A log is **9** feet long. Lee wants to cut it into **4** pieces of equal size. How many cuts must he make?

_____

6. A corral is in the shape of a square. There are **5** fence posts equally spaced on each side of the corral. How many fence posts are there in all?

_____

7. A garden is divided into **3** sections. There are three times as many pepper plants as cucumber plants and twice as many tomato plants as pepper plants. If there are **8** cucumber plants, how many tomato plants are there?

_____

8. Five students compared their heights. Rose was the shortest. Stan was **5** feet tall. Pearl was not the tallest. Tyler was taller than Vincent, but not as tall as Pearl. Who is the tallest?

_____

Name _____

Least Common Multiple, Least Common Denominator

These two fractions have **unlike denominators**.

$$\frac{3}{4} \qquad \frac{1}{6}$$

To add or subtract the fractions, you first need to find a **common denominator**.

1. Find multiples of each denominator.

> The denominator of $\frac{3}{4}$ is **4**.
>
> The denominator of $\frac{1}{6}$ is **6**.

Find multiples of **4** and **6**. Do not list **0**.

Multiples of **4**:
4, 8, 12, 16, 20, 24, . . .

Multiples of **6**:
6, 12, 18, 24, 30, 36, . . .

2. Compare the lists of multiples. Circle the numbers that are the same in both lists. These are **common multiples**.

Multiples of **4**:
4, 8, ⑫ 16, 20, ㉔ . . .

Multiples of **6**:
6, ⑫ 18, ㉔ 30, 36, . . .

12 is the least number in both lists. It is called the **least common multiple (LCM)**.

3. Write equivalent fractions. Use the **LCM** as the **least common denominator (LCD)**.

$$\frac{3 \times 3}{4 \times 3} = \frac{9}{12}$$

$$\frac{1 \times 2}{6 \times 2} = \frac{2}{12}$$

Then add or subtract.

$$\frac{9}{12} + \frac{2}{12} = \frac{11}{12}$$

Write two common multiples of each pair of numbers. Then write the least common multiple.

> Multiples of **4**: **4, 8, 12, 16, 20, 24, 28, 32, 36, 40, 44, 48, 52, 56,** . . .
>
> Multiples of **5**: **5, 10, 15, 20, 25, 30, 35, 40, 45, 50, 55, 60, 65, 70, 75, 80,** . . .
>
> Multiples of **8**: **8, 16, 24, 32, 40, 48, 56, 64, 72, 80, 88, 96, 104,** . . .
>
> Multiples of **10**: **10, 20, 30, 40, 50, 60, 70, 80, 90, 100, 110, 120,** . . .

1. **4** and **5**
Common multiples: _____

Least common multiple: _____

4 and **8**
Common multiples: _____

Least common multiple: _____

2. **4** and **10**
Common multiples: _____

Least common multiple: _____

5 and **8**
Common multiples: _____

Least common multiple: _____

3. **5** and **10**
Common multiples: _____

Least common multiple: _____

8 and **10**
Common multiples: _____

Least common multiple: _____

Find the least common denominator of two mixed numbers the same way you find the least common denominator of two fractions.

Find the **LCD** of $4\frac{1}{5}$ and $2\frac{5}{6}$.

Multiples of **5: 5, 10, 15, 20, 25, (30), 35, . . .**

Multiples of **6: 6, 12, 18, 24, (30), 36, . . .**

The **LCD** of $4\frac{1}{5}$ and $2\frac{5}{6}$ is **30**.

Write multiples of each denominator. Then find the LCD.

4. $2\frac{2}{3}$ _____

  $5\frac{1}{4}$ _____

  LCD _____

5. $1\frac{2}{5}$ _____

  $6\frac{1}{3}$ _____

  LCD _____

6. $4\frac{3}{10}$ _____

  $4\frac{2}{5}$ _____

  LCD _____

Solve.

7. A set of wrenches contains these sizes: $\frac{1}{4}$, $\frac{1}{2}$, $\frac{3}{4}$, and **1** inch. You need wrenches to fit bolts of these sizes: $\frac{1}{8}$, $\frac{2}{8}$, $\frac{3}{8}$, $\frac{4}{8}$, $\frac{5}{8}$, $\frac{6}{8}$, $\frac{7}{8}$, and $\frac{8}{8}$ inch. What size wrenches should you add to the set?

_____

 Quick Check

Write the answer in simplest form.

Work Space

8. $\frac{5}{8} + \frac{2}{8}$

9. $2\frac{7}{10} + \frac{9}{10}$

10. $1\frac{3}{4} + 4\frac{3}{4}$

11. $\begin{array}{r} \frac{7}{8} \\ -\frac{1}{8} \\ \hline \end{array}$

12. $\begin{array}{r} 7\frac{11}{12} \\ -\frac{5}{12} \\ \hline \end{array}$

13. $\begin{array}{r} 3\frac{5}{9} \\ -3\frac{2}{9} \\ \hline \end{array}$

Find the LCD for the fractions or mixed numbers.

14. $\frac{7}{12}$ and $\frac{1}{3}$

15. $1\frac{3}{10}$ and $2\frac{1}{8}$

16. $3\frac{1}{4}$ and $2\frac{2}{5}$

____

____

____

Name _____

Before you can add fractions with **unlike denominators**, you need to write the fractions as equivalent fractions with like denominators.

Find $\frac{3}{4} + \frac{1}{6}$

$\frac{3}{4} = \frac{9}{12}$

$\frac{1}{6} = \frac{2}{12}$

1. Find the least common denominator (LCD) of **4** and **6**.

$$\frac{3}{4} = \frac{}{12}$$
$$+\frac{1}{6} = +\frac{}{12}$$

The LCM of **4** and **6** is **12**.

2. Write equivalent fractions for $\frac{3}{4}$ and $\frac{1}{6}$. Then add.

$$\frac{3}{4} = \frac{9}{12}$$
$$+\frac{1}{6} = \frac{2}{12}$$
$$\overline{\frac{11}{12}}$$

Think: **3 × 4 = 12**. Multiply the numerator by 3.

Think: **2 × 6 = 12**. Multiply the numerator by 2.

Add. Write the sum in simplest form.

1. $\frac{1}{2} = \frac{}{4}$ $\frac{2}{5} = \frac{}{15}$ $\frac{1}{6} = \frac{}{12}$ $\frac{5}{6} = \frac{}{24}$

$+\frac{1}{4} = +\frac{1}{4}$ $+\frac{1}{3} = +\frac{}{15}$ $+\frac{1}{4} = +\frac{}{12}$ $+\frac{1}{8} = +\frac{}{24}$

2. $\frac{2}{3}$ $\frac{1}{10}$ $\frac{1}{9}$ $\frac{4}{5}$

$+\frac{1}{9}$ $+\frac{3}{4}$ $+\frac{5}{6}$ $+\frac{2}{3}$

3. $\frac{2}{3}$ $\frac{1}{2}$ $\frac{3}{5}$ $\frac{3}{10}$

$+\frac{1}{4}$ $+\frac{2}{5}$ $+\frac{1}{4}$ $+\frac{1}{2}$

4. $\frac{1}{6}$ $\frac{5}{12}$ $\frac{3}{10}$ $\frac{3}{5}$

$+\frac{7}{10}$ $+\frac{1}{2}$ $+\frac{5}{8}$ $+\frac{2}{9}$

To find the sum of three fractions,
you follow the same steps.

$$\left(\frac{1}{2} + \frac{1}{3}\right) + \frac{1}{6}$$

1. Find the LCD of **2**, **3**, and **6**.

$$\frac{1}{2} = \frac{}{6}$$
$$\frac{1}{3} = \frac{}{6}$$
$$+\frac{1}{6} = \frac{}{6}$$

The LCM of
2, 3, and **6** is **6**.

2. Write equivalent fractions.
   Add. Write the sum in simplest form.

$$\frac{1}{2} = \frac{3}{6}$$
$$\frac{1}{3} = \frac{2}{6}$$
$$+\frac{1}{6} = \frac{1}{6}$$
$$\frac{6}{6} = 1 \leftarrow \text{simplest form}$$

Write the sum in simplest form.

5. $\left(\frac{1}{8} + \frac{3}{8}\right) + \frac{2}{8} = \underline{\hspace{1cm}}$ $\frac{1}{3} + \left(\frac{2}{3} + \frac{1}{3}\right) = \underline{\hspace{1cm}}$ $\left(\frac{1}{2} + \frac{3}{4}\right) + \frac{1}{8} = \underline{\hspace{1cm}}$

6. $\left(\frac{4}{5} + \frac{2}{5}\right) + \frac{3}{5} = \underline{\hspace{1cm}}$ $\frac{3}{10} + \left(\frac{3}{5} + \frac{1}{2}\right) = \underline{\hspace{1cm}}$ $\frac{2}{3} + \left(\frac{1}{6} + \frac{2}{9}\right) = \underline{\hspace{1cm}}$

Problem Solving
Reasoning   Solve.

7. In the Lincoln School, $\frac{1}{6}$ of the students are on the track
   team and $\frac{1}{4}$ of the students are on the tennis team. No students
   play on both teams. What fraction of the students are on the
   two teams altogether? $\underline{\hspace{1cm}}$

Test Prep ★ Mixed Review

8 Which expression does not have the value
of 6?

A $600 \div (2 + 8)$

B $(6 \div 3) \times 2 + 2$

C $60 \div (2 \times 5)$

D $(6 - 3) + (12 \div 4)$

9 Which two numbers have a product of
about 400?

F 400 and 3

G 320 and 2

H 26 and 15

J 24 and 30

Adding Mixed Numbers with Unlike Denominators

When you add mixed numbers with unlike denominators, you must find a common denominator for the fractions before you add. Write the sum in simplest form.

$$3\frac{1}{4} = 3\frac{2}{8}$$
$$+ 1\frac{3}{8} = 1\frac{3}{8}$$
$$4\frac{5}{8}$$

$$2\frac{3}{4} = 2\frac{6}{8}$$
$$+ 4\frac{5}{8} = 4\frac{5}{8}$$
$$6\frac{11}{8} = 7\frac{3}{8} \leftarrow \text{simplest form}$$

Add. Write the sum in simplest form.

1.
$$6\frac{2}{3}$$
$$+ 4\frac{1}{6}$$

$$2\frac{3}{4}$$
$$+ 1\frac{1}{2}$$

$$5\frac{1}{6}$$
$$+ 3\frac{3}{4}$$

2.
$$5\frac{7}{8}$$
$$+ 7\frac{3}{4}$$

$$6\frac{5}{9}$$
$$+ 5\frac{5}{6}$$

$$6\frac{7}{8}$$
$$+ 7\frac{1}{2}$$

3.
$$16\frac{11}{12}$$
$$+ 7\frac{1}{4}$$

$$3\frac{2}{3}$$
$$+ 2\frac{1}{4}$$

$$2\frac{3}{4}$$
$$+ 1\frac{2}{3}$$

4.
$$8\frac{5}{18}$$
$$+ 5\frac{5}{9}$$

$$14\frac{11}{24}$$
$$+ 9\frac{1}{3}$$

$$1\frac{7}{10}$$
$$+ 6\frac{3}{4}$$

5.
$$9\frac{3}{4}$$
$$+ 8\frac{2}{3}$$

$$5\frac{2}{3}$$
$$+ 6\frac{1}{5}$$

$$6\frac{7}{8}$$
$$+ 3\frac{5}{6}$$

To find the sum of three mixed numbers, follow these steps.

Add $6\frac{1}{2} + 1\frac{3}{4} + 7\frac{2}{3}$

1. Find the LCD.

The LCM of **2**, **4**, and **3** is **12**.

2. Use the LCD and write equivalent fractions.

$\frac{1}{2} = \frac{6}{12} \qquad \frac{3}{4} = \frac{9}{12} \qquad \frac{2}{3} = \frac{8}{12}$

3. Add the fractions.
Then add the whole numbers.
Write your answer in simplest form.

$$6\frac{1}{2} \rightarrow 6\frac{6}{12}$$
$$1\frac{3}{4} \rightarrow 1\frac{9}{12}$$
$$+\,7\frac{2}{3} \rightarrow 7\frac{8}{12}$$
$$\overline{\qquad\qquad 14\frac{23}{12} = 15\frac{11}{12}}$$

Write the sum in simplest form.

6. $1\frac{1}{3} + 1\frac{2}{3} + 5\frac{1}{3} =$ _____

$3\frac{1}{4} + 1\frac{3}{4} + 2\frac{1}{4} =$ _____

7. $2\frac{5}{6} + 4\frac{1}{2} + 1\frac{5}{12} =$ _____

$5\frac{2}{3} + 8\frac{4}{9} + 4\frac{1}{3} =$ _____

8. $9\frac{3}{8} + 2\frac{1}{4} + 6\frac{2}{3} =$ _____

$3\frac{1}{2} + 1\frac{3}{10} + 6\frac{1}{2} =$ _____

Problem Solving Reasoning — **Write the next three numbers in the pattern.**

9. $1,\ 1\frac{3}{4},\ 2\frac{1}{2},\ 3\frac{1}{4},\ 4,$ _____

10. $2\frac{1}{2},\ 2\frac{3}{4},\ 3,\ 3\frac{1}{4},\ 3\frac{1}{2},$ _____

11. $4\frac{5}{8},\ 5\frac{3}{4},\ 6\frac{7}{8},\ 8,\ 9\frac{1}{8},$ _____

12. $3\frac{5}{8},\ 6,\ 8\frac{3}{8},\ 10\frac{3}{4},\ 13\frac{1}{8},$ _____

Test Prep ★ Mixed Review

13 $n - 189 = 215$
What is the value of the variable n?

A 26

B 36

C 404

D 414

14 **Which number is greatest?**

F 4^4

G 3,000

H 3^5

J 20×10^2

Name _____

Before you can subtract fractions with **unlike denominators,** you need to write the fractions as equivalent fractions with like denominators.

Find $\frac{3}{4} - \frac{1}{6}$

$\frac{3}{4} = \frac{9}{12}$

$\frac{1}{6} = \frac{2}{12}$

1. Find the LCD of **4** and **6**.

$\frac{3}{4} = \frac{}{12}$ ←

$-\frac{1}{6} = \frac{}{12}$ ←

The LCM of **4** and **6** is **12**.

2. Write equivalent fractions. Subtract. Simplify if necessary.

$\frac{3}{4} = \frac{9}{12}$

$-\frac{1}{6} = \frac{2}{12}$

$\frac{7}{12}$

Subtract. Write the difference in simplest form.

1.

$\frac{3}{4} = \frac{}{4}$

$-\frac{1}{2} = \frac{}{4}$

$\frac{5}{8} = \frac{}{8}$

$-\frac{1}{4} = \frac{}{8}$

$\frac{3}{4} = \frac{}{16}$

$-\frac{5}{16} = \frac{}{16}$

$\frac{8}{15} = \frac{}{30}$

$-\frac{3}{10} = \frac{}{30}$

2.

$\frac{9}{11}$

$-\frac{1}{2}$

$\frac{1}{3}$

$-\frac{1}{7}$

$\frac{3}{5}$

$-\frac{1}{2}$

$\frac{1}{6}$

$-\frac{1}{15}$

3.

$\frac{4}{5}$

$-\frac{7}{12}$

$\frac{3}{4}$

$-\frac{3}{10}$

$\frac{9}{10}$

$-\frac{1}{4}$

$\frac{3}{8}$

$-\frac{1}{6}$

4.

$\frac{4}{5}$

$-\frac{2}{3}$

$\frac{7}{10}$

$-\frac{1}{5}$

$\frac{3}{4}$

$-\frac{2}{5}$

$\frac{1}{2}$

$-\frac{3}{10}$

Write the sum or difference in simplest form.

5. $\dfrac{2}{8}$ $\dfrac{1}{8}$ $\dfrac{3}{5}$ $\dfrac{4}{9}$

$+\dfrac{1}{4}$ $+\dfrac{5}{12}$ $+\dfrac{3}{20}$ $+\dfrac{3}{10}$

---

6. $\dfrac{5}{12}$ $\dfrac{3}{8}$ $\dfrac{5}{16}$ $\dfrac{5}{8}$

$-\dfrac{1}{3}$ $-\dfrac{1}{5}$ $+\dfrac{1}{4}$ $-\dfrac{1}{2}$

| Problem Solving |
| Reasoning |

Solve.

7. A cook estimates that mixing $4\dfrac{3}{4}$ pounds of flour with

$2\dfrac{7}{8}$ pounds of flour will create about **8** pounds of flour.

Is the cook's estimate reasonable? Explain.

 ## Quick Check

Add. Write the sum in simplest form.

Work Space

8. $\dfrac{2}{8}$ **9.** $\dfrac{5}{16}$ **10.** $\dfrac{2}{3}$

$+\dfrac{5}{12}$ $+\dfrac{1}{4}$ $+\dfrac{1}{6}$

---

11. $2\dfrac{5}{6}$ **12.** $4\dfrac{4}{5}$ **13.** $3\dfrac{6}{8}$

$+3\dfrac{4}{9}$ $+7\dfrac{2}{5}$ $+6\dfrac{1}{2}$

Subtract. Write the difference in simplest form.

14. $\dfrac{1}{4} - \dfrac{1}{6}$ **15.** $\dfrac{4}{5} - \dfrac{1}{2}$ **16.** $\dfrac{4}{8} - \dfrac{1}{6}$

---

104   Unit 4 Lesson 10

Name _____

Subtracting from Whole Numbers

Sometimes when you subtract, you must rename **1** as a fraction.
Here are some different ways to rename **1**.

$$1 = \frac{2}{2} \qquad 1 = \frac{3}{3} \qquad 1 = \frac{4}{4} \qquad 1 = \frac{5}{5} \qquad 1 = \frac{6}{6} \qquad 1 = \frac{7}{7} \qquad 1 = \frac{8}{8}$$

To subtract a fraction or a mixed number from a whole number,
rename the whole number as a mixed number, then subtract.

Find $4 - \frac{1}{6}$.

1. Rename the whole number as a mixed number.

$$\begin{array}{rl} 4 & = 3\frac{6}{6} \\ -\frac{1}{6} & = -\frac{1}{6} \end{array}$$

$$\begin{aligned} 4 &= 3 + 1 \\ &= 3 + \frac{6}{6} \\ &= 3\frac{6}{6} \end{aligned}$$

2. Subtract.

$$\begin{array}{rl} 4 & = 3\frac{6}{6} \\ -\frac{1}{6} & = -\frac{1}{6} \\ \hline & 3\frac{5}{6} \end{array}$$

Subtract. Write the difference in simplest form.

1.

$$\begin{array}{r} 7 \\ -1\frac{3}{4} \\ \hline \end{array} \qquad \begin{array}{r} 3 \\ -1\frac{2}{7} \\ \hline \end{array} \qquad \begin{array}{r} 7 \\ -5\frac{1}{4} \\ \hline \end{array} \qquad \begin{array}{r} 6 \\ -2\frac{1}{2} \\ \hline \end{array}$$

2.

$$\begin{array}{r} 8 \\ -\frac{2}{5} \\ \hline \end{array} \qquad \begin{array}{r} 4 \\ -\frac{1}{6} \\ \hline \end{array} \qquad \begin{array}{r} 1 \\ -\frac{3}{8} \\ \hline \end{array} \qquad \begin{array}{r} 2 \\ -\frac{1}{3} \\ \hline \end{array}$$

3.

$$\begin{array}{r} 10 \\ -4\frac{1}{2} \\ \hline \end{array} \qquad \begin{array}{r} 9 \\ -1\frac{4}{7} \\ \hline \end{array} \qquad \begin{array}{r} 6 \\ -5\frac{1}{3} \\ \hline \end{array} \qquad \begin{array}{r} 4 \\ -1\frac{7}{9} \\ \hline \end{array}$$

4.

$$\begin{array}{r} 3 \\ -\frac{1}{6} \\ \hline \end{array} \qquad \begin{array}{r} 6 \\ -\frac{2}{8} \\ \hline \end{array} \qquad \begin{array}{r} 8 \\ -\frac{2}{5} \\ \hline \end{array} \qquad \begin{array}{r} 7 \\ -\frac{4}{10} \\ \hline \end{array}$$

Copyright © Houghton Mifflin Company. All rights reserved.

Unit 4 Lesson 11 **105**

Add or subtract. Write the sum or difference in simplest form.

5.

$6\frac{3}{4}$
$- 1$
_____

8
$- 5\frac{2}{3}$
_____

$7\frac{3}{5}$
$+ 5$
_____

6.

$6\frac{5}{7}$
$- \frac{3}{7}$
_____

$8\frac{3}{4}$
$+ 7$
_____

5
$- 2\frac{5}{6}$
_____

7.

7
$- 3\frac{2}{3}$
_____

$4\frac{5}{8}$
$+ 4$
_____

9
$- 5\frac{7}{8}$
_____

Problem Solving Reasoning Solve.

8. What number must be subtracted from **9** to have a difference of **$4\frac{5}{9}$**? _____

9. What number can be added to **$3\frac{2}{3}$** to have a sum of about **$4\frac{1}{2}$**? _____

10. What number must be added to **$3\frac{1}{2}$** to have a sum of **7**? _____

11. What number can be added to **$5\frac{3}{8}$** to get about **$9\frac{1}{2}$**? _____

Test Prep ★ Mixed Review

12 There are approximately 3500 seats in the community theater. The 12 sections are the same size. About how many seats are in each section?

A 200

B 250

C 275

D 300

13 What is the value of the expression $5^2 - (72 - 6 \times 9)$?

F 594

G 25

H 7

J 5

Name _____

Subtracting Mixed Numbers with Renaming

Sometimes, you need to rename when you subtract mixed numbers.

Find $3\frac{1}{4} - 1\frac{2}{4}$

1. Rename $3\frac{1}{4}$.

$$3\frac{1}{4} = 3 + \frac{1}{4}$$
$$= 2 + 1 + \frac{1}{4}$$
$$= 2 + \left(\frac{4}{4} + \frac{1}{4}\right)$$
$$= 2 + \frac{5}{4}$$

2. Subtract the fractions.

$$3\frac{1}{4} = 2\frac{5}{4}$$
$$- 1\frac{3}{4} = 1\frac{3}{4}$$
$$\overline{\frac{2}{4}}$$

3. Subtract the whole numbers. Simplify.

$$3\frac{1}{4} = 2\frac{5}{4}$$
$$- 1\frac{3}{4} = 1\frac{3}{4}$$
$$\overline{1\frac{2}{4} = 1\frac{1}{2}}$$

Rename the mixed number.

1. $5\frac{5}{6} = 4\frac{}{6}$ $\qquad$ $8\frac{5}{7} = 7\frac{}{7}$ $\qquad$ $6\frac{5}{12} = 5\frac{}{12}$ $\qquad$ $9\frac{5}{6} = 8\frac{}{6}$

2. $6\frac{2}{5} = 5\frac{}{5}$ $\qquad$ $5\frac{2}{9} = 4\frac{}{9}$ $\qquad$ $6\frac{2}{8} = 5\frac{}{8}$ $\qquad$ $2\frac{4}{5} = 1\frac{}{5}$

3. $2\frac{4}{9} = $ _____ $\qquad$ $3\frac{5}{8} = $ _____ $\qquad$ $4\frac{1}{4} = $ _____ $\qquad$ $3\frac{4}{5} = $ _____

Subtract. Write the difference in simplest form.

4.
$$3\frac{1}{8}$$
$$- 1\frac{5}{8}$$
$\qquad$
$$6\frac{2}{9}$$
$$- 3\frac{7}{9}$$
$\qquad$
$$5\frac{4}{7}$$
$$- 2\frac{6}{7}$$
$\qquad$
$$6\frac{1}{3}$$
$$- 1\frac{2}{3}$$

5.
$$8\frac{3}{5}$$
$$- 4\frac{4}{5}$$
$\qquad$
$$6\frac{3}{9}$$
$$- 2\frac{5}{9}$$
$\qquad$
$$7\frac{1}{8}$$
$$- 2\frac{5}{8}$$
$\qquad$
$$5\frac{1}{7}$$
$$- 1\frac{4}{7}$$

6.
$$4\frac{1}{4}$$
$$- 2\frac{3}{4}$$
$\qquad$
$$6\frac{1}{5}$$
$$- 1\frac{4}{5}$$
$\qquad$
$$3\frac{1}{3}$$
$$- 1\frac{2}{3}$$
$\qquad$
$$4\frac{1}{9}$$
$$- 1\frac{4}{9}$$

Subtract. Write the difference in simplest form.

7.
$$4\frac{3}{8}$$
$$-1\frac{5}{8}$$
_____

$$8\frac{1}{6}$$
$$-3\frac{5}{6}$$
_____

$$7\frac{1}{3}$$
$$-2\frac{2}{3}$$
_____

$$10\frac{4}{5}$$
$$-4\frac{3}{5}$$
_____

8.
$$9\frac{3}{10}$$
$$-3\frac{7}{10}$$
_____

$$6\frac{1}{2}$$
$$-1\frac{1}{2}$$
_____

$$6\frac{1}{8}$$
$$-4\frac{3}{8}$$
_____

$$3\frac{1}{10}$$
$$-2\frac{3}{10}$$
_____

Problem Solving Reasoning — Solve.

9. On Saturday Jamie rode her bike $2\frac{7}{10}$ miles from her house to soccer practice. After riding $1\frac{9}{10}$ miles on the way back home, she got a flat tire. How far was Jamie from her house when she got the flat tire? _____

10. How far had Jamie ridden altogether on Saturday before she got the flat tire? _____

11. Jamie's tire was fixed and she rode back home. How far did she ride in all on Saturday? _____

Test Prep ★ Mixed Review

12. At a farm stand, Tanya bought $1\frac{1}{16}$ lb of snow peas, $2\frac{1}{4}$ lb of potatoes, $4\frac{1}{16}$ lb of broccoli, and $2\frac{3}{4}$ lb of carrots. Which two vegetables together weigh about 7 lb?

A snow peas and potatoes

B broccoli and carrots

C snow peas and broccoli

D potatoes and carrots

13. What is the prime factorization of 54 in exponent form?

F $2 \times 3 \times 9$

G 2×3^3

H $2^3 \times 3$

J 2×3^2

Name _____

When you subtract mixed numbers with unlike denominators, you must find a common denominator for the fractions before you subtract.

The LCM of **6** and **3** is **6**.

$$4\frac{5}{6} = 4\frac{5}{6}$$
$$-1\frac{2}{3} = 1\frac{4}{6}$$
$$\overline{\hspace{1.5cm}3\frac{1}{6}}$$

$$9\frac{1}{6} = \quad 9\frac{1}{6} \rightarrow \quad 8\frac{7}{6}$$
$$-1\frac{2}{3} = -1\frac{4}{6} \rightarrow -1\frac{4}{6}$$
$$\overline{\hspace{3cm}7\frac{3}{6} = 7\frac{1}{2}} \leftarrow \text{simplest form}$$

Not enough to subtract. So, rename the whole number. $9 = 8\frac{6}{6}$

$$9\frac{1}{6} = 8\frac{7}{6}$$

Subtract. Write the difference in simplest form.

1.
$$7\frac{1}{4}$$
$$-2\frac{5}{6}$$

$$8\frac{1}{2}$$
$$-1\frac{2}{3}$$

$$9\frac{1}{4}$$
$$-5\frac{1}{2}$$

2.
$$6\frac{1}{3}$$
$$-5\frac{4}{6}$$

$$10\frac{1}{2}$$
$$-2\frac{4}{5}$$

$$12\frac{2}{3}$$
$$-6\frac{3}{4}$$

3.
$$5\frac{1}{2}$$
$$-3\frac{3}{4}$$

$$15\frac{1}{8}$$
$$-7\frac{3}{4}$$

$$9\frac{2}{3}$$
$$-2\frac{5}{6}$$

4.
$$10\frac{1}{2}$$
$$-4\frac{7}{8}$$

$$11\frac{1}{4}$$
$$-6\frac{5}{8}$$

$$12\frac{1}{3}$$
$$-4\frac{2}{3}$$

Circle the expression that has the greater difference.

5. $4\frac{1}{3} - 2\frac{1}{6}$ or $4\frac{1}{3} - 2\frac{1}{2}$ $\qquad$ $5\frac{2}{5} - 4\frac{1}{2}$ or $5\frac{2}{3} - 4\frac{1}{2}$

6. $3\frac{7}{8} - 3\frac{1}{8}$ or $3\frac{3}{4} - 3\frac{1}{8}$ $\qquad$ $8\frac{1}{4} - 3\frac{3}{5}$ or $8\frac{1}{4} - 3\frac{3}{4}$

Subtract. Write the difference in simplest form.

7. $4\frac{1}{2}$ $10\frac{3}{4}$ $6\frac{2}{5}$

     $-1\frac{5}{6}$ $-5\frac{1}{6}$ $-2\frac{5}{6}$

8. $5\frac{3}{4}$ $2\frac{1}{4}$ $9\frac{3}{4}$

     $-2\frac{1}{3}$ $-1\frac{5}{8}$ $-3\frac{5}{6}$

Problem Solving Reasoning   Solve.

9. Anna has $3\frac{1}{4}$ yd of fabric. She plans to use $2\frac{1}{2}$ yd for curtains. Does she have enough left to make 2 pillows that each use $\frac{5}{8}$ yd of fabric? Explain.

 Quick Check

Subtract. Write the difference in simplest form.

Work Space

10. 4 **11.** 7 **12.** 8

     $-3\frac{6}{7}$ $-5\frac{5}{8}$ $-4\frac{1}{4}$

13. $4\frac{7}{12}$ **14.** $8\frac{1}{5}$ **15.** $10\frac{3}{8}$

     $-3\frac{11}{12}$ $-2\frac{4}{5}$ $-5\frac{7}{8}$

16. $3\frac{2}{5}$ **17.** $15\frac{1}{3}$ **18.** $12\frac{2}{8}$

     $-1\frac{1}{4}$ $-2\frac{5}{6}$ $-7\frac{5}{12}$

Name _____

Sometimes it is helpful to use a diagram such as a number line to solve problems.

In this lesson, you will use a number line to help you solve problems involving the comparison, addition, and subtraction of whole numbers, fractions, and mixed numbers.

Tips to Remember

1. Understand	2. Decide	3. Solve	4. Look back

- Ask yourself whether you have solved a problem like this before.
- When you can, make predictions about the answer. Then compare your answer and your prediction.
- When solving the problems, use the number lines to help you find equivalent fractions.
- Check your answer by doing the actual computation.

Solve. Use the number lines.

1. Mario and his friends ordered **3** pizzas. Each pizza was sliced into **8** pieces. They ate **21** slices. How much pizza did they eat? Write your answer as a mixed number.

   Think: Which number line will you use? Between which two whole numbers is $\frac{21}{8}$?

   _____

   Answer _____

2. Alana walked $\frac{3}{4}$ mile to the library. Later she walked $\frac{7}{8}$ mile to the ice cream store. How far did she walk in all?

   Think: Which fraction is equivalent to $\frac{3}{4}$? Is the distance walked greater than **1** mile?

   _____

   _____

   Answer _____

Solve. Use the number lines.

3. Tamika sliced an apple into **8** equal pieces and ate **6** of them. Mary sliced an apple into **4** equal pieces. Mary and Tamika ate the same amount. How many pieces did Mary eat?

_____

4. Shira, Tess, and Uri wanted to see who could run the farthest in ten minutes. Shira ran $\frac{5}{8}$ mile, Tess ran $\frac{5}{6}$ mile, and Uri ran $\frac{3}{4}$ mile. Who ran the farthest?

_____

5. A cake recipe calls for a total of **3** cups of flour. The baker has already included $1\frac{1}{3}$ cups. How many more cups of flour must be added?

_____

6. A math book is $\frac{3}{4}$ inch thick. A social studies book is $1\frac{1}{2}$ inches thick. Will these books fit one on top of the other in a space that is **2** inches high?

_____

7. Look back at problem 4. Explain how you arrived at your answer. Who ran the second farthest? Who ran the least distance?

_____

_____

_____

8. Look back at problem 5. Explain the method you used to solve the problem. Tell which number line you used. What operations did you use to find the answer?

_____

_____

_____

Use multiplication to write three equivalent fractions.

1. $\dfrac{2}{3}$ _____, _____, _____

2. $\dfrac{24}{48}$ _____, _____, _____

Write each mixed number as a fraction and each fraction as a mixed number.

3. $1\dfrac{2}{3} =$ _____

4. $2\dfrac{4}{5} =$ _____

5. $\dfrac{11}{8} =$ _____

6. $\dfrac{20}{9} =$ _____

Write each fraction or mixed number in simplest form.

7. $\dfrac{8}{32} =$ _____

8. $\dfrac{12}{15} =$ _____

9. $2\dfrac{9}{18} =$ _____

10. $4\dfrac{24}{40} =$ _____

Add or subtract. Write each answer in simplest form.

11. $\dfrac{3}{5} + \dfrac{1}{5}$

12. $\dfrac{5}{8} - \dfrac{4}{8}$

13. $1\dfrac{3}{4} + \dfrac{1}{4}$

14. $2\dfrac{9}{10} - 1\dfrac{3}{10}$

15. $\dfrac{1}{4} + \dfrac{3}{8}$

16. $\dfrac{9}{10} - \dfrac{3}{5}$

17. $2\dfrac{5}{8} + 3\dfrac{1}{12}$

18. $5\dfrac{1}{2} - 4\dfrac{1}{3}$

19. $6 - \dfrac{3}{5}$

20. $8 - \dfrac{5}{8}$

21. $5 + 3\dfrac{5}{9}$

22. $4\dfrac{1}{8} + 1$

On another sheet of paper, draw a number line to represent a 12-mile race. Then use the number line to solve each problem.

23. Tina stopped for water after $4\dfrac{3}{4}$ miles. How far was she from the finish? _____

24. Benny stopped for water after running $10\dfrac{1}{2}$ miles. How far was Benny from the finish? _____

1 Which picture shows another name for $\frac{2}{3}$?

A

B

C

D

2 What is the cost of buying 1 ear of corn?

F 40¢   H 25¢

G 30¢   J 15¢

Use these spools to answer questions 3 and 4.

Red   Blue   White

$2\frac{1}{4}$ yd $1\frac{7}{8}$ yd $2\frac{1}{2}$ yd

3 Which list shows the spools of ribbon in greatest to least order?

A red, blue, white

B red, white, blue

C white, blue, red

D white, red, blue

4 About how much ribbon is there altogether?

F Between 6 yards and 7 yards

G Between 5 yards and 6 yards

H Between 4 yards and 5 yards

J Fewer than 4 yards

5 A recipe calls for 6 pounds of potatoes to make 12 servings of potato salad? How many pounds of potatoes are needed to make 60 servings?

A 17 pounds   C 30 pounds   E Not here

B 20 pounds   D 32 pounds

6 What is the value of the variable n?
$4 \times (2 \times 9) = (4 \times n) \times 9$

F 72   H 9   K 2

G 36   J 4

7 Which statement is true about the numbers 5 and 35?

A Their GCF is 105.

B One is a prime factor of the other

C Both are prime numbers

D Both are composite numbers.

E Both are even numbers.

8 The number of people who came to the hockey game does not round to 30,000 to the nearest ten thousand. How many people came to the hockey game?

F 24,956   H 26,459   K 29,456

G 25,496   J 26,945

9 You write two numbers on a piece of paper. Their difference is 2,416. One of the numbers is 5,482. What could the other number be?

A 2,982   C 7,599   E 7,898

B 2,066   D 7,808

10 You buy a dozen rolls that cost $.25 each and 4 bagels that cost $.45 each. Which expression below shows your total cost?

F ($.25) + 4 × $.45

G (12 × $.25) × (4 + $.45)

H (12 × $.25) + (4 × $.45)

J (12 × $25) + (4 × $45)

K Not here

UNIT 5 • TABLE OF CONTENTS

Multiplication and Division of Fractions and Mixed Numbers

We will be using this vocabulary:

reciprocals two numbers whose product is **1**

pictograph a graph in which pictorial symbols are used to represent multiples of a number

bar graph a representation of numbers or numerical facts that uses lengths of bars to show information

Dear Family,

During the next few weeks, our math class will be learning and practicing the multiplication and division of fractions and mixed numbers.

You can expect to see homework that provides practice with multiplying whole numbers and fractions. Here is a sample you may want to keep handy to give help if needed.

Multiplying Whole Numbers and Fractions

Example: Find $8 \times \dfrac{3}{4}$.

To multiply a whole number and a fraction, first write the whole number as a fraction. To write a whole number as a fraction, write it over **1**.

$$8 \times \frac{3}{4} = \frac{8}{1} \times \frac{3}{4}$$

Then multiply the numerators and multiply the denominators.

$$\frac{8}{1} \times \frac{3}{4} = \frac{24}{4}$$

When working with fractions, write the answer in simplest form. One way to write a fraction in simplest form is to divide. Find the greatest common factor and divide both the numerator and the denominator by it.

$$\frac{24 \div 4}{4 \div 4} = \frac{6}{1} = 6$$

During this unit, students will need to continue practicing multiplication and division facts.

Sincerely,

Name _____

Multiplying Whole Numbers and Fractions

You can write a division equation to show **6** apples separated into **2** groups with **3** apples in each group.

$$6 \div 2 = 3$$

Each of the **2** groups has $\frac{1}{2}$ of the total number of apples. You can write a multiplication sentence to show this.

$$\frac{1}{2} \times 6 = 3$$

Here is how you multiply a whole number and a fraction:

1. Write the whole number as a fraction. Multiply the numerators.

$$\frac{4}{1} \times \frac{2}{5} = \frac{4 \times 2}{?}$$

2. Multiply the denominators.

$$\frac{4}{1} \times \frac{2}{5} = \frac{4 \times 2}{5}$$
$$= \frac{8}{5}$$

3. Write your answer in simplest form.

$$\frac{4}{1} \times \frac{2}{5} = \frac{4 \times 2}{5}$$
$$= \frac{8}{5} \text{ or } 1\frac{3}{5}$$

Multiply. Write each product in simplest form.

1. $\frac{1}{2} \times 8 =$ _____ $\frac{1}{4} \times 12 =$ _____ $6 \times \frac{2}{3} =$ _____

2. $\frac{1}{6} \times 18 =$ _____ $\frac{1}{5} \times 10 =$ _____ $\frac{3}{8} \times 9 =$ _____

3. $\frac{1}{3} \times 15 =$ _____ $20 \times \frac{1}{4} =$ _____ $11 \times \frac{1}{3} =$ _____

4. $\frac{3}{4} \times 8 =$ _____ $14 \times \frac{5}{7} =$ _____ $\frac{2}{5} \times 25 =$ _____

5. $3 \times \frac{4}{7} =$ _____ $\frac{2}{9} \times 4 =$ _____ $\frac{1}{4} \times 24 =$ _____

Multiply. Write each product in simplest form.

6. $5 \times \dfrac{3}{5} =$ _____ 　　　$8 \times \dfrac{1}{6} =$ _____ 　　　$\dfrac{2}{5} \times 13 =$ _____

7. $\dfrac{1}{4} \times 16 =$ _____ 　　　$\dfrac{5}{8} \times 4 =$ _____ 　　　$24 \times \dfrac{1}{12} =$ _____

8. $6 \times \dfrac{3}{4} =$ _____ 　　　$\dfrac{1}{6} \times 20 =$ _____ 　　　$42 \times \dfrac{1}{4} =$ _____

9. $10 \times \dfrac{3}{5} =$ _____ 　　　$3 \times \dfrac{8}{9} =$ _____ 　　　$\dfrac{1}{8} \times 12 =$ _____

10. $\dfrac{1}{3} \times 17 =$ _____ 　　　$\dfrac{3}{4} \times 5 =$ _____ 　　　$2 \times \dfrac{3}{10} =$ _____

11. $4 \times \dfrac{4}{5} =$ _____ 　　　$\dfrac{7}{8} \times 6 =$ _____ 　　　$4 \times \dfrac{3}{16} =$ _____

Problem Solving Reasoning | Solve.

12. Jake spent a $\dfrac{1}{2}$ hour doing homework. Rosa spent **35** minutes doing homework. Who spent more time doing homework?

Explain. _____

_____

_____

13. The first quarter of a football game lasted **45** minutes. The second quarter lasted $\dfrac{3}{5}$ of an hour. Which quarter took less time?

Explain. _____

_____

_____

_____

14. Latrice enjoys sewing and has $1\dfrac{1}{3}$ yards of fabric. If she uses $\dfrac{2}{3}$ of the fabric to make a pillow, how much fabric will she use?

Explain. _____

_____

_____

_____

Test Prep ★ Mixed Review

15 A shop printed 8^3 posters. What is 8^3 equivalent to?

 A 24

 B 64

 C 512

 D 1,000

16 A small car travels 32 miles on a gallon of gas. *About* how much gas will the car use on a trip of 232 miles?

 F less than 15 gallons

 G between 15 and 20 gallons

 H between 25 and 30 gallons

 J more than 30 gallons

Modeling Multiplication of Fractions

Suppose you ate $\frac{3}{4}$ of $\frac{1}{2}$ of a pan of corn bread.

You actually ate $\frac{3}{8}$ of the whole pan of corn bread.

$$\frac{3}{4} \text{ of } \frac{1}{2} = \frac{3}{8}$$

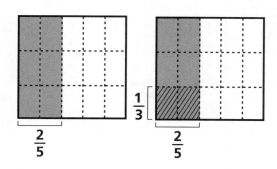

$\frac{1}{3}$

$\frac{2}{5}$ $\frac{2}{5}$

Suppose you cut another whole pan of corn bread into **15** pieces as shown in the model on the left.

What is $\frac{1}{3}$ of $\frac{2}{5}$ of the corn bread?

$$\frac{1}{3} \text{ of } \frac{2}{5} = \frac{2}{15}$$

Finding a fraction of a fraction is the same as multiplying a fraction by a fraction.

Here's how to multiply $\frac{3}{4} \times \frac{1}{2}$.

1. Multiply the numerators to find the numerator of the product.

2. Multiply the denominators to find the denominator of the product.

$$\frac{3}{4} \text{ of } \frac{1}{2} = \frac{3}{4} \times \frac{1}{2}$$

$$\frac{3}{4} \times \frac{1}{2} = \frac{3}{?}$$

$$\frac{3}{4} \times \frac{1}{2} = \frac{3}{8}$$

Multiply. Use the model to check your answer.

1.

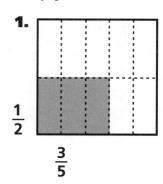

$\frac{1}{2}$

$\frac{3}{5}$

$$\frac{1}{2} \times \frac{3}{5} = \underline{\hspace{1cm}}$$

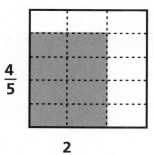

$\frac{4}{5}$

$\frac{2}{3}$

$$\frac{4}{5} \times \frac{2}{3} = \underline{\hspace{1cm}}$$

Multiply. Use the model to check your answer.

2. $\dfrac{1}{2} \times \dfrac{1}{3} =$ _____

  $\dfrac{2}{3} \times \dfrac{2}{5} =$ _____

3. $\dfrac{1}{3} \times \dfrac{1}{4} =$ _____

  $\dfrac{2}{3} \times \dfrac{2}{3} =$ _____

4. $\dfrac{1}{2} \times \dfrac{3}{4} =$ _____

  $\dfrac{3}{4} \times \dfrac{3}{4} =$ _____

5. $\dfrac{2}{5} \times \dfrac{1}{3} =$ _____

  $\dfrac{1}{3} \times \dfrac{1}{3} =$ _____

6. $\dfrac{1}{4} \times \dfrac{3}{4} =$ _____

 $\dfrac{3}{5} \times \dfrac{1}{2} =$ _____

| Problem Solving |
| Reasoning |

Solve.

7. When you multiply two whole numbers the product is equal to or greater than either of the factors. Is this true or false? Explain with examples.

_____

_____

8. When you multiply two fractions, is the product greater than or less than either of the factors. Give an example.

_____

_____

Test Prep ★ Mixed Review

9 Which number makes the equation true?
$31 - n = 26$

A 2

B 3

C 4

D 5

10 Which number completes the table?

n	3	40	500
$n \times 500$	1,500	20,000	?

F 2,500

G 25,000

H 250,000

J 2,500,000

Name _____

Remember, to multiply fractions:

1. Multiply the numerators to find the numerator of the product.

2. Multiply the denominators to find the denominator of the product.

3. Write your answer in simplest form.

$\frac{5}{6} \times \frac{3}{4} = \frac{15}{24}$ or $\frac{5}{8}$ ← simplest form $\frac{7}{8} \times \frac{4}{3} = \frac{28}{24}$ or $1\frac{1}{6}$ ← simplest form

---

Multiply.

1. $\frac{5}{8} \times \frac{3}{4} =$ _____ $\frac{2}{9} \times \frac{4}{3} =$ _____ $\frac{7}{6} \times \frac{1}{4} =$ _____

2. $\frac{2}{3} \times \frac{5}{7} =$ _____ $\frac{1}{10} \times \frac{1}{2} =$ _____ $\frac{3}{5} \times \frac{7}{5} =$ _____

Multiply. Write each product in simplest form.

3. $\frac{2}{3} \times \frac{7}{8} =$ _____ $\frac{4}{9} \times \frac{1}{2} =$ _____ $\frac{6}{7} \times \frac{3}{4} =$ _____

4. $\frac{5}{6} \times \frac{2}{3} =$ _____ $\frac{2}{7} \times \frac{1}{3} =$ _____ $\frac{1}{9} \times \frac{3}{7} =$ _____

5. $\frac{3}{5} \times \frac{1}{2} =$ _____ $\frac{4}{7} \times \frac{3}{4} =$ _____ $\frac{8}{9} \times \frac{5}{8} =$ _____

6. $\frac{4}{5} \times \frac{2}{9} =$ _____ $\frac{8}{9} \times \frac{3}{4} =$ _____ $\frac{1}{9} \times \frac{1}{8} =$ _____

7. $\frac{1}{3} \times \frac{8}{9} =$ _____ $\frac{2}{3} \times \frac{7}{9} =$ _____ $\frac{3}{4} \times \frac{2}{5} =$ _____

8. $\frac{4}{5} \times \frac{7}{8} =$ _____ $\frac{3}{4} \times \frac{6}{7} =$ _____ $\frac{7}{8} \times \frac{2}{9} =$ _____

9. $\frac{3}{4} \times \frac{2}{3} =$ _____ $\frac{4}{9} \times \frac{2}{7} =$ _____ $\frac{1}{9} \times \frac{1}{4} =$ _____

Multiply. Write each product in simplest form.

10. $\frac{3}{5} \times 5 =$ _____ $6 \times \frac{2}{3} =$ _____ $\frac{1}{4} \times 10 =$ _____

11. $\frac{1}{6} \times \frac{9}{5} =$ _____ $\frac{6}{5} \times \frac{5}{3} =$ _____ $\frac{5}{8} \times \frac{1}{5} =$ _____

12. $\frac{3}{4} \times \frac{3}{4} =$ _____ $\frac{5}{3} \times \frac{9}{10} =$ _____ $3 \times \frac{3}{2} =$ _____

Problem Solving
Reasoning Solve.

13. Joseph and his friends baked 48 cookies. They ate $\frac{1}{6}$ of them. How many cookies did Joseph and his friends eat? _____

14. Lisa lives $\frac{3}{5}$ mile from school. She walks $\frac{1}{2}$ of this distance to get to the bus stop. How far is it from her home to the bus stop? _____

 ## Quick Check

Multiply. Write the answer in simplest form.

15. $\frac{1}{2} \times 5$ **16.** $\frac{2}{3} \times 4$ **17.** $6 \times \frac{3}{4}$

_____   _____   _____

Use the picture. Multiply.

18.   **19.**   **20.**

$\frac{2}{5} \times \frac{2}{3}$ $\frac{1}{2} \times \frac{1}{3}$ $\frac{2}{3} \times \frac{1}{8}$

_____   _____   _____

Multiply. Write the answer in simplest form.

21. $\frac{1}{3} \times \frac{1}{4}$ **22.** $\frac{6}{8} \times \frac{2}{3}$ **23.** $\frac{3}{8} \times \frac{8}{9}$

_____   _____   _____

Here is how you can multiply with a mixed number. Write any mixed numbers or whole numbers as fractions. Then multiply the fractions.

$$6 \times 1\frac{1}{2} = \frac{6}{1} \times \frac{3}{2}$$

$$= \frac{18}{2} \text{ or } 9$$

Here is another way to multiply fractions and mixed numbers:

1. Divide any numerator and any denominator by their GCF.

2. Multiply.

3. Then simplify if possible.

$$6 \times 1\frac{1}{2} = \frac{\overset{3}{\cancel{6}}}{1} \times \frac{3}{\underset{1}{\cancel{2}}}$$

$$= \frac{9}{1} \text{ or } 9$$

The GCF of **6** and **2** is **2**.
$6 \div 2 = 3$ and $2 \div 2 = 1$.

$$\frac{3}{8} \times 1\frac{5}{9} = \frac{\overset{1}{\cancel{3}}}{\underset{4}{\cancel{8}}} \times \frac{\overset{7}{\cancel{14}}}{\underset{3}{\cancel{9}}}$$

$$= \frac{7}{12}$$

The GCF of **3** and **9** is **3**.
$3 \div 3 = 1$ and $9 \div 3 = 3$.
The GCF of **14** and **8** is **2**.
$14 \div 2 = 7$ and $8 \div 2 = 4$.

Write the mixed number as a fraction.

1. $3\frac{5}{9} =$ _____ $2\frac{3}{20} =$ _____ $5\frac{1}{4} =$ _____ $2\frac{5}{12} =$ _____ $2\frac{1}{14} =$ _____

Multiply. Write the product in simplest form.

2. $3 \times 3\frac{5}{9} =$ _____ $5\frac{1}{4} \times 8 =$ _____ $1\frac{1}{2} \times 3 =$ _____

3. $\frac{7}{8} \times \frac{8}{7} =$ _____ $5\frac{1}{2} \times \frac{1}{4} =$ _____ $4\frac{2}{3} \times \frac{1}{10} =$ _____

4. $5 \times 2\frac{3}{20} =$ _____ $2\frac{5}{12} \times 6 =$ _____ $5 \times 1\frac{3}{4} =$ _____

5. $\frac{2}{5} \times 2\frac{1}{2} =$ _____ $3\frac{1}{9} \times \frac{4}{7} =$ _____ $2 \times 2\frac{3}{8} =$ _____

Multiply. Write each product in simplest form.

6. $7 \times 2\frac{3}{21} =$ _____ $5\frac{1}{4} \times \frac{1}{2} =$ _____ $\frac{1}{3} \times 2\frac{1}{6} =$ _____

7. $2\frac{2}{3} \times \frac{3}{4} =$ _____ $3\frac{1}{5} \times \frac{3}{4} =$ _____ $10\frac{1}{2} \times 1\frac{1}{2} =$ _____

8. $6\frac{1}{5} \times \frac{5}{6} =$ _____ $\frac{2}{5} \times 6\frac{1}{4} =$ _____ $4 \times 3\frac{1}{8} =$ _____

9. $5\frac{3}{8} \times 4 =$ _____ $6\frac{3}{4} \times \frac{4}{5} =$ _____ $6\frac{2}{5} \times 5 =$ _____

10. $\frac{1}{5} \times 3\frac{1}{3} =$ _____ $7\frac{3}{4} \times \frac{3}{10} =$ _____ $2 \times 9\frac{5}{6} =$ _____

| Problem Solving |
| Reasoning |

Use the recipe to solve the problems.

11. Write the amount of the ingredients you would need to make **3** dozen muffins.

_____

_____

_____

_____

Muffins
Makes 1 dozen muffins

$1\frac{3}{4}$ cups flour

$\frac{1}{3}$ cup sugar

2 teaspoons baking powder

1 egg

$\frac{3}{4}$ cup milk

$1\frac{1}{4}$ cup cooking oil

$\frac{3}{4}$ cup blueberries

12. How much flour would you need to make $1\frac{1}{2}$ dozen muffins?

_____

Test Prep ★ Mixed Review

13 Which expression shows the prime factorization of 60?

A $2^2 \times 3 \times 5$

B $2 \times 3 \times 5^2$

C 6×10

D $1 \times 2 \times 3 \times 4 \times 5$

14 You are at the post office. The bank is $\frac{3}{4}$ mile away. The cleaner is $\frac{2}{3}$ mile away. How much closer are you to the cleaner than to the bank?

F $1\frac{5}{12}$ mile   **H** $\frac{1}{6}$ mile

G $\frac{5}{7}$ mile   **J** $\frac{1}{12}$ mile

Name _____

Fractions and Properties

The properties of addition and multiplication can help you find sums and products of fractions. Look at the examples below.

Addition Properties	Multiplication Properties
The Commutative Property	**The Commutative Property**
When the order of the addends is changed, the sum remains the same. $\frac{3}{8} + \frac{5}{8} = \frac{5}{8} + \frac{3}{8}$	When the order of the factors is changed, the product remains the same. $\frac{3}{8} \times \frac{5}{8} = \frac{5}{8} \times \frac{3}{8}$
The Associative Property	**The Associative Property**
When the grouping of the addends is changed, the sum remains the same. $\left(\frac{1}{5} + \frac{1}{4}\right) + \frac{1}{2} = \frac{1}{5} + \left(\frac{1}{4} + \frac{1}{2}\right)$	When the grouping of the factors is changed, the product remains the same. $\left(\frac{1}{5} \times \frac{1}{4}\right) \times \frac{1}{2} = \frac{1}{5} \times \left(\frac{1}{4} \times \frac{1}{2}\right)$
The Adding Zero Property	**The Multiplying by One Property**
When you add 0 to any number, the sum is that number. $\frac{1}{2} + 0 = \frac{1}{2}$ $\qquad$ $0 + 1\frac{1}{4} = 1\frac{1}{4}$	When you multiply any number by 1, the product is that number. $\frac{1}{2} \times 1 = \frac{1}{2}$ $\qquad$ $1 \times 2\frac{1}{6} = 2\frac{1}{6}$

Complete the equation. Then circle *C*, *A*, or *Z* to tell which property of addition is being shown. (You may circle more than one letter.)

1. $\left(\frac{2}{3} + \frac{1}{6}\right) + \frac{5}{6} = \frac{2}{3} + \left(\underline{\hspace{1cm}} + \frac{5}{6}\right)$ *C A Z* $\qquad$ $1\frac{2}{5} + \underline{\hspace{1cm}} = 1\frac{2}{5}$ *C A Z*

2. $\frac{5}{8} + \frac{1}{4} = \underline{\hspace{1cm}} + \frac{5}{8}$ *C A Z* $\qquad$ $1\frac{1}{4} + \left(\frac{1}{8} + \frac{3}{4}\right) = \left(1\frac{1}{4} + \underline{\hspace{1cm}}\right) + \frac{1}{8}$ *C A Z*

Complete the equation. Then circle *C*, *A*, or *O* to tell which property of multiplication is being shown. (You may circle more than one letter.)

3. $\frac{1}{3} \times \frac{1}{2} = \frac{1}{2} \times \underline{\hspace{1cm}}$ *C A O* $\qquad$ $2 \times \left(1\frac{1}{2} \times \frac{5}{8}\right) = \left(\underline{\hspace{1cm}} \times 1\frac{1}{2}\right) \times \frac{5}{8}$ *C A O*

4. $1 \times \underline{\hspace{1cm}} = 3\frac{2}{3}$ *C A O* $\qquad$ $\left(\frac{1}{2} \times 1\right) \times \frac{9}{10} = \underline{\hspace{1cm}} \times \frac{1}{2}$ *C A O*

You can use the Multiplying by One Property to find equivalent fractions.

Some equivalent fractions for the number **1** are:

$$\frac{1}{1}, \frac{2}{2}, \frac{3}{3}, \frac{4}{4}, \frac{5}{5}, \frac{6}{6}, \frac{7}{7}, \frac{8}{8}$$

You can use any name for **1** and the property will still be true.

Examples: $\frac{1}{4} \times 1 = \frac{1}{4}$ $\qquad$ $\frac{1}{4} \times \frac{2}{2} = \frac{2}{8}$

Multiplying $\frac{1}{4}$ by **1** and by $\frac{2}{2}$ does not change the value of $\frac{1}{4}$,

because $\frac{1}{4}$ and $\frac{2}{8}$ are equivalent fractions.

Complete the equation with a name for 1.

5. $\frac{1}{2} \times$ _____ $= \frac{2}{4}$ $\qquad$ $\frac{6}{7} \times$ _____ $= \frac{12}{14}$ $\qquad$ $\frac{3}{4} \times$ _____ $= \frac{9}{12}$ $\qquad$ $\frac{5}{8} \times$ _____ $= \frac{20}{32}$

Complete the equation to find an equivalent fraction.

6. $\frac{6}{7} \times \frac{4}{4} = \frac{}{28}$ $\qquad\qquad$ $\frac{4}{10} \times \frac{}{} = \frac{}{20}$ $\qquad\qquad$ $\frac{6}{9} \times \frac{}{} = \frac{12}{}$

7. $\frac{1}{5} \times \frac{}{} = \frac{2}{10}$ $\qquad\qquad$ $\frac{2}{5} \times \frac{}{} = \frac{10}{}$ $\qquad\qquad$ $\frac{3}{4} \times \frac{}{} = \frac{}{12}$

8. $\frac{3}{4} \times \frac{}{} = \frac{}{16}$ $\qquad\qquad$ $\frac{3}{5} \times \frac{}{} = \frac{12}{}$ $\qquad\qquad$ $\frac{5}{6} \times \frac{}{} = \frac{30}{}$

Problem Solving
Reasoning

Solve using mental math.

9. $\frac{250}{250} \times \frac{37}{90} = a$ $\qquad\qquad$ $\left(\frac{1}{2} + \frac{47}{56}\right) + \frac{1}{2} = w$ $\qquad\qquad$ $p + \left(\frac{81}{84} - \frac{81}{84}\right) = \frac{75}{79}$

_____ $= a$ $\qquad\qquad$ _____ $= w$ $\qquad\qquad$ _____ $= p$

Test Prep ★ Mixed Review

10 Which number makes $1 + 99 = n + 1$ a true equation?

A 101

B 99

C 98

D 97

11 The school nurse measured four students. Taisha is 48 in. tall. Chan is 52 in. tall. Alaina and Mario are each 56 in. tall. What is their average height?

F 48 in. $\qquad\qquad$ H 53 in.

G 52 in. $\qquad\qquad$ J 56 in.

Name _____

This pictograph shows the enrollment in the intermediate grades in the Watkins School. Each figure represents a particular number of children.

In this lesson you will need to use the graph to compare and draw conclusions about the data.

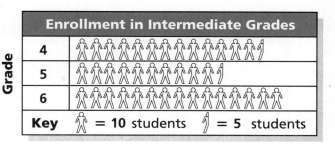

Tips to Remember

1. Understand	2. Decide	3. Solve	4. Look back

- Ask yourself whether you have solved a problem like this before.
- Think about strategies you have learned, and use them to help you solve a problem.
- When using a pictograph, remember to use the key.

Use the pictograph to solve the problem.

1. How many students are in each grade? Explain how you got your answer.

Think: How can the key and multiplication help you find the answer?

_____

_____

_____

_____

Answer_____

_____

_____

2. If the same graph were drawn with each symbol representing **15** students, then how many symbols would be needed to show the grades?

Think: Should you use division or multiplication to find how many symbols are needed?

_____

_____

Answer_____

_____

_____

Use the appropriate graph to solve the problem.

Students Who Like Pizza

Grade 4	🧍🧍🧍🧍🧍🧍🧍
Grade 5	🧍🧍🧍🧍🧍🧍🧍🧍
Grade 6	🧍🧍🧍🧍🧍🧍🧍🧍
Key	🧍 = **10** students
	🧍 = **5** students

Pizzas Preferences

3. What is the total number of students who like pizza? Which graph did you use?

_____

_____

4. How many students like to eat their pizza with a topping other than cheese?

_____

_____

5. How many more fifth graders like pizza than fourth graders?

_____

6. If you were to draw a pictograph for the bar graph, what symbol would you use and how many students would it represent?

_____

_____

Extend Your Thinking

7. Write a problem about the bar graph. Solve the problem.

_____

_____

_____

_____

8. Look back at the pictograph. Could each whole symbol stand for **15** children? Explain your answer.

_____

_____

_____

Name _____

Reciprocals

Two numbers whose product is **1** are called **reciprocals** of each other.

$3 \times \dfrac{1}{3} = \dfrac{3 \times 1}{3} = \dfrac{3}{3} = 1$ 3 and $\dfrac{1}{3}$ are reciprocals.

$\dfrac{3}{5} \times \dfrac{5}{3} = \dfrac{3 \times 5}{5 \times 3} = \dfrac{15}{15} = 1$ $\dfrac{3}{5}$ and $\dfrac{5}{3}$ are reciprocals.

$4\dfrac{1}{2} \times \dfrac{2}{9} = \dfrac{9}{2} \times \dfrac{2}{9} = \dfrac{9 \times 2}{2 \times 9} = \dfrac{18}{18} = 1$ $4\dfrac{1}{2}$ and $\dfrac{2}{9}$ are reciprocals.

You can write the reciprocal of any number.
• First, write any whole number or mixed number as a fraction.
• Then reverse the numerator and denominator.

$$\dfrac{2}{3} \rightarrow \dfrac{3}{2}$$
$$\dfrac{1}{4} \rightarrow \dfrac{4}{1} \text{ or } 4$$
$$8 = \dfrac{8}{1} \rightarrow \dfrac{1}{8}$$
$$3\dfrac{1}{5} = \dfrac{16}{5} \rightarrow \dfrac{5}{16}$$

reciprocals

Write the reciprocal of each number.

1. $\dfrac{1}{2}$ _____   7 _____ $4\dfrac{1}{3}$ _____ $\dfrac{2}{9}$ _____

2. $\dfrac{4}{5}$ _____ $2\dfrac{1}{16}$ _____ $\dfrac{3}{4}$ _____ $\dfrac{1}{7}$ _____

3. $5\dfrac{5}{6}$ _____ $\dfrac{1}{5}$ _____ $\dfrac{17}{20}$ _____   25 _____

4. $\dfrac{1}{9}$ _____ $\dfrac{5}{9}$ _____   2 _____ $4\dfrac{2}{3}$ _____

5. 9 _____ $1\dfrac{1}{2}$ _____ $\dfrac{9}{10}$ _____ $\dfrac{1}{4}$ _____

6. $\dfrac{11}{12}$ _____ $\dfrac{1}{13}$ _____   15 _____ $6\dfrac{4}{5}$ _____

Complete the equation. Write your answer in simplest form.

7. $3 \times \dfrac{1}{3} =$ _____ $2 \times$ _____ $= 1$ _____ $\times \dfrac{1}{3} = 1$ $4 \times$ _____ $= 1$

8. $5 \times \dfrac{1}{5} =$ _____ $10 \times$ _____ $= 1$ _____ $\times \dfrac{1}{6} = 1$ $\dfrac{1}{8} \times$ _____ $= 1$

9. $7 \times \dfrac{1}{7} =$ _____ $6 \times$ _____ $= 1$ _____ $\times \dfrac{1}{9} = 1$ $12 \times$ _____ $= 1$

Problem Solving
Reasoning

Solve.

10. What number is its own reciprocal?

_____

11. What number has no reciprocal?

_____

 Quick Check

Multiply. Write the answer in simplest form.

Work Space

12. $3 \times 1\dfrac{5}{6}$ **13.** $\dfrac{3}{4} \times 1\dfrac{4}{9}$ **14.** $3\dfrac{1}{8} \times \dfrac{12}{25}$

_____   _____   _____

Use the properties to find the values.

15. $\left(11 \times \dfrac{3}{10}\right) + \left(11 \times \dfrac{7}{10}\right)$ _____

16. $\dfrac{3}{3} + \dfrac{2}{2} + \dfrac{0}{9}$ _____

17. $\dfrac{2}{3} \times \dfrac{7}{7}$ _____

Find the reciprocal to complete.

18. $\dfrac{1}{2} \times$ _____ $= 1$

19. _____ $\times 10 = 1$

20. $2\dfrac{1}{3} \times$ _____ $= 1$

Name _____

Dividing on the Number Line

This number line shows halves.

$$0 \quad 1 \quad 2 \quad 3 \quad 4 \quad 5 \quad 6$$

$$\frac{0}{2} \quad \frac{1}{2} \quad \frac{2}{2} \quad \frac{3}{2} \quad \frac{4}{2} \quad \frac{5}{2} \quad \frac{6}{2} \quad \frac{7}{2} \quad \frac{8}{2} \quad \frac{9}{2} \quad \frac{10}{2} \quad \frac{11}{2} \quad \frac{12}{2}$$

To find the number of halves in **6**, you can count the number of halves on the number line or in **6** objects:

$$6 \div \frac{1}{2} = 12$$

Since there are **2** halves in each whole, you could also multiply by the reciprocal of $\frac{1}{2}$.

$$6 \times \frac{2}{1} \text{ or } 6 \times 2 = 12 \quad \text{So, there are } \textbf{12} \text{ halves in } \textbf{6}.$$

Complete the number sentence. Write your answer in simplest form.

1. $3 \div \frac{1}{2} =$ _____

$3 \times 2 =$ _____

2. $5 \div \frac{1}{2} =$ _____

$5 \times 2 =$ _____

3. $4 \div \frac{1}{2} =$ _____

$4 \times 2 =$ _____

4. $7 \div \frac{1}{2} =$ _____

$7 \times 2 =$ _____

Use the number line and the pictures.
Complete the number sentence.

$$0 \quad 1 \quad 2 \quad 3 \quad 4$$

$$\frac{0}{4} \quad \frac{1}{4} \quad \frac{2}{4} \quad \frac{3}{4} \quad \frac{4}{4} \quad \frac{5}{4} \quad \frac{6}{4} \quad \frac{7}{4} \quad \frac{8}{4} \quad \frac{9}{4} \quad \frac{10}{4} \quad \frac{11}{4} \quad \frac{12}{4} \quad \frac{13}{4} \quad \frac{14}{4} \quad \frac{15}{4} \quad \frac{16}{4} \quad \frac{17}{4} \quad \frac{18}{4}$$

5. $1 \div \frac{1}{4} =$ _____

$1 \times 4 =$ _____

6. $3 \div \frac{1}{4} =$ _____

$3 \times 4 =$ _____

7. $2 \div \frac{1}{4} =$ _____

$2 \times 4 =$ _____

8. $4 \div \frac{1}{4} =$ _____

$4 \times 4 =$ _____

---

9. $1 \div \frac{1}{3} =$ _____

$4 \div \frac{1}{3} =$ _____

10. $1 \div \frac{1}{8} =$ _____

$3 \div \frac{1}{8} =$ _____

11. $1 \div \frac{1}{5} =$ _____

$4 \div \frac{1}{5} =$ _____

12. $1 \div \frac{1}{6} =$ _____

$3 \div \frac{1}{6} =$ _____

Copyright © Houghton Mifflin Company. All rights reserved.

Unit 5 Lesson 8 **131**

You can use a number line to find how many three-fourths are in $\frac{18}{4}$.

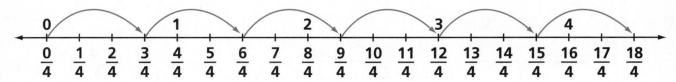

Count the number of three-fourths shown on the number line or in the fraction models.

$$\frac{18}{4} \div \frac{3}{4} = 6$$

You can also multiply by the reciprocal of $\frac{3}{4}$:

$$\frac{\overset{6}{\cancel{18}}}{\cancel{4}} \times \frac{\cancel{4}}{\cancel{3}} = 6$$

So, there are 6 three-fourths in $\frac{18}{4}$.

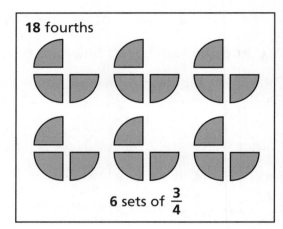

18 fourths

6 sets of $\frac{3}{4}$

Complete. Write your answer in simplest form.

13. $\frac{6}{4} \div \frac{3}{4} =$ _____

$\frac{6}{4} \times \frac{4}{3} =$ _____

14. $\frac{15}{4} \div \frac{3}{4} =$ _____

$\frac{15}{4} \times \frac{4}{3} =$ _____

15. $3 \div \frac{3}{4} =$ _____

$3 \times \frac{4}{3} =$ _____

16. $6 \div \frac{3}{4} =$ _____

$6 \times \frac{4}{3} =$ _____

| Problem Solving |
| Reasoning |

Solve. Draw a number line or a picture to help.

17. A grocer is dividing a **10**-pound block of cheese into pieces weighing $\frac{1}{4}$ pound each. How many pieces will be created from the block?

_____

18. At Ryan's school, the school day lasts **6** hours. Each period of the day is $\frac{2}{3}$ hour long. How many periods are in one school day?

_____

Test Prep ★ Mixed Review

19 Marta is 5 years older than Josh. If a is Josh's age, which expression shows Marta's age?

A $a - 5$

B $a + 5$

C $a \div 5$

D $a \times 5$

20 A flower weighs $6\frac{3}{4}$ ounces. Which point is $6\frac{3}{4}$ on the number line?

F A

G B

H C

J D

Name _____

Dividing by a Fraction

To divide by a fraction, multiply by the reciprocal of that fraction.

Examples

reciprocals

$$3 \div \frac{1}{2} = 3 \times 2$$
$$= 6$$

reciprocals

$$\frac{5}{6} \div \frac{1}{2} = \frac{5}{\overset{3}{6}} \times \overset{1}{2}$$
$$= \frac{5}{3} \text{ or } 1\frac{2}{3}$$

reciprocals

$$\frac{5}{6} \div \frac{2}{3} = \frac{5}{\underset{2}{6}} \times \frac{\overset{1}{3}}{2}$$
$$= \frac{5}{4} \text{ or } 1\frac{1}{4}$$

Divide. Write each quotient in simplest form.

1. $\frac{2}{3} \div \frac{5}{8} =$ _____ $\frac{1}{3} \div \frac{8}{24} =$ _____ $\frac{4}{15} \div \frac{28}{30} =$ _____

2. $\frac{4}{5} \div \frac{7}{15} =$ _____ $\frac{3}{5} \div \frac{15}{27} =$ _____ $\frac{4}{17} \div \frac{1}{34} =$ _____

3. $\frac{5}{7} \div \frac{3}{5} =$ _____ $\frac{2}{3} \div \frac{3}{4} =$ _____ $\frac{7}{4} \div \frac{1}{3} =$ _____

4. $\frac{2}{3} \div \frac{1}{2} =$ _____ $\frac{8}{9} \div \frac{4}{7} =$ _____ $\frac{5}{3} \div \frac{5}{9} =$ _____

5. $\frac{7}{8} \div \frac{5}{8} =$ _____ $\frac{4}{5} \div \frac{3}{4} =$ _____ $\frac{6}{7} \div \frac{5}{6} =$ _____

6. $\frac{4}{9} \div \frac{2}{3} =$ _____ $\frac{1}{9} \div \frac{2}{5} =$ _____ $\frac{7}{8} \div \frac{4}{7} =$ _____

7. $\frac{5}{2} \div \frac{5}{6} =$ _____ $\frac{1}{6} \div \frac{3}{2} =$ _____ $\frac{3}{7} \div \frac{3}{10} =$ _____

To divide a fraction by a whole number, multiply the fraction by the reciprocal of the whole number.

$$\frac{14}{9} \div 3 = \frac{14}{9} \times \frac{1}{3} \text{ or } \frac{14}{27}$$

Divide. Write each quotient in simplest form.

8. $\frac{3}{8} \div 5 =$ _____ $\frac{8}{9} \div 4 =$ _____ $\frac{1}{3} \div 9 =$ _____

Divide. Write each quotient in simplest form.

9. $\dfrac{5}{6} \div \dfrac{7}{8} =$ _____ $\dfrac{1}{2} \div 7 =$ _____ $4 \div \dfrac{3}{10} =$ _____

10. $\dfrac{4}{5} \div \dfrac{3}{7} =$ _____ $\dfrac{7}{8} \div 3 =$ _____ $6 \div \dfrac{2}{5} =$ _____

11. $\dfrac{2}{3} \div 12 =$ _____ $\dfrac{4}{9} \div 2 =$ _____ $\dfrac{7}{3} \div 6 =$ _____

12. $8 \div \dfrac{4}{5} =$ _____ $10 \div \dfrac{1}{3} =$ _____ $\dfrac{1}{4} \div \dfrac{7}{12} =$ _____

| Problem Solving |
| Reasoning |

Solve.

13. Jill is making a decoration. She cuts an **8**-foot ribbon into pieces that are each $\dfrac{3}{4}$ foot long. The remaining piece of ribbon is shorter than the others. How long is it? _____

14. Sam has $\dfrac{2}{3}$ of a piece of poster board. He cuts the poster board into **6** equal-size pieces. What part of the whole poster board is each smaller piece? _____

15. Suppose you are dividing a fraction by a whole number. Will your answer be less than or greater than the dividend? Give an example.

_____

✓ Quick Check

Use the number line to complete. Divide. Write each quotient in simplest form.

Work Space

16. $2 \div \dfrac{1}{3}$ _____   **17.** $4 \div \dfrac{1}{3}$ _____   **18.** $3 \div \dfrac{1}{3}$ _____

Divide. Write each quotient in simplest form.

19. $\dfrac{1}{2} \div \dfrac{3}{8}$ **20.** $\dfrac{2}{10} \div 4$ **21.** $\dfrac{10}{12} \div \dfrac{4}{6}$

_____   _____   _____

Name _____

Dividing by a Mixed Number

Tom, Carey, Dave, and Kim had $1\frac{1}{2}$ quarts of orange juice to divide equally. How much of the juice will each person get?

To divide mixed numbers and whole numbers:

1. Write any mixed numbers or whole numbers as fractions.

$$1\frac{1}{2} \div 4 = \frac{3}{2} \div \frac{4}{1}$$

2. Divide as you do with fractions.

$$1\frac{1}{2} \div 4 = \frac{3}{2} \div \frac{4}{1}$$
$$= \frac{3}{2} \times \frac{1}{4}$$
$$= \frac{3}{8}$$

Each person will get $\frac{3}{8}$ quart of the juice.

Write the mixed number as a fraction.

1. $1\frac{1}{2} =$ _____ $4\frac{1}{3} =$ _____ $3\frac{2}{3} =$ _____ $2\frac{1}{6} =$ _____

2. $10\frac{1}{4} =$ _____ $8\frac{1}{3} =$ _____ $4\frac{6}{7} =$ _____ $9\frac{1}{8} =$ _____

Divide. Write the quotient in simplest form.

3. $5 \div 4\frac{1}{3} =$ _____ $8 \div 2\frac{2}{3} =$ _____ $7 \div 1\frac{1}{2} =$ _____

4. $4 \div 3\frac{3}{4} =$ _____ $3\frac{1}{7} \div 4 =$ _____ $5\frac{1}{4} \div 3 =$ _____

5. $2\frac{1}{4} \div 8 =$ _____ $4\frac{6}{7} \div 4 =$ _____ $8\frac{2}{3} \div \frac{1}{2} =$ _____

6. $2\frac{1}{4} \div \frac{4}{9} =$ _____ $1\frac{1}{4} \div 1\frac{1}{2} =$ _____ $\frac{10}{3} \div 3\frac{1}{3} =$ _____

7. $9 \div 1\frac{2}{3} =$ _____ $6 \div 4\frac{3}{5} =$ _____ $\frac{1}{8} \div 7 =$ _____

8. $3\frac{5}{8} \div 6 =$ _____ $5\frac{1}{3} \div 1\frac{1}{9} =$ _____ $2\frac{1}{7} \div 1\frac{1}{2} =$ _____

Waffles
Makes 12 small squares

2 eggs

2 cups flour

$\frac{1}{2}$ cup vegetable oil

$1\frac{3}{4}$ cups milk

1 tablespoon sugar

4 teaspoons baking powder

$\frac{1}{4}$ teaspoon salt

Apple Crisp
Serves 24

16 cups sliced apples

$2\frac{2}{3}$ cups packed brown sugar

2 cups flour

2 cups oats

$1\frac{1}{3}$ cups margarine

3 teaspoons cinnamon

3 teaspoons nutmeg

9. If one batch of waffles makes **12** small squares, then **2** times each ingredient will make _____ small squares. Using $\frac{1}{2}$ of each ingredient will make _____ small squares. To make **36** small squares, use _____ times each ingredient. To make **8** small squares, use _____ times each ingredient.

10. If one recipe of apple crisp serves **24**, then **2** times each ingredient will serve _____. To serve _____, use $\frac{1}{2}$ of each ingredient. To serve 6, use _____ times each ingredient. To serve 36, use _____ times each ingredient.

Test Prep ★ Mixed Review

11. Davio helped his father $\frac{1}{2}$ hour before lunch and $\frac{9}{10}$ hour after lunch. How long did he help his father?

A $\frac{4}{10}$ hour   **C** $1\frac{2}{5}$ hours

B $\frac{5}{11}$ hour   **D** $1\frac{1}{2}$ hours

12. Davio sleeps $\frac{3}{8}$ of the 24 hours in a day. How many hours of the day is Davio asleep?

F $23\frac{5}{8}$ **H** 12

G $24\frac{3}{8}$ **J** 9

Fractions and the Order of Operations

You can simplify an expression that includes fractions and more than one operation. Follow the same order of operations that you follow when you work with whole numbers:

1. Do the operations inside parentheses first.

$$\frac{1}{4} + \left(\frac{1}{2}\right)^2 \times \left(\frac{1}{6} + \frac{2}{3}\right)$$

$$\boxed{\frac{1}{6} + \frac{2}{3} = \frac{5}{6}}$$

2. Simplify exponents.

$$\frac{1}{4} + \left(\frac{1}{2}\right)^2 \times \frac{5}{6}$$

$$\boxed{\left(\frac{1}{2}\right)^2 = \frac{1}{2} \times \frac{1}{2} \text{ or } \frac{1}{4}}$$

3. Multiply and divide from left to right.

$$\frac{1}{4} + \frac{1}{4} \times \frac{5}{6}$$

$$\boxed{\frac{1}{4} \times \frac{5}{6} = \frac{5}{24}}$$

4. Add and subtract from left to right.

$$\frac{1}{4} + \frac{5}{24}$$

$$\frac{11}{24}$$

Complete to simplify each expression.

1. $\frac{3}{8} + \frac{5}{8} \div \frac{1}{2}$

$\frac{3}{8} +$ _____

_____

2. $2 - \left(\frac{1}{3}\right)^2 + \frac{5}{9}$

$2 -$ _____ $+ \frac{5}{9}$

_____ $+ \frac{5}{9} = 2\frac{4}{9}$

3. $\left(\frac{2}{5} + \frac{3}{5}\right) \times \left(\frac{9}{10} - \frac{1}{5}\right)$

_____ $\times$ _____

_____

Simplify each expression.

4. $2 \times \left(\frac{11}{12} - \frac{7}{12}\right) =$ _____

5. $1 - \left(\frac{2}{5}\right)^2 =$ _____

6. $\frac{7}{8} - \frac{1}{4} \div 2 =$ _____

7. $1\frac{1}{3} + 2 \times \frac{1}{2} - \frac{1}{4} =$ _____

8. $7\frac{1}{6} - \frac{5}{6} \div \frac{1}{6} + \frac{2}{3} =$ _____

$\left(\frac{1}{2} \times \frac{1}{3}\right)^2 =$ _____

$\frac{5}{6} \div \frac{1}{6} \times \frac{1}{4} =$ _____

$2\frac{1}{2} \div \left(\frac{1}{4} + \frac{1}{8}\right) =$ _____

$\left(\frac{3}{4}\right)^2 - \frac{1}{4} \times \frac{3}{4} =$ _____

$\frac{1}{2} \times 3 + \frac{1}{3} \times \left(\frac{1}{2}\right)^2 =$ _____

Circle the expression that best represents the problem. Then solve.

9. Kara rode her bike $\frac{3}{4}$ mile east from her house to the park. Then she rode $\frac{1}{4}$ mile west to her friend's house. Then she rode $1\frac{1}{4}$ miles east to the library. How far was Kara from her home?

$$\frac{3}{4} + \left(\frac{1}{4} + 1\frac{1}{4}\right)$$

$$\frac{3}{4} - \frac{1}{4} + 1\frac{1}{4}$$

$$\frac{3}{4} - \left(1\frac{1}{4} + \frac{1}{4}\right)$$

_____

10. The Ming family lives on **8** acres. Their house, garage, and barn cover $\frac{1}{4}$ acre, and **2** acres are planted with hay. The rest of their property is pasture. How many acres of pasture do the Mings have?

$$8 + \frac{1}{4} - 2$$

$$8 - \frac{1}{4} + 2$$

$$8 - \left(\frac{1}{4} + 2\right)$$

_____

Solve.

11. The roof of a birdhouse is made of two square pieces of wood that are $4\frac{1}{2}$ inches long on a side. You are buying cedar shingles to cover the whole roof. What is the area of the roof to be shingled? _____

12. Toya needs $2\frac{1}{2}$ yards of fabric for curtains. She needs $\frac{3}{4}$ yard of the same kind of fabric for each of **3** pillows. How much fabric does she need in all? _____

 Quick Check

Divide. Write each quotient in simplest form.

13. $6 \div 3\frac{3}{8}$ **14.** $\frac{5}{6} \div 2\frac{1}{3}$ **15.** $3\frac{3}{5} \div 6\frac{3}{4}$

_____   _____   _____

Work Space

Write the value of each expression.

16. $8 \times \frac{4}{7} + \frac{3}{7}$ **17.** $\left(\frac{0}{8} \div \frac{8}{8}\right) \times \frac{1}{8}$ **18.** $\frac{4}{5} \times \left(1 \div \frac{1}{4}\right)$

_____   _____   _____

Sometimes problems that seem difficult to solve may be easier to understand using other numbers.

To solve these problems, try substituting simpler numbers. Then use the same method with the actual numbers.

Problem

Martin has $760 to invest in the stock market. How many shares of a stock selling at 47\frac{1}{2}$ each can he buy?

---

1 **Understand**   As you reread, ask yourself questions.

• What do you know?

**Martin has $760.
He wants to buy shares of stock that cost 47\frac{1}{2}$ each.**

What do you need to find?

_____

---

2 **Decide**   Choose a method for solving.

• Try the strategy Solve a Simpler Problem.

• What operation is involved?_____

Write a problem using simpler numbers.

_____

---

3 **Solve**   Use the numbers from your simpler problem to write an expression

• Solve the simpler problem.

_____

• Solve the original problem.

_____

---

4 **Look back**   Think about your answer.

Explain how the estimate helps check the actual answer.

_____

Use the **Solve a Simpler Problem** strategy or any other strategy you may have learned.

1. A shelf is $32\frac{1}{2}$ inches long. If each trophy is $3\frac{3}{4}$ inches wide, how many trophies can be lined up side by side on the shelf?

Think: What simpler problem would help?

_____

Answer_____

_____

2. A cookie recipe calls for $1\frac{2}{3}$ cups of flour for each dozen cookies. How many cups of flour are needed for $7\frac{1}{2}$ dozen cookies?

Think: What simpler number can you use for $1\frac{2}{3}$?

_____

Answer_____

3. In 1998 the population of the United States was **270,312,000**. The estimated population of the United States for the year 2020 is **322,052,000**. By how much is the population expected to increase?

_____

4. Beth bought some **33¢** and some **23¢** stamps. The number of **33¢** stamps was twice the number of **23¢** stamps. She paid **$4.45** in all for the stamps. How many of each did she buy?

_____

_____

5. In 1997, **86,588,369** people visited zoos and **35,781,485** people visited aquariums. What was the total annual attendance for both zoos and aquariums?

_____

6. Peter picked $5\frac{1}{2}$ pecks of pickled peppers. If there are **8** quarts in a peck, how many quarts of pickled peppers did Peter pick?

_____

7. During a rainstorm, $3\frac{3}{4}$ inches of rain fell in $2\frac{1}{2}$ hours. What was the average number of inches of rain that fell per hour?

_____

8. Gina wants to buy **48** shares of a stock that is selling for $\$14\frac{3}{4}$ each. How much money does she need to buy this stock?

_____

Write each product or quotient in simplest form.

1. $10 \times \frac{2}{5} = $ _____

2. $\frac{5}{9} \times \frac{3}{4} = $ _____

3. $\frac{2}{3} \times \frac{3}{8} = $ _____

4. $2\frac{3}{5} \times \frac{2}{3} = $ _____

5. $2\frac{2}{3} \times 6 = $ _____

6. $1\frac{5}{6} \times 2\frac{1}{2} = $ _____

7. $4 \div \frac{1}{4} = $ _____

8. $\frac{3}{8} \div \frac{1}{9} = $ _____

9. $\frac{4}{5} \div 6 = $ _____

10. $2\frac{3}{4} \div \frac{5}{8} = $ _____

11. $4 \div 1\frac{2}{3} = $ _____

12. $5\frac{1}{2} \div 1\frac{4}{5} = $ _____

Complete each equation.

13. $\frac{2}{3} \times \frac{4}{5} = \frac{4}{5} \times $ _____

14. $\frac{2}{5} + 5\frac{1}{3} = $ _____ $+ \frac{2}{5}$

15. $0 + \frac{5}{6} = $ _____

16. $\frac{1}{2} \times \left(\frac{5}{6} \times 2\right) = \left(\frac{1}{2} \times \right.$ _____ $\left.\right) \times 2$

17. $\frac{2}{3} + \left(\frac{5}{6} + \frac{5}{8}\right) = \left($ _____ $+ \frac{5}{6}\right) + \frac{5}{8}$

Use the graph to answer the question.

18. Two-thirds of the cans collected on Monday came from fifth-grade students. How many cans did fifth-grade students collect on Monday? _____

Number Of Cans Collected	
Mon.	🛢🛢🛢🛢🛢🛢
Tues.	🛢🛢
Wed.	🛢🛢🛢🛢
Thurs.	🛢🛢🛢
Fri.	🛢🛢🛢
Key	🛢 = 10 cans

Solve by using simpler numbers.

19. One-fourth of the **20,000** people in a stadium are in lower-deck seats. How many people are in lower-deck seats? _____

Solve.

20. What number is the reciprocal of $2\frac{1}{2}$? _____

A toy store recorded how much time customers played with some toys. Use the results to answer questions 1 and 2.

Toy	Number of Hours
Squeaky Toy	10
Art Chest	12
Giant Ball	19
Spinning Top	8
Walking Doll	7

1 According to the survey, which toy did people seem least interested in?

A Squeaky Toy   **C** Spinning Top

B Art Chest   **D** Walking Doll

2 The store manager drew a pictograph of the data.

Total Play Time for Toys	
Squeaky Toy	🕐 🕐 🌗
Art Chest	🕐 🕐 🕐
Giant Ball	🕐 🕐 🕐 🕐 🕐
Spinning Top	🕐 🕐
Walking Doll	?
Key 🕐 = 4 hours	

How many 🕐 are needed for the Walking Doll?

F 1   **H** $1\frac{3}{4}$

G $1\frac{1}{4}$ **J** 2

3 Which expression is equivalent to $n \times (47 + 76)$?

A $47 \times n \times 76$

B $47 + 76 + n$

C $(n \times 47) + (n \times 76)$

D $(47 \times n) + 76$

4 Which expression equals 80?

F $(2 \times 4) + (2 \times 36)$

G 5×2^3

H $2 \times 2 \times 2 \times 2 \times 10$

J $2 \times 2 \times 2 \times 5$

5 The product of two numbers is $\frac{9}{10}$. One of the numbers is $\frac{5}{6}$. What is the other number?

A $4\frac{1}{2}$ **C** $\frac{25}{27}$

B $1\frac{2}{25}$ **D** $\frac{1}{15}$

6 Briana lives $\frac{3}{5}$ mile east of school. Dean lives on the same street $\frac{1}{2}$ mile west of school. Which shows the distance in miles between the students?

F $\frac{4}{10}$ **H** $\frac{4}{7}$ **K** Not here

G $\frac{9}{10}$ **J** $1\frac{1}{10}$

7 Each day a man jogs $\frac{1}{2}$ mile. After 5 days, how many miles will he have jogged?

A $\frac{1}{2}$ **C** $4\frac{1}{2}$ **E** $5\frac{1}{2}$

B $2\frac{1}{2}$ **D** 5

8 A ribbon is $\frac{6}{12}$ foot long. Jason cuts a piece $\frac{4}{12}$ foot long from it. Which fraction shows how much ribbon is left in simplest form?

F $\frac{10}{12}$ foot   **H** $\frac{2}{12}$ foot   **K** Not here

G $\frac{1}{6}$ foot   **J** $\frac{2}{6}$ foot

UNIT 6 • TABLE OF CONTENTS

Decimals

Dear Family,

During the next few weeks, our math class will be learning about decimals.

You can expect to see homework that provides practice with multiplying decimals. Here is a sample you may use to give help if needed.

We will be using this vocabulary:

decimal a number such as **0.5** (five tenths) and **3.67** (three and sixty-seven hundredths); a decimal is sometimes called a decimal fraction

factor a number to be multiplied

order to arrange numbers in a certain way, such as from least to greatest or greatest to least

powers of 10 numbers such as $10^1 = 10$, $10^2 = 100$, $10^3 = 1,000$, and so on

Multiplying Decimals by Decimals

Multiply decimals the way you multiply whole numbers. Then show the same number of decimal places in your answer as there are in the factors.

Example: Find **1.4 × 2.9.**

Multiply decimals just as you would multiply whole numbers.

$$\begin{array}{r} 1.4 \\ \times\ 2.9 \\ \hline 126 \\ +\ 280 \\ \hline 406 \end{array}$$

Then show the same number of decimal places in your answer as there are in the factors.

$$\begin{array}{r} 1.4 \\ \times\ 2.9 \\ \hline 126 \\ +\ 280 \\ \hline 4.06 \end{array}$$

1.4 ← one decimal place
× 2.9 ← one decimal place
4.06 ← two decimal places

Example: Find **0.28 × 0.95.**

$$\begin{array}{r} 0.28 \\ \times\ 0.95 \\ \hline 140 \\ +\ 2520 \\ \hline 0.2660 \end{array}$$

0.28 ← two decimal places
× 0.95 ← two decimal places
0.2660 ← four decimal places

During this unit, students will need to continue practicing multiplication and addition facts.

Sincerely,

In our base ten system, each place in a number is 10 times greater than the value of the place to its right. Each place is also $\frac{1}{10}$ of the value of the place to its left. You can extend a place-value chart to include place values less than **1**.

Thousands	Hundreds	Tens	Ones		Tenths	Hundredths	Thousandths
3	5	7	2	.	6	9	4

A decimal point separates the ones and tenths places.

You can write this number in different ways:

- **Standard Form: 3,572.694**
- **Expanded Form: 3,000 + 500 + 70 + 2 + 0.6 + 0.09 + 0.004**
- **Word Form:**
  three *thousand*, five *hundred* seventy-two **and** six hundred ninety-four *thousandths*
- **Short Word Form: 3** *thousand*, **5** *hundred* **72 and 694** *thousandths*

Decimals that name the same amount are **equivalent decimals**.

0.5	=	0.50	=	0.500
5 *tenths*		50 *hundredths*		500 *thousandths*

Other Examples

3.1 three **and** one *tenth*   **4.05** 4 and **5** *hundredths*   **4.050** 4 and **50** *thousandths*

Write the word form.

1. 0.3 _____   0.07 _____

2. 0.90 _____   4.15 _____

Write the short word form.

3. 0.20 _____   0.10 _____

4. 0.103 _____   3.017 _____

Write each decimal.

5. seven tenths _____   6 hundredths _____

6. 48 hundredths _____   three thousandths _____

7. fifty-one thousandths _____   eight hundred four thousandths _____

8. 2 and 6 tenths _____   12 and 25 hundredths _____

To compare decimals, you can use a number line.
The decimal farther to the right is greater.

You can also compare digits with the same place value.

Think: **1.0 > 0.6**

To compare **0.25** and **0.205,** write a zero in the hundredths place so that both numbers have the same number of decimal places.

0.25**0** ◯ 0.205

Compare the digits in each place value from left to right.

5 hundredths > 0 hundredths, so **0.250 > 0.205**

Match each number with a point on the number line.

9. 0.25 _____   0.12 _____   0.31 _____   0.13 _____   0.19 _____

10. 0.29 _____   0.36 _____   0.38 _____   0.40 _____   0.17 _____

Compare. Write <, >, or =.

11. 0.3 ◯ 0.13   0.12 ◯ 0.012   1.56 ◯ 0.516   0.010 ◯ 0.01

12. 3.28 ◯ 3.820   0.054 ◯ 0.45   1.008 ◯ 0.08   1.25 ◯ 2.95

Write the decimals in order from least to greatest.

13. 0.127, 0.72, 1.270 _____   0.71, 0.43, 0.74 _____

14. 1.295, 2.085, 0.925 _____   0.487, 0.58, 0.009 _____

Problem Solving Reasoning   Solve.

15. What is the greatest decimal less than **1** that you can write using the digits **0, 1, 2, 3,** and **4** only once? The least decimal? _____

Test Prep ★ Mixed Review

16 What is the standard numeral for **8 billion 8 million?**

A 8,008,000

B 8,080,000

C 8,008,000,000

D 8,080,000,000

17 What is the value of $400 \times 10 \div a$ when $a = 10$?

F 4

G 40

H 400

J 4000

Name _____

Comparing and Ordering Decimals and Fractions

You can write fractions and mixed numbers as decimals.

$$\frac{4}{10} = 0.4 \leftarrow 4 \text{ tenths} \qquad 21\frac{5}{100} = 21.05 \leftarrow 21 \text{ and } 5 \text{ hundredths}$$

It is often helpful to know decimal equivalents for common fractions.

$$0.5 = \frac{5}{10} \rightarrow \frac{1}{2} \quad \boxed{\text{Simplest Form}} \qquad 0.25 = \frac{25}{100} \rightarrow \frac{1}{4} \quad 0.6 = \frac{1}{10} \rightarrow \frac{3}{5}$$

To compare a fraction and a decimal, first write them in the same form.

Compare $\frac{1}{2}$ and **0.7**.	Compare $\frac{3}{100}$ and **0.03**.	Compare $4\frac{7}{10}$ and **3.2**
$\frac{1}{2} = \frac{5}{10} \rightarrow 0.5$	$\frac{3}{100} = 0.03$	$4 > 3$, so $4\frac{7}{10} > 3.2$
$0.5 < 0.7$, so $\frac{1}{2} < 0.7$		

Use fractions, mixed numbers, and decimals to name points on the number line. Write each missing number.

1.

| 2 | $2\frac{1}{10}$ | $2\frac{2}{10}$ | $2\frac{3}{10}$ | ____ | $2\frac{5}{10}$ | $2\frac{6}{10}$ | ____ | $2\frac{8}{10}$ | $2\frac{9}{10}$ | 3 | $3\frac{1}{10}$ | $3\frac{2}{10}$ |

| 2.0 | 2.1 | | 2.3 | 2.4 | 2.5 | 2.6 | | 2.8 | 2.9 | 3.0 | | 3.2 |

____ (under $2\frac{2}{10}$) ____ (under 2.8 area) ____ (under 3.1 area)

2.

| 0 | $\frac{1}{100}$ | $\frac{2}{100}$ | $\frac{3}{100}$ | $\frac{4}{100}$ | ____ | $\frac{6}{100}$ | ____ | $\frac{8}{100}$ | $\frac{9}{100}$ | $\frac{10}{100}$ | $\frac{11}{100}$ | $\frac{12}{100}$ |

| 0 | 0.01 | 0.02 | | 0.04 | 0.05 | 0.06 | | 0.08 | 0.09 | 0.10 | 0.11 | |

____ ____ ____

Write each fraction or mixed number as a decimal.

3. $\frac{17}{100} = $ _____ $\frac{83}{100} = $ _____ $15\frac{30}{100} = $ _____ $1\frac{52}{100} = $ _____

4. $2\frac{73}{1,000} = $ _____ $\frac{19}{1,000} = $ _____ $9\frac{142}{1,000} = $ _____ $\frac{1}{1,000} = $ _____

Write each decimal as a fraction or as a mixed number.

5. 0.64 = _____   0.90 = _____   3.45 = _____   0.29 = _____

6. 7.050 = _____   0.218 = _____   4.003 = _____   13.084 = _____

Write each decimal as a fraction in simplest form.

7. 0.1 = _____   0.500 = _____   0.25 = _____   0.75 = _____   0.8 = _____

8. 0.2 = _____   0.40 = _____   2.60 = _____   4.250 = _____   10.6 = _____

Compare. Write >, <, or = .

9.   0.75 $\bigcirc$ 0.08   1.79 $\bigcirc$ $2\frac{4}{5}$ 36.007 $\bigcirc$ 36.040 $10\frac{1}{2}$ $\bigcirc$ 10.5

10. $1\frac{111}{1,000}$ $\bigcirc$ 1.111   12.9 $\bigcirc$ $12\frac{85}{100}$ $\frac{3}{5}$ $\bigcirc$ 0.07 $\frac{1}{4}$ $\bigcirc$ 0.35

List in order from greatest to least.

11. $\frac{1}{2}$, 0.75, 10.5, 0.40 _____ $\frac{4}{5}$, $\frac{110}{100}$, $3\frac{1}{2}$, 1.01 _____

12. 0.33, $\frac{3}{10}$, $\frac{1}{4}$, $\frac{400}{1,000}$ _____   0.63, 0.07, $2\frac{3}{4}$, $2\frac{4}{5}$ _____

Solve.

13. Mel bought $2\frac{4}{5}$ lb of fruit. His sister bought more.

Which amount might she have bought, **2.75** lb or $2\frac{9}{10}$ lb? _____

Test Prep ★ Mixed Review

14 Which expression is equivalent to
$2 \times 2 \times 7 \times 7 \times 7$?

 A 22,777

 B $2^2 + 7^3$

 C $2^2 \times 7^3$

 D $2^2 \div 7^3$

15 A theater has 27 rows with n seats in each row. Which expression shows how many seats there are in all?

 F $27 \div n$

 G $27 \times n$

 H $27 - n$

 J $27 + n$

Name _____

You can use what you know about rounding whole numbers to help you round decimals.

Round **4.715** to the nearest hundredth.
- First, look at the digit to the right of the place you are rounding to.

- If the digit is equal to or greater than **5**, *round up*. If the digit is less than **5**, *round down*.

Round to hundredths.

↓

4.715

↑

Look at thousandths. 5 = 5 So, round up.

4.715 rounds to **4.72**.

Other Examples

- Round **76.37** to the nearest whole number. 3 < 5, so round down to **76**.

- Round **16.87** to the nearest tenth. 7 > 5, so round up to **16.9**

You can use rounding to estimate decimal sums and differences.

Estimate by rounding.

Round to the nearest whole number.

12.85	→	13
+ 16.29	→	+ 16
		29

Round to the nearest tenth.

43.657	→	43.7
− 11.931	→	− 11.9
		31.8

Round each number to the given place.

		Ones	Tenths	Hundredths
1.	1.734	_____	_____	_____
2.	0.005	_____	_____	_____
3.	6.817	_____	_____	_____
4.	9.906	_____	_____	_____
5.	12.522	_____	_____	_____
6.	4.278	_____	_____	_____
7.	25.486	_____	_____	_____
8.	20.111	_____	_____	_____
9.	0.090	_____	_____	_____
10.	5.977	_____	_____	_____
11.	7.771	_____	_____	_____
12.	0.012	_____	_____	_____

Estimate each sum or difference by rounding each number to the given place.

13. nearest whole number	4.38 − 3.91	7.98 −1.05	0.09 + 1.58	14.351 − 12.910
14. nearest tenth	8.057 − 4.138	13.84 + 1.50	38.557 + 9.941	24.010 − 7.284
15. nearest hundredth	0.243 + 0.178	0.677 + 0.475	1.890 − 0.321	2.083 + 0.906
16. nearest tenth	3.00 − 2.19	0.999 + 0.819	4.150 − 4.092	0.05 + 0.09

Problem Solving Reasoning

Sometimes an estimate is enough to solve a problem. Sometimes an exact answer is needed. Write *estimate* or *exact* to tell what is needed to solve the problem.

17. Suppose you and two friends go to a movie. How much will you pay for **1** ticket?

_____

18. Did the cashier give you the correct change?

_____

19. How much money should you bring to pay for **3** tickets and snacks?

_____

20. How many people attended the movie?

_____

✓ Quick Check

Write each decimal.

Work Space

21. three hundredths _____   **22.** seven and two tenths _____

23. 7 and **29** thousandths _____

Write <, >, or =.

24. $\frac{6}{10}$ ◯ 0.06   **25.** 2.7 ◯ $2\frac{70}{100}$ **26.** $\frac{452}{1000}$ ◯ 4.52

Use rounding to estimate the sum or difference to the nearest tenth.

27. 4.99 + 3.57 _____   **28.** 24.002 − 1.87_____

29. 12.643 + 1.24 + 10.17 _____

Name _____

Remember to line up the decimal points when adding
or subtracting decimals. Sometimes you may need to
write zeros before you add or subtract.

Add: **5.38 + 0.496**

$$\begin{array}{r} \overset{1}{5.38}0 \\ + 0.496 \\ \hline 5.876 \end{array}$$

Subtract: **16 − 3.98**

$$\begin{array}{r} 1\overset{5}{\cancel{6}}.\overset{\overset{9}{\cancel{10}}}{\cancel{0}}\overset{10}{\cancel{0}} \\ - 3.9\,8 \\ \hline 12.02 \end{array}$$

Estimate first. Then add.

1.

1.75	5.274	2.6	8.536	21.6
2.60	0.63	0.314	0.17	7.05
+ 3.90	+ 0.8	+ 4.15	+ 0.683	+ 0.874

2. 2.837 + 5.42 = _____   39.7 + 16.985 = _____

3. 584 + 25.3 = _____   4.06 + 2.385 + 0.4 = _____

4. 17.2 + 3.5 + 4.73 = _____   5.55 + 5.5 + 0.5 = _____

5. 16 + 3.80 = _____   63 + 58.75 = _____

Estimate first. Then subtract.

6.

52.68	6.90	9.36	92.8	32.0
− 5.40	− 5.40	− 3.42	− 15.34	− 25.85

7.

4.385	15.0	9.0	7.425	734.0
− 2.63	− 8.64	− 3.625	− 3.8	− 16.85

8. 5.8 − 4.25 = _____   15.74 − 3.618 = _____

9. 38 − 3.65 = _____   74 − 52.80 = _____

10. 49.5 − 37.837 = _____   74.36 − 36 = _____

Write each missing digit.

11.
$$
\begin{array}{r}
0.04 \\
+\ 0.6\_ \\
\hline
0.\_1
\end{array}
\qquad
\begin{array}{r}
0.45 \\
+\ 0.\_6 \\
\hline
1.2\_
\end{array}
\qquad
\begin{array}{r}
0.\_\_ \\
+\ 0.06 \\
\hline
0.44
\end{array}
\qquad
\begin{array}{r}
0.09 \\
+\ 0.\_\_ \\
\hline
0.75
\end{array}
\qquad
\begin{array}{r}
0.\_\_\_ \\
+\ 0.216 \\
\hline
0.294
\end{array}
$$

Estimate. Write a decimal point in each addend to make the number sentence true.

12. 433 + 131 = 135.33   676 + 28 = 34.76

13. 384 + 297 = 68.1   729 + 531 = 78.21

14. 18 + 395 = 41.3   3785 + 293 = 407.8

15. 8076 + 5997 = 867.57   136 + 4987 = 18.587

| Problem Solving Reasoning | Solve. |

16. The odometer in Mr. Gregory's new car showed **345.6** miles before a trip and **1,400.5** miles after the trip. How many miles long was the trip?

_____

17. Janice read a chart at the airport weather station: "Weekly rainfall for the three-week period from March 6 through March 26: **6.4** centimeters, **3.27** centimeters, **4.3** centimeters." Was the total rainfall more or less than **14** centimeters? How much more or less?

_____

18. Steve had a temperature of **39°C** in the morning. By evening his temperature had gone down to **37.6°C**. By how many degrees did Steve's temperature change during the day? If normal body temperature is **36.9°C**, did Steve still have a fever?

_____

Test Prep ★ Mixed Review

19 What is the value of the expression $24 \div c - 6$ when $c = 4$?

A 0

B 8

C 14

D 22

20 You ate $\frac{1}{4}$ of a pizza. Your sister ate $\frac{1}{6}$ of the pizza. How much of the pizza is left?

F $\frac{7}{12}$ H $\frac{7}{10}$

G $\frac{5}{12}$ J $\frac{1}{2}$

Name _____

To solve a problem, you may need to begin with a conjecture about the answer.

When you make a conjecture, you make a "first guess" about the answer. Then you verify or check to see if it is correct.

Problem

Mark has some nickels and some dimes. He has 10 coins in all. The total amount of money he has is 80¢. How many nickels does he have? How many dimes does he have?

---

1 Understand As you reread, ask yourself questions.

• What do you know about the coins Mark has?

  Mark has 10 coins. Some are nickels. Some are dimes. Together the coins are worth 80¢.

• What information do you already know that is not given in the problem?

  A nickel is worth 5¢. A dime is worth 10¢.

What information do you need to find out?

_____

---

2 Decide Choose a method for solving.
Try the strategy Conjecture and Verify.

• What will your first guess be?   Are there 10 coins?

  Nickels: 5   Dimes: 5   _____

---

3 Solve Verify your conjecture. Try again if you need to.

First Guess		Try Again
Nickels: 5	Value: 25¢	_____
Dimes: 5	Value: 50¢	_____
Total: 10	75¢	_____

---

4 Look back Check your answer. Write the answer below.

Answer:_____

• How did your first guess help you make another try?

_____

_____

Use the Conjecture and Verify strategy or any other
strategy you have learned.

1. Maria and Mike have **$65** between them. Maria has **3** times as much money as Mike. How much money does Mike have? How much does Maria have?

Think: Should you divide **$65** into **3** or **4** parts?

_____

Answer _____

_____

2. Sheryl has **7** more videotapes than Wayne. Together they have **43** videotapes. How many videotapes does Wayne have? How many videotapes does Sheryl have?

Think: Should you add **7** to **43** or subtract **7** from **43**?

_____

Answer _____

_____

3. I'm thinking of two numbers. When I add them, their sum is **25**. When I multiply them, their product is **100**. What are the numbers?

_____

4. John drives **3.48** miles each way to and from work. About how far does he drive in two days?

_____

5. Anne wants to buy a sweater for **$39.99**. She also wants to buy **2** pairs of gloves costing **$5.99** each. She has **$50**. Does she have enough money?

_____

6. Shirley has quarters, nickels, and dimes in her piggy bank. She has **10** quarters, **20** dimes, and **40** nickels. How much money does Shirley have?

_____

7. Bob has some pennies, nickels, and dimes. He has **10** coins in all. The total amount of money he has is **40¢**. How many of each coin does he have?

_____

8. Jim has some pennies, dimes, and quarters. He has **20** coins in all. The total amount of money is **$2.00**. How many of each coin does he have?

_____

9. I'm thinking of two decimals. Their sum is **15.2**, and when the smaller is subtracted from the larger, their difference is **6.4**. What are the two decimals?

_____

10. Keiko has **4** pieces of wood with a total length of **19** feet. Three of the pieces are the same length, and one piece is **4** feet long. How long are the other pieces?

_____

Multiplying Whole Numbers and Decimals

Each time Jim rides his bike to and from the store, his odometer increases by **0.7** kilometer. How far does he ride in **3** trips?

To solve the problem, you can write **0.7** as a fraction, multiply, and change the answer to a decimal.

Think:

$$2\frac{1}{10}$$
$$10\overline{)21}$$
$$\underline{20}$$

$$3 \times 0.7 = 3 \times \frac{7}{10} \quad \boxed{3 \times 7 = 21}$$

$$= \frac{21}{10}$$

$$= 2\frac{1}{10} \text{ or } 2.1$$

You can also multiply using a decimal. Multiply as with whole numbers. Then write the decimal point in the product.

$$\begin{array}{r} 0.7 \\ \times\ 3 \\ \hline 2.1 \end{array}$$ — 1 decimal place

The product must have as many decimal places as there are in the factors.

Find **3 × 0.82**. Multiply with a fraction.

$$3 \times 0.82 = 3 \times \frac{82}{100} \quad \boxed{3 \times 82 = 246}$$

$$= \frac{246}{100}$$

$$= 2\frac{46}{100} \text{ or } 2.46$$

Multiply with a decimal.

$$\begin{array}{r} 0.82 \\ \times\ 3 \\ \hline 2.46 \end{array}$$ — 2 decimal places

There are a total of **2** decimal places in the factors. So, there are **2** decimal places in the product.

Multiply.

1.
0.3	0.8	0.3	0.2	0.3	0.4	0.5	0.9
× 5	× 9	× 8	× 9	× 9	× 6	× 7	× 7

2.
0.5	0.1	0.9	0.2	0.4	0.7	0.9	0.6
× 5	× 7	× 6	× 6	× 7	× 7	× 9	× 6

Multiply.

3.
0.03	0.31	0.11	0.75	0.03	0.33
× 5	× 2	× 7	× 5	× 7	× 8

4.
0.72	0.49	0.38	0.45	0.21	0.14
× 3	× 7	× 2	× 8	× 9	× 4

Write the number of decimal places the product will have.

5. One factor is a whole number and the other is a decimal in tenths. _____

6. One factor is a whole number and the other is a decimal in hundredths. _____

Find **8 × 0.421.**
Multiply with a fraction.

$$8 \times 0.421 = 8 \times \frac{421}{1,000}$$

8 × 421 = 3,368

$$= \frac{3,368}{1,000}$$

$$= 3\frac{368}{1,000} \text{ or } 3.368$$

Multiply with a decimal.

$$\begin{array}{r} 0.421 \\ \times\ 8 \\ \hline 3.368 \end{array}$$ } — 3 decimal places

There is a total of **3** decimal places in the factors. So, there are **3** decimal places in the product.

Multiply.

7.
$$\begin{array}{r} 0.695 \\ \times\ 9 \\ \hline \end{array}$$
$$\begin{array}{r} 0.213 \\ \times\ 8 \\ \hline \end{array}$$
$$\begin{array}{r} 0.165 \\ \times\ 6 \\ \hline \end{array}$$
$$\begin{array}{r} 0.982 \\ \times\ 3 \\ \hline \end{array}$$
$$\begin{array}{r} 0.821 \\ \times\ 5 \\ \hline \end{array}$$
$$\begin{array}{r} 7.060 \\ \times\ 2 \\ \hline \end{array}$$

8.
$$\begin{array}{r} 4.70 \\ \times\ 56 \\ \hline \end{array}$$
$$\begin{array}{r} 0.26 \\ \times\ 89 \\ \hline \end{array}$$
$$\begin{array}{r} 73 \\ \times\ 7.8 \\ \hline \end{array}$$
$$\begin{array}{r} 136 \\ \times\ 0.45 \\ \hline \end{array}$$
$$\begin{array}{r} 4.8 \\ \times\ 96 \\ \hline \end{array}$$
$$\begin{array}{r} 86 \\ \times\ 0.72 \\ \hline \end{array}$$

9.
$$\begin{array}{r} 38.07 \\ \times\ 48 \\ \hline \end{array}$$
$$\begin{array}{r} 7,375 \\ \times\ 0.086 \\ \hline \end{array}$$
$$\begin{array}{r} 37.7 \\ \times\ 46 \\ \hline \end{array}$$
$$\begin{array}{r} 4.098 \\ \times\ 89 \\ \hline \end{array}$$
$$\begin{array}{r} 458 \\ \times\ 0.36 \\ \hline \end{array}$$
$$\begin{array}{r} 1,004 \\ \times\ 9.5 \\ \hline \end{array}$$

Problem Solving
Reasoning

Solve.

10. Arnold bought **4** tickets to a play. Each ticket cost **$7.50.**

How much did he spend altogether? _____

11. Do you think the product of **3 × 8.3** is greater than or equal to **0.3 × 83**? Explain.

Test Prep ★ Mixed Review

12 What is $\frac{2}{3}$ of 6 days?

A 4 days

B $5\frac{1}{3}$ days

C $6\frac{2}{3}$ days

D 9 days

13 One piece of rope is $2\frac{1}{2}$ feet long and the other is $3\frac{3}{8}$ feet long. What is the combined length of the two pieces?

F $5\frac{6}{8}$ ft

H $6\frac{1}{8}$ ft

G $5\frac{7}{8}$ ft

J $6\frac{7}{8}$ ft

Multiplying Decimals by Decimals

These examples will help you place the decimal point in a product.

$$\frac{3}{10} \times \frac{9}{10} = \frac{27}{100}$$

| Think: *hundredths* means **2** decimal places |

↓ ↓ ↓

$$0.3 \times 0.9 = 0.27$$

$$\frac{83}{100} \times \frac{3}{10} = \frac{249}{1,000}$$

| Think: *thousandths* means **3** decimal places |

↓ ↓ ↓

$$0.83 \times 0.3 = 0.249$$

$$\frac{21}{10} \times \frac{7}{10} = \frac{147}{100}$$

↓ ↓ ↓

$$2.1 \times 0.7 = 1.47$$

You can use what you know about whole numbers to multiply decimals.

1. Multiply as you would whole numbers.

$$\begin{array}{r} 1.6 \\ \times\, 0.8 \\ \hline 128 \end{array}$$

2. Find the total number of decimal places in the two factors.

$$\begin{array}{rl} \overset{4}{1.6} & \text{1 place} \\ \times\, 0.8 & +\ \text{1 place} \\ \hline 128 & \text{2 places} \end{array}$$

3. Write the decimal point in the product.

$$\begin{array}{rl} \overset{4}{1.6} & \\ \times\, 0.8 & \\ \hline 1.28 & \leftarrow \text{2 places} \end{array}$$

Complete.

1. If there is one decimal place in each of two factors, then how many decimal places will the product have?

_____

2. If there is one decimal place in one factor and two decimal places in the other factor, then how many decimal places will the product have?

_____

Sometimes you need to write one or more zeros in the product before you can place the decimal point.

$$\begin{array}{rl} 0.4 & \text{1 place} \\ \times\, 0.2 & \text{1 place} \end{array} \Big\rangle \text{2 places}$$
$$\overline{0.08}$$

$$\begin{array}{rl} 0.06 & \text{2 places} \\ \times\, 0.3 & \text{1 place} \end{array} \Big\rangle \text{3 places}$$
$$\overline{0.018}$$

Multiply.

3.
$$\begin{array}{r} 3.74 \\ \times\, 0.8 \\ \hline \end{array} \qquad \begin{array}{r} 8.29 \\ \times\, 0.9 \\ \hline \end{array} \qquad \begin{array}{r} 65.3 \\ \times\, 0.7 \\ \hline \end{array} \qquad \begin{array}{r} 4.28 \\ \times\, 1.2 \\ \hline \end{array} \qquad \begin{array}{r} 93.1 \\ \times\, 2.9 \\ \hline \end{array}$$

4.
$$\begin{array}{r} 72.9 \\ \times\, 3.8 \\ \hline \end{array} \qquad \begin{array}{r} 8.34 \\ \times\, 4.7 \\ \hline \end{array} \qquad \begin{array}{r} 67.5 \\ \times\, 5.3 \\ \hline \end{array} \qquad \begin{array}{r} 5.83 \\ \times\, 0.93 \\ \hline \end{array} \qquad \begin{array}{r} 96.2 \\ \times\, 0.89 \\ \hline \end{array}$$

5.
$$\begin{array}{r} 0.02 \\ \times\, 0.4 \\ \hline \end{array} \qquad \begin{array}{r} 0.6 \\ \times\, 0.1 \\ \hline \end{array} \qquad \begin{array}{r} 0.4 \\ \times\, 0.6 \\ \hline \end{array} \qquad \begin{array}{r} 0.03 \\ \times\, 0.5 \\ \hline \end{array} \qquad \begin{array}{r} 0.02 \\ \times\, 3 \\ \hline \end{array} \qquad \begin{array}{r} 0.01 \\ \times\, 0.3 \\ \hline \end{array}$$

If you estimate before you multiply, you will know whether your answer makes sense. Estimating the product will also help you place the decimal point correctly. Find each product. Estimate first.

6. 67.3
  × 0.4

 Estimate: 70.0
× 0.4 ⎱ 2 decimal
28.00 ⎰ places

96.7
× 0.2

831.4
× 0.9

172.9
× 0.1

719.2
× 0.6

7. 23.9
  × 1.6

63.1
× 1.5

95.7
× 2.7

2.6
× 0.82

3.3
× 2.02

4.1
× 8.01

Problem Solving
Reasoning

Solve.

8. Mary bought some bagels and some rolls. The bagels cost **$.40** each and the rolls cost **$.25**. If she spent **$3.90** in all for **12** items, how many of each did she buy?

_____

9. One recipe for bagels uses **0.45** bag of flour. A recipe for rolls uses **1.5** times as much. Does the recipe for rolls use more or less than $\frac{3}{4}$ bag of flour?

_____

✓ Quick Check

Add or subtract.

Work Space

10. 0.06 + 0.95

11. 13.904 + 9.88

12. 55 − 16.75

_____   _____   _____

13.   10.16
      25.071
    + 9.5

14. $20.56
    − 11.19

15. 57.083 − 39.17

_____

Multiply.

16.   65
      × 0.09

17. 9.16
    × 42

18. 9.50
     × 116

Multiply. Be sure to place the decimal point in each answer.

19. 0.07
    × 0.06

20. 6.98
    × 0.25

21. 1.17
    × 9.9

Multiplying and Dividing by Powers of Ten

When you multiply **10** by itself any number of times, the product is called a **power of 10.** You can write a power of **10** using an exponent.

$10 = 10^1$ $10 \times 10 = 10^2$ or **100** $10 \times 10 \times 10 = 10^3$ or **1,000**

Write each power of 10 using an exponent and in standard form.

1. $10 \times 10 \times 10 \times 10 =$ _____ _____

2. $10 \times 10 \times 10 \times 10 \times 10 =$ _____ _____

3. $10 \times 10 \times 10 \times 10 \times 10 \times 10 =$ _____ _____

You can use patterns to help you find the product of a number and a power of **10.**

$63 \times 10 = 630$	$0.75 \times 10 = 7.5$	$0.059 \times 10 = 0.59$
$63 \times 100 = 6,300$	$0.75 \times 100 = 75$	$0.059 \times 100 = 5.9$
$63 \times 1,000 = 63,000$	$0.75 \times 1,000 = 750$	$0.059 \times 1,000 = 59$

Write 2 or 3 to complete each statement.

4. The exponent _____ tells you how many zeros to write when you find

the product of a whole number and **10** to the third power.

5. You can multiply a number by **100** mentally. Just move the decimal

point in the number to the right _____ places.

Multiply using patterns.

6. $73 \times 10 =$ _____ $31 \times 100 =$ _____ $5.21 \times 10 =$ _____

7. $0.43 \times 1,000 =$ _____ $0.107 \times 10^3 =$ _____ $0.006 \times 10^2 =$ _____

8. $17.28 \times 10 =$ _____ $0.093 \times 1,000 =$ _____ $42.178 \times 10^2 =$ _____

9. $0.037 \times 1,000 =$ _____ $5.401 \times 100 =$ _____ $400,000 \times 10 =$ _____

You can also use patterns to divide by powers of **10**.

290 ÷ 10 = 29	65,000 ÷ 10 = 6,500	4.3 ÷ 10 = 0.43
290 ÷ 100 = 2.9	65,000 ÷ 100 = 650	4.3 ÷ 100 = 0.043
290 ÷ 1,000 = 0.29	65,000 ÷ 1,000 = 65	4.3 ÷ 1,000 = 0.0043

Divide. Use patterns to help you.

10. 63 ÷ 10 = _____ $0.59 ÷ 10^1$ _____   4.71 ÷ 10 = _____

11. 0.01 ÷ 1,000 = _____ $34.8 ÷ 10^3 =$ _____   0.651 ÷ 100 = _____

12. 500,000 ÷ 1,000 = _____ $3,240.27 ÷ 10^2 =$ _____ $77 ÷ 10^3 =$ _____

Write *true* **or** *false* **for each statement.**

13. When you divide a number by a power of **10,** the decimal point in the

number moves to the right. _____

14. The exponent tells how many places to move the decimal point

when multiplying or dividing by a power of **10.** _____

Problem Solving Reasoning   **Solve.**

15. The highest point in Louisiana is Driskill Mountain. It is about **530** ft
high. The highest point in New York, Mount Marcy, is about **10** times as
high. About how high is Mount Marcy?

_____

16. True or false? $43 \times 10^2 = 430,000 ÷ 10^2$. Explain.

_____

Test Prep ★ Mixed Review

17 A carton of books weighed $7\frac{1}{2}$ pounds.
What is the total weight of 10 identical
cartons?

   A $17\frac{1}{2}$ lb

   B 75 lb

   C 77 lb

   D 150 lb

18 If 1 centimeter is about $\frac{2}{5}$ inches, then
how many centimeters are there in 1 foot
(12 inches)?

   F $\frac{2}{5}$

   G $2\frac{1}{2}$

   H $4\frac{4}{5}$

   J 30

Name _____

Dividing by Whole Numbers

To divide a decimal by a whole number:

1. Divide as you would with whole numbers.

2. Then place the decimal point in the quotient directly above the decimal point in the dividend. Write zeros as placeholders as necessary.

3. Multiply to check, since multiplication is the inverse of division.

Examples

Check:

```
   8.3          8.3
7)58.1         × 7
 − 56 ↓       58.1
   2 1
 − 2 1
     0
```

Write zeros as placeholders

Check:

```
              0.08         0.08
           4)0.32          × 4
            − 32          0.32
               0
```

Check:

```
   1.402       1.402
6)8.412          × 6
 −6 ↓         8.412
  2 4
 −2 4
   012
  −12
     0
```

Divide and check.

1. 6)5.4   7)41.3   8)6.32   5)9.75   9)3.843

2. 2)0.342   3)2.88   4)8.44   6)1.44   3)0.639

3. 2)0.846   7)0.266   4)0.852   2)0.684   7)0.889

Place the decimal point in the quotient to make each
equation true. Use estimation to help you.

4. $17.5 \div 5 = 3\ 5$ $27.2 \div 8 = 3\ 4$ $205.2 \div 6 = 3\ 4\ 2$

Divide and check.

5. $6\overline{)2.46}$ $2\overline{)0.258}$ $3\overline{)5.49}$ $8\overline{)7.76}$ $5\overline{)1.730}$

6. $2\overline{)1.92}$ $9\overline{)1.134}$ $7\overline{)6.216}$ $3\overline{)7.743}$ $6\overline{)0.222}$

Problem Solving
Reasoning

Solve.

7. The grams of fat in **1** tbs of salad
dressings are: Blue cheese **1.5** g,
French **1.4** g, Italian **1.3** g, mayonnaise
1.7 g, thousand island **1.0** g. What is
the average amount of fat in **1** tbs of
each of these salad dressings?

_____

8. The Cheese Shop sells **5** pounds of
Italian cheese for **$14.50**. At that rate,
what is the cost of **1** pound?

_____

9. Shaun mailed **100** letters for a charity.
The cost of the mailing was **$40**. How
much did it cost to mail each
envelope?

_____

10. Barbara spent **$80.78** for groceries
one week. What was her average cost
per day for the groceries?

_____

Test Prep ★ Mixed Review

11 Your cousin worked for $2\frac{3}{4}$ hours on
Monday and $2\frac{2}{3}$ hours on Tuesday. How
many hours is that in all?

  A $4\frac{5}{7}$ **C** $5\frac{1}{12}$

  B $4\frac{7}{12}$ **D** $5\frac{5}{12}$

12 Gina bought a used bicycle for $139. She
made a down payment of $40. At $11 a
week, how long will it take her to pay the
rest?

  F 11 weeks

  G 10 weeks

  H 9 weeks

  J 8 weeks

Name _____   **Writing Zeros in the Dividend**

Sometimes you must write one or more zeros in the
dividend to continue dividing.

Divide: $4\overline{)2.7}$

1. Divide. Write a zero in
   the hundredths place in
   the dividend.

| 2. Divide again. Write a zero
     in the thousandths place
     in the dividend. | 3. Divide a third time. |

Think: 27 ÷ 4 is
about 6.

$$\begin{array}{r} 0.6 \\ 4\overline{)2.70} \\ -24 \\ \hline 30 \end{array}$$

Think: 30 ÷ 4 is
about 7.

$$\begin{array}{r} 0.67 \\ 4\overline{)2.700} \\ -24 \\ \hline 30 \\ -28 \\ \hline 20 \end{array}$$

$$\begin{array}{r} 0.675 \\ 4\overline{)2.700} \\ -24 \\ \hline 30 \\ -28 \\ \hline 20 \\ -20 \\ \hline 0 \end{array}$$

Check:

$$\begin{array}{r} 0.675 \\ \times\ \ 4 \\ \hline 2.700 \end{array}$$

Here is another example: $2 \div 5 = $
$$\begin{array}{r} 0.4 \\ 5\overline{)2.0} \\ -20 \\ \hline 0 \end{array}$$

Divide. Write zeros in the dividend if necessary.

1. $5\overline{)2.7}$ $4\overline{)3.5}$ $2\overline{)9.1}$ $8\overline{)5.2}$

2. $8\overline{)19}$ $5\overline{)24}$ $2\overline{)27}$ $4\overline{)19}$

3. $24\overline{)9}$ $24\overline{)15}$ $10\overline{)62.4}$ $16\overline{)12.4}$

Copyright © Houghton Mifflin Company. All rights reserved.

Solve.

4. June has **38** friends coming to a party. She expects to seat her friends at tables with **4** at each table. How many tables does she need?

_____

5. June and her sister share the expenses equally. The party costs **$63**. How much does each sister pay?

_____

6. Favors for the party can be purchased in packages of **4** or **8**. A package of **4** costs **$9.60** and a package of **8** costs **$22**. Which package is the better buy?

_____

7. Juice for the party costs **$3.12** for **8** cartons. How much will one more carton cost?

_____

 ## Quick Check

Multiply or divide.

8. 9.53×10 _____

9. 0.8742×10^3 _____

10. 100×0.039 _____

11. $3.7 \div 10^2$ _____

12. $10\overline{)0.98}$

13. $100\overline{)56}$

14. $5\overline{)29.5}$

15. $9\overline{)610.2}$

16. $6\overline{)0.804}$

Divide. Write zeros in the dividend if necessary.

17. $4\overline{)9.6}$

18. $8\overline{)23}$

19. $36\overline{)86.4}$

Work Space

Name _____

Dividing a Decimal by a Decimal

You can use what you know about dividing by a whole
number to divide by a decimal.

> Multiplying the **divisor** and the **dividend** by the same number
> does not change the quotient.

Multiply the divisor and dividend by **10**.	Multiply the divisor and dividend by **100**.

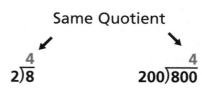

Find the quotient: 2.6)8.06

1. Change the divisor to a
whole number. Multiply
by **10**.

$$2.6.)\overline{8.06}$$

10 × 2.6 = 26

2. Multiply the dividend by
the same number, **10**.

$$2.6.)\overline{8.0.6}$$

10 × 8.06 = 80.6

3. Divide and place the
decimal point in the
quotient.

```
       3.1
26)80.6
  -78
    2 6
   -2 6
      0
```

Rewrite each. Multiply the divisor and dividend by 10, 100, or 1,000.

1. 0.34)42.5   0.003)2.61   1.5)4.87   0.2)1.32

_____ _____ _____ _____

2. 0.009)0.15   16.2)31   4.28)2.7   0.8)15

_____ _____ _____ _____

Find the quotient.

3. 0.3)1.44   0.5)0.385   0.2)1.78   0.4)1.84

4. 0.21)5.46   3.5)17.5   6.1)32.33   1.24)0.4712

Divide. Remember to place the decimal point in the quotient.

5. $0.8\overline{)1.12}$ $0.5\overline{)16.55}$ $0.9\overline{)4.86}$ $0.21\overline{)5.46}$

6. $0.039\overline{)0.2496}$ $0.047\overline{)2.632}$ $0.005\overline{)0.515}$ $0.07\overline{)4.62}$

7. $0.252\overline{)47.88}$ $0.2\overline{)0.13}$ $0.36\overline{)1.872}$ $0.007\overline{)7.28}$

| Problem Solving |
| Reasoning |

Solve.

8. Moira is measuring yarn for the hair on a puppet. Each piece must be **0.5** in. long. How many pieces can she cut from a length of yarn that measures **26** in.?

_____

9. A bicycle club rode **38.7** kilometers in **4.5** hours. What was the average number of kilometers they rode each hour?

_____

10. Karen bought **10** stamps. Some cost **$.32** and some cost **$.20**. She spent **$2.84**. How many of each did she buy?

_____

Test Prep ★ Mixed Review

11 A pencil is $\frac{18}{8}$ inches long. What is another way to write $\frac{18}{8}$ in.?

  A $\frac{6}{4}$ in.   **C** $2\frac{1}{8}$ in.

  B $1\frac{1}{2}$ in.   **D** $2\frac{1}{4}$ in.

12 Which number has a 6 in the hundredths place, a 5 in the tenths place, and a 7 in the thousandths?

  F 0.567

  G 0.576

  H 0.657

  J 0.675

Interpreting Remainders

Sometimes you will need to decide whether to write a remainder as a whole number, fraction, or decimal.

Whole Number Remainder	**Divide.**	**Write the answer.**
A baker is putting 43 muffins in boxes. She puts 4 muffins in one box. How many boxes will she use?	$$\begin{array}{r} 10\ \text{R3} \\ 4\overline{)43} \\ 4\downarrow \\ \hline 03 \end{array}$$ ← remainder	There will be **10** boxes of **4** muffins, with **3** muffins left over. She needs 11 boxes. Write the remainder as a whole number.

Fraction Remainder	**Divide.**	**Write the answer.**
You need to cut a **43**-inch board into **4** equal-size pieces. How long will each piece be?	$$\begin{array}{r} 10\frac{3}{4} \\ 4\overline{)43} \\ 4\downarrow \\ \hline 03 \end{array}$$ ← remainder	Each piece will be $10\frac{3}{4}$ inches long. Write the remainder as a fraction.

Decimal Remainder	**Divide.**	**Write the answer.**
Four friends divide the cost of dinner. The bill was **$43.00**. How much did each friend pay?	$$\begin{array}{r} 10.75 \\ 4\overline{)43.00} \\ 4 \\ \hline 03\ 0 \\ 2\ 8 \\ \hline 20 \\ 20 \\ \hline 0 \end{array}$$ Write zeros in the dividend to continue dividing.	Each friend paid **$10.75**. Write the remainder as a decimal.

Divide. Explain how the quotient should be written.

1. A piece of ribbon **39** feet long is cut into **6** equal pieces. How long is each piece?

_____

2. Each dress requires **2** yards of fabric. How many dresses can be made from **7** yards of material?

_____

3. Three children are to share **$5.00** equally. How much does each child get?

_____

4. There are **14** students going on a field trip. Each car can carry **4** students and an adult driver. How many cars are needed?

_____

Solve. Explain how the quotient should be written.

5. Maurice made this chart to record what he spent each day last week in the cafeteria.

Monday $7.05
Tuesday $4.28
Wednesday $5.26
Thursday $3.99
Friday $6.21

What was the average amount he spent per day?

_____

6. Six friends spent **$99** for lunch one day. What is each person's share of the bill?

_____

7. Kate is making a bookcase with shelves **3** feet long. She has a board **7** feet long. How many shelves can she cut from the board?

_____

8. You bring **12** apples for **36** members of the band. How should you cut the apples so each member gets one piece?

_____

9. Doug is using yarn to tie packages. He has **15** feet of yarn and **12** packages. He wants to use the same length for each package. How long should he make each piece?

_____

10. Mr. Jefferson is delivering pies to a bake sale. He can fit **3** pies in each box. How many boxes does he need for 17 pies?

_____

Test Prep ★ Mixed Review

11 A pickup truck is 19 feet long. A sports car is only 13.7 feet long. About how much shorter is the sports car?

A 35 ft

B 25 ft

C 15 ft

D 5 ft

12 Which decimal is equivalent to the fraction $\frac{3}{100}$?

F 300

G 3

H 0.30

J 0.03

Simplify: $0.8 \times (6.1 + 4.7) + 0.2$

Remember the Order of Operations:

• Work inside parentheses first.

• Multiply and divide from left to right.

• Add and subtract from left to right.

$0.8 \times (6.1 + 4.7) + 0.2$

$0.8 \times 10.8 + 0.2$

$8.64 + 0.2$

8.84

Simplify. Tell whether the answer would change if the parentheses were removed.

1. $(3.9 \times 2.8) + 4.2 =$ _____ $3.9 \times (2.8 + 4.2) =$ _____

2. $(19.7 - 3.1) \times 2.8 =$ _____ $19.7 - (3.1 \times 2.8) =$ _____

3. $(6.24 \div 3) \times 2 =$ _____ $6.24 \div (3 \times 2) =$ _____

Write decimal points as needed to make the equation true. Estimate first to help you place the decimal point.

4. $(41 \times 202) \div 2 = 41.41$ $41 \times (202 \div 2) = 4.141$

5. $(252 \times 39) - 203 = 96.25$ $252 \times (39 - 203) = 47.124$

6. $(436 + 189) \times 417 = 260.625$ $436 + (189 \times 417) = 514.813$

Remember that the properties and rules for whole numbers are the same for decimals. Name the property shown.

7. $(1.5 + 6.9) + 28 = (6.9 + 1.5) + 28$ _____

8. $5.37 \times 0 = 0$ _____ $0 + 14.38 = 14.38$ _____

9. $(73.4 + 2) \times 3.1 = (73.4 \times 3.1) + (2 \times 3.1)$ _____

10. $(28.115 + 79) \times 0 = 0$ _____

11. $0.032 \times 1 = 0.032$ _____

Complete each equation. Name the property you used.

11. $12 \times (2.9 + 1.8) = (12 \times \underline{\hspace{1cm}}) + (12 \times 1.8)$ _____

12. $1.53 \times (10 \times 2.4) = (2.4 \times 1.53) \times \underline{\hspace{1cm}}$ _____

13. $50 + 2.37 + 0 = 2.37 + \underline{\hspace{1cm}} + 50$ _____

14. $8 + (9.3 + \underline{\hspace{1cm}}) = 17.3$ _____

Problem Solving Reasoning	**Solve. Evaluate each expression to find the total cost.**

15. $3a + 3d$ _____

17. $2b + 2a$ _____

16. $2a + c$ _____

18. $c + 3d$ _____

School Supplies		
a	$2.50	notebook
b	$.55	marker
c	$1.49	package of pencils
d	$.79	pad of paper

Variables

 Quick Check

First multiply to make the divisor a whole number. Then find the quotient.

Work Space

19. $6.1\overline{)32.33}$ **20.** $0.36\overline{)1.872}$ **21.** $0.039\overline{)0.2496}$

Write the remainder as a whole number, a fraction, and a decimal rounded to the nearest hundredth.

22. $3\overline{)89}$ **23.** $8\overline{)413}$ **24.** $4\overline{)301}$

_____   _____   _____

Simplify.

25. $0.7 \times (0.8 + 1.2)$ _____   **26.** $3.2 \div 4 + 3 \times 0.5$ _____

27. $(16.8 - 8.1) - 2.9$ _____

28. What number makes the equation true?

$3 \times 6.2 = (3 \times 6.0) + (n \times 0.2)$ _____

Name_____

Sometimes you need to do more than one step to solve a problem.

In this lesson, you will use the price list to solve multi-step problems.

Menu	
Lemonade	$.85
Hamburger	$2.49
Hot dog	$1.69
Salad	$.99

Tips to Remember

1. Understand 2. Decide 3. Solve 4. Look back

- Think about the action in the problem. Is there more than one action? Which operation best represents each action— addition, subtraction, multiplication, or division?
- Try to break the problem into parts.
- Think about strategies you have learned, and use them to help solve a problem.

Solve. Use the price list above.

1. You had **$5.** You bought a hamburger and a lemonade. How much money did you have left?

Think: Should you add or subtract the prices of the lemonade and hamburger?

_____

Answer_____

2. You want to buy **1** hot dog, **1** salad, and **1** lemonade. You have **$3.25** in your pocket. Do you have enough money?

Think: Do you need to find an exact answer or is an estimate enough to answer the question?

_____

Answer_____

3. Mr. Lee bought lunch for his family. He bought **4** lemonade drinks, **2** hamburgers, **2** hot dogs, and **2** salads. How much change did he receive from **$15.00?**

_____

4. Mrs. Washington purchased **4** hot dogs and **2** lemonade drinks. Would **2** hamburgers and **2** lemonades have been cheaper?

_____

Solve. Use the price list.

The Snack Bar			
Hamburger	$2.49	Salad	$0.99
Superburger	$2.99	Frosty Shake	$1.29
Hot dog	$1.69	Lemonade	$0.85

5. You want to buy **2** frosty shakes. You have only **$1.75** in your pocket. How much more do you need?

_____

6. How much more does it cost to buy a superburger and a frosty shake than a hamburger and a lemonade?

_____

7. There is **0.25** lb of ground beef in a hamburger and **0.35** lb of ground beef in a superburger. How many pounds of ground beef are needed to make **16** hamburgers and **20** super-burgers?

_____

8. The Snack Bar bought a package of **48** hot dogs for **$24**, and two packages of **24** rolls for **$7.20** each. One day all the hot dogs were sold. How much profit did The Snack Bar make on hot dogs?

_____

9. The Green family stopped at The Snack Bar for lunch. They bought **2** salads, a superburger, and **3** of the same drink. The bill came to **$7.52**. Which drink did they buy?

_____

10. Yuko ordered a superburger, a salad, and a frosty shake. When she paid the cashier, she received **2** quarters, **2** dimes, and **3** pennies. How much money had she given the cashier?

_____

Extend Your Thinking

11. Look back at problem **8**. What is The Snack Bar's cost of buying a hot dog and a roll? Explain how you found your answer.

_____

_____

_____

12. Look back at problem **9**. Explain how you found your answer.

_____

_____

_____

Identify the place value of each underlined digit.

1. 5.<u>4</u> _____

2. 341.6<u>4</u> _____

3. 700.00<u>9</u> _____

_____   _____   _____

Compare. Write <, > or =.

4. 1.9 ◯ 1.09

5. 13.5 ◯ 13.55

6. 476.99 ◯ 476.990

Write each fraction or mixed number as a decimal. Write each decimal as a fraction or mixed number.

7. $\frac{5}{100}$ _____

8. $1\frac{43}{100}$ _____

9. 0.3 _____

10. 2.035 _____

Estimate each sum or difference by rounding each number to the given place.

11. one
$$\begin{array}{r} 46.49 \\ + 3.6 \\ \hline \end{array}$$

12. hundredth
$$\begin{array}{r} 8.455 \\ - 0.384 \\ \hline \end{array}$$

13. tenth
$$\begin{array}{r} 36.071 \\ - 3.04 \\ \hline \end{array}$$

Estimate each sum or difference. Then add or subtract.

14.
$$\begin{array}{r} 4.7 \\ - 0.8 \\ \hline \end{array}$$

15.
$$\begin{array}{r} 3.06 \\ + 4.7 \\ \hline \end{array}$$

16.
$$\begin{array}{r} 50.56 \\ + 29.6 \\ \hline \end{array}$$

17.
$$\begin{array}{r} 650.10 \\ - 3.04 \\ \hline \end{array}$$

18.
$$\begin{array}{r} 58.005 \\ + 4.77 \\ \hline \end{array}$$

Multiply.

19.
$$\begin{array}{r} 0.8 \\ \times 8 \\ \hline \end{array}$$

20.
$$\begin{array}{r} 0.53 \\ \times 61 \\ \hline \end{array}$$

21.
$$\begin{array}{r} 6.55 \\ \times 0.54 \\ \hline \end{array}$$

22.
$$\begin{array}{r} 10.05 \\ \times 0.7 \\ \hline \end{array}$$

23.
$$\begin{array}{r} 0.46 \\ \times 100 \\ \hline \end{array}$$

Divide and check.

24. $7\overline{)45.5}$

25. $6\overline{)2.7}$

26. $25\overline{)0.3}$

27. $100\overline{)40.6}$

28. $3.7\overline{)8.51}$

Use the Guess and Check strategy. Solve.

29. The total weight of the Sarah's packages is **3.69** kg. One package weighs twice as much as the other. How much does each package weigh? _____

Name _____

1 Tan spent $4.80 on stamps. Each stamp cost $0.32. How many stamps did he buy?

A 13   C 32   E Not here

B 15   D 48

2 The movie is shown every 3 hours. It is $2\frac{1}{3}$ hours long. What part of an hour is the movie not being shown?

F $\frac{3}{4}$ h   H $\frac{2}{3}$ h   K $\frac{1}{4}$ h

G $\frac{1}{3}$ h   J $\frac{1}{2}$ h

3 Nancy earned $38,790.65 last year. Which shows the amount written in words?

A Three million eight thousand seven hundred ninety dollars and sixty-five cents

B Thirty-eight million seven hundred ninety thousand dollars and sixty-five cents

C Thirty-eight thousand seven hundred dollars and sixty-five cents

D Thirty-eight thousand seven hundred ninety dollars and sixty-five cents

4 Bobby scored 35 points on each of his spelling tests. He has a total of 385 points. Which equation could be used to find the number of spelling tests Bobby has taken?

F $385 \times 35 = n$

G $35 \div n = 385$

H $35 \times 385 = n$

J $385 \div 35 = n$

5 Hannah has saved $8.58 to buy a hat that costs $13.99. Which is a reasonable estimate of how much money she still needs to save in order to buy the hat?

A $6.00   C $13.99

B $8.58   D $15.00

6 Ian read that the moon is about 250,000 miles from Earth. Which expression is equivalent to 250,000?

A 2.5×10^6

B 2.5×10^5

C 2.5×10^4

D 2.5×10^3

The table shows the normal precipitation for a city in California during the first six months of the year. Use the table to answer questions 7–10.

Normal Precipitation in Inches

Jan.	Feb.	Mar.	Apr.	May	June
3.1	3.3	2.3	1.2	0.2	0.1

7 Which measurement gives the average normal precipitation in inches for the six months?

A 0.1   C 1.7

B 1.1   D 3.3

8 What would the average normal precipitation be if the measurement for Jan. was 3.7 inches instead of 3.1 inches?

F 1.8 inches   H 1.6 inches

G 1.7 inches   J 1.5 inches

9 Which point on the number line shows the normal precipitation for March?

A A   C C

B B   D D

10 Which two months each have normal precipitation of less than $\frac{1}{2}$ inch?

F May and June   H January and June

G April and May   J February and March

UNIT 7 • TABLE OF CONTENTS

Measurement

Dear Family,

During the next few weeks, our math class will be learning about measurement.

You can expect to see homework that provides practice with changing from one unit of measure to another. Here is a sample you may want to keep handy to give help if needed.

Customary Units of Length

The inch (in.), foot (ft), yard (yd), and mile (mi) are customary units of length.

Example 19 in. = _?_ ft _____ in.

Refer to the chart to find **1 ft = 12 in.**

Then divide **19** by **12**.

```
  1 R7
12)19
```
So, **19** in. = **1 ft 7 in.**

| 1 ft = 12 in. |
| 3 ft = 1 yd |
| 1 mi = 5,280 ft |

Example 5,280 ft = _?_ yd

Refer to the chart to find **3 ft = 1 yd.**

Then divide **5,280** by **3**.

```
  1,760
3)5,280
```
So, **5,280** ft = **1,760** yd.

| 1 ft = 12 in. |
| 3 ft = 1 yd |
| 1 mi = 5,280 ft |

During this unit, students will need to continue practicing addition, subtraction, multiplication, and division facts.

Sincerely,

The basic unit of length in the metric system is the **meter (m).**

10 millimeters (mm) = 1 centimeter (cm)
10 centimeters (cm) = 1 decimeter (dm)
10 decimeters (dm) = 1 meter (m)

The length of a baseball bat is about **1** meter.
The diameter of a baseball is about **1** decimeter.
The width of your fingernail is about **1** centimeter.
The thickness of a dime is about **1** millimeter.

The metric system is based on **10.** To change from one unit to another, multiply or divide by **10, 100,** or **1,000.**

- To change from a longer unit to a shorter unit, multiply.

5 m = ? cm
5 m = 500 cm

| Think: 1 m = 100 cm |
| 5 × 100 = 500 |

- To change from a shorter unit to a longer unit, divide.

50 mm = ? cm
50 mm = 5 cm

| Think: 10 mm = 1 cm |
| 50 ÷ 10 = 5 |

- Remember to add all the like units together.

8 m 5 dm = ? dm
8 m 5 dm = 85 dm

| Think: 1 m = 10 dm |
| (8 × 10) + 5 = 85 |

Think: 80 dm + 5 dm

Choose the best unit for measuring.
Write *mm, dm, cm,* or *m.*

1. length of pencil _____   thickness of coin _____

2. height of adult _____   width of this page _____

3. thickness of paper clip _____   height of school building _____

Complete.

4. 3 m = _____ cm   60 mm = _____ cm   7 m 3 dm = _____ dm

5. 7 dm = _____ cm   4,000 mm = _____ m   4 dm 9 cm = _____ cm

6. 5,000 mm = _____ dm   8 m = _____ mm   3 cm 4 mm = _____ mm

7. 300 cm = _____ m   4 dm = _____ mm   3 dm 8 cm = _____ cm

8. 20 cm = _____ mm   200 mm = _____ cm   5 m 2 dm = _____ dm

9. 20 dm = _____ m   5 m = _____ mm   4 cm 7 mm = _____ mm

In the metric system, **kilometers (km)** are used to measure greater distances. A kilometer is about the length of **9** football fields.

1 kilometer (km) = 1,000 meters.

Solve.

10. About how many times do you need to walk around

your schoolyard to walk **1** km? _____

11. About how many minutes does it take to walk **1** km? _____

12. Estimate each distance.

a. from your home to your school   b. from your school to the nearest

_____ km   grocery store _____ km

13. Name a place that is about **1** kilometer from your school. _____

Complete.

14. 2 km = _____ m   3 km = _____ m   5 km 175 m = _____ m

15. 5,000 m = _____ km   4,000 m = _____ km   8 km 9 m = _____ m

Problem Solving Reasoning   Solve.

16. The wingspan of a butterfly is **77** mm. Its height is **7** cm.

Which is greater, its wingspan or its height? _____

17. Mario is **140** cm tall. His brother is **1** m **62** cm tall. His sister is

1,090 mm tall. Who is the tallest? _____

18. The prefixes *deci*, *centi*, *milli*, and *kilo* are used to form other metric units of

length. Predict what each prefix means. Then use a dictionary to verify your

prediction. _____

Test Prep ★ Mixed Review

19. A watch regularly sells for $47.99. In a sale, the price of the watch has been reduced by $\frac{1}{3}$. *About* how much money do you save if you buy the watch on sale?

A $15   C $25
B $20   D $30

20. When you take money out of an ATM you need to enter a secret number. Suppose the last 3 digits of your code number are divisible by 4, 6, and 8. Which code number could you have?

F 457-621   H 457-216
G 457-612   J 457-126

Metric Units of Capacity and Mass

Capacity is the amount a container will hold. The basic unit of capacity in the metric system is the liter (**L**). It is about the size of a quart. A smaller unit of capacity is the **milliliter (mL)**.

---

1 liter (L) = 1,000 milliliters (mL)

The basic unit of **mass** in the metric system is the **gram (g)**. It is about the weight of a paper clip.

To measure the mass of very light objects, use **milligrams (mg)**.

To measure the mass of heavy objects, use **kilograms (kg)**.

To measure very great masses, use **metric tons (T)**.

1,000 milligrams (mg) = 1 gram (g)
1,000 grams (g) = 1 kilogram (kg)
1,000 kilograms (kg) = 1 metric ton (T)

Choose the most reasonable estimate of capacity.

1. a glass of water	**25** mL	**250** mL	**25** L
2. a sink	**30** L	**300** mL	**300** L
3. a spoon	**100** mL	**10** L	**10** mL
4. a soup bowl	**20** L	**200** mL	**200** L

Choose the best unit for measuring the mass. Write *mg*, *g*, *kg*, or *T*.

5. pine needle _____   school bus _____

6. dime _____   person _____

7. book _____   key _____

8. pencil _____   car _____

9. seed _____   basketball _____

Complete.

10. 3 L = _____ mL   2,000 mL = _____ L   1 L 400 mL = _____ mL

11. 5,000 mL = _____ L   15 L = _____ mL   4 L 25 mL = _____ mL

12. 5,000 g = _____ kg   8,000 kg = _____ T   2 g = _____ mg

13. 2 T = _____ kg   1 T = _____ g   42,000 mg = _____ g

Compare. Write > or <.

14. 400 L $\bigcirc$ 5,000 mL   1,500 mL $\bigcirc$ 2 L   1 L $\bigcirc$ 580 mL

15. 4,390 g $\bigcirc$ 2 kg   8,976 kg $\bigcirc$ 8 T   30,000 mg $\bigcirc$ 3 kg

Problem Solving Reasoning	Solve.

16. Which has a greater mass, a 3-kilogram box or a **300**-milligram box? Explain. _____

_____

17. How many **200**-milliliter paper cups can be filled from a **2**-liter pitcher of lemonade?

_____

18. A recipe for fruit punch requires **1** L of ginger ale, **750** mL of lemonade, and **500** mL of pineapple juice. Jon made twice this amount. How much punch did he make?

_____

19. Sarah is using **800**-g bags of sand to fill a sandbox that can hold **5** kg of sand. How many bags will she need to completely fill the sandbox?

_____

Test Prep ★ Mixed Review

20 When Arnie was asked how long he spent on his project, he answered that he spent the reciprocal of $\frac{4}{7}$ hour. How long did he spend on the project?

A $\frac{4}{7}$ h   **C** $1\frac{4}{7}$ h

B $\frac{3}{4}$ h   **D** $1\frac{3}{4}$ h

21 In the morning, 3,151 people got on the train at Dover. In the afternoon, 19 more people got off the train at Dover than had gotten on in the morning. How many people got off the train in Dover?

F 3,032   **H** 3,232

G 3,170   **J** 3,270

Name _____

You can use decimals to write measures in the metric system.
The line segment below is **108** mm or **10.8** cm long.

You can use what you know about multiplying and dividing by
10, **100**, or **1,000** to change from one unit to another.

Longer to shorter
unit, multiply. ➡️

10.8 cm = ? mm
10.8 cm = **108** mm

Think: 1 cm = **10** mm
To multiply a decimal by **10**, move the
decimal point one place to the right.

Shorter to longer
unit, divide. ➡️

10.8 cm = ? m
10.8 cm = **0.108** m

Think: 1 m = **100** cm
To divide a decimal by **100**, move the
decimal point two places to the left.

Complete to change units.

1. 4.35 m

_____ dm

_____ cm

_____ mm

2. 2.36 m

_____ dm

_____ cm

_____ mm

3. _____ m

5.725 dm

_____ cm

_____ mm

4. _____ m

_____ dm

890 cm

_____ mm

Complete.

5. 15.6 m = _____ dm

6. 4.2 kg = _____ T

7. 53 cm = _____ dm

8. 0.8 L = _____ mL

9. 0.06 T = _____ kg

250 mL = _____ L

6.83 m = _____ mm

9.1 kg = _____ g

0.74 g = _____ mg

402 mm = _____ m

7 g = _____ kg

1.8 dm = _____ mm

6.4 cm = _____ m

2.09 m = _____ cm

67 m = _____ km

Write a decimal point to make each statement reasonable.

10. The speed of a jet plane averaged **9 6 8 4 5** kilometers per hour.

11. Some children are **1 2 5** meters tall.

12. The weight of an **11**-year-old student is about **3 7 6** kilograms.

13. The height of a classroom door is **2 0 0 0** decimeters.

14. A baseball player threw a ball a distance of **4 5 6 7 8** meters.

Compare. Write > or <.

15. 0.27 dm $\bigcirc$ 27 cm   3.4 kg $\bigcirc$ 3,004 g   5,620 mL $\bigcirc$ 6 L

16. 420 mg $\bigcirc$ 4.2 g   2,500 m $\bigcirc$ 0.25 km   7.8 cm $\bigcirc$ 70 mm

17. 1.1 L $\bigcirc$ 926 mL   0.8 g $\bigcirc$ 9,000 mg   100.5 dm $\bigcirc$ 10.5 m

---

Problem Solving Reasoning | **Use the information in the box to solve.**

> A **$1** bill has a mass of **1** gram.
> A **$1** bill is **0.1** millimeter thick.

18. A new car costs **$15,000**. How many kilograms of $1 bills would it take to buy this car? If the $1 bills are stacked one on top of another, how many centimeters tall would the stack be?

_____

19. Suppose you saved a **$1** bill each day for **10** years, except for February 29. What would be the mass of your savings in grams? How many meters tall would the stack of your savings be?

_____

 Quick Check

Complete.

20. 3,000 mm = _____ m   **21.** 4 dm 5 cm = _____ cm

22. 6 km 25 m = _____ m

Compare. Write > or <.

23. 430 g $\bigcirc$ 1 kg   **24.** 2,500 mL $\bigcirc$ 2 L

25. 1,800 mg $\bigcirc$ 9 g

Complete.

26. 0.6 L = _____ mL   **27.** 3.2 kg = _____ mg

28. 0.25 cm = _____ m

Work Space

Name _____

The airline time table shows 4 daily nonstop flights from New York City to Lake Placid, New York.

In this lesson, you will solve problems by reading a time table or a graph.

Flight #	From: NYC	To: Lake Placid
23	8:41 A.M.	10:00 A.M.
55	10:35 A.M.	11:59 A.M.
79	2:59 P.M.	4:15 P.M.
92	6:35 P.M.	8:05 P.M.

Tips to Remember

1. Understand	2. Decide	3. Solve	4. Look back

- Compare the labels on the table or graph with the words and numbers in the problem.
- Use a list to organize the facts you need from the table or graph.
- Reread the problem carefully. Ask yourself questions about any part that you do not understand. Reread to find answers.

Use the airline time table to solve the problems.

1. How much time is there between the departures of Flight 55 and Flight 79?

Think: How much time is there between 10:35 A.M. and 12:00 noon? Between 12:00 noon and 2:59 P.M.?

_____

Answer: _____

2. How much longer does Flight 92 take than Flight 23?

Think: How can you rewrite **10:00** so that you will be able to subtract the minutes?

_____

_____

Answer: _____

3. How long does Flight 79 take?

_____

_____

4. Jane arrived at the airport **2** hours and **15** minutes early for Flight 55. Did she get there before the earlier flight departed? Expain how you know.

_____

_____

Solve. Use the graph.

Students in a class in Canada made this **double-line graph** to show the high and low temperatures in their town.

The double-line graph allows you to compare the two sets of data on one graph. Use the key to find the high and low temperatures.

High and Low Temperatures
(for 5 days)

Key
High ●——●
Low ●——●

5. On which day was the difference between the high and low temperature the greatest? How much was this difference?

_____

_____

6. The class calculated the average temperature for the week. What was the average?

_____

7. The high temperature of the day on Monday occurred at **11:39** A.M. The low temperature occurred at **10:51** P.M. How much time passed between the high and the low temperatures of the day?

_____

8. The low temperature of the day on Friday occurred at **2:15** A.M. The high temperature occurred **10** hours and **30** minutes later. At what time did the high temperature occur?

_____

Extend Your Thinking

9. Describe the **trend** or direction that the temperatures are moving for both the highs and the lows for the **5** days. What season do you think comes next?

_____

_____

10. Look back at problem **6**. Explain the method you used to solve the problem. Describe another method you might have used.

_____

_____

_____

Standard units of length in the customary system are the
inch (in.), **foot (ft)**, **yard (yd)**, and **mile (mi)**.

You can change from one unit to another by using this
information.

12 inches (in.) = **1** foot (ft)
3 feet = **1** yard (yd)
36 inches = **1** yard
5,280 feet = **1** mile (mi)
1,760 yards = **1** mile

- To change from a longer
  unit to shorter, multiply.

  3 ft = ? in.
  3 ft = 36 in.

  Think: 1 ft = 12 in.
  3 × 12 = 36

- To change from a shorter
  unit to longer, divide.

  12 ft = ? yd
  12 ft = 4 yd

  Think: 3 ft = 1 yd
  12 ÷ 3 = 4

- You may need to write a
  remainder using the smaller
  unit.

  42 in. = ? ft ? in.
  42 in. = 3 ft 6 in.

  Think: 12 in. = 1 ft
  42 ÷ 12 = 3 R6

Choose the best unit for measuring. Write *in., ft, yd,* or *mi*.

1. length of your finger _____   width of a sidewalk _____

2. height of classroom _____   width of a $1 bill _____

3. distance from school to home _____   length of a soccer field _____

Complete.

4. 7 ft = _____ in.   24 ft = _____ yd   72 in. = _____ yd

5. 60 in. = _____ ft   2 mi = _____ ft   15 yd = _____ ft

6. 108 in. = _____ yd   5 ft = _____ in.   36 ft = _____ yd

7. 5 yd = _____ ft   144 in. = _____ ft   15,840 ft = _____ mi

8. 30 in. = _____ ft _____ in.   10 ft = _____ yd _____ ft

9. 6,000 ft = _____ mi _____ ft   125 in.= _____ ft _____ in.

You may need to regroup when you add customary units.

1. Add inches.

$$\begin{array}{r} 4 \text{ ft} \quad 7 \text{ in.} \\ + 3 \text{ ft} \quad 8 \text{ in.} \\ \hline 15 \text{ in.} \end{array}$$

> Think:
> 7 + 8 = 15

2. Regroup. 15 in. = 1 ft 3 in.

$$\begin{array}{r} \overset{1}{} \\ 4 \text{ ft} \quad 7 \text{ in.} \\ + 3 \text{ ft} \quad 8 \text{ in.} \\ \hline 3 \text{ in.} \end{array}$$

3. Add feet.

$$\begin{array}{r} \overset{1}{} \\ 4 \text{ ft} \quad 7 \text{ in.} \\ + 3 \text{ ft} \quad 8 \text{ in.} \\ \hline 8 \text{ ft} \quad 3 \text{ in.} \end{array}$$

You may also need to regroup when you subtract customary units.

1. Regroup. 6 yd = 5 yd 3 ft

$$\begin{array}{r} \overset{5}{\cancel{6}} \text{ yd} \quad \overset{4}{\cancel{1}} \text{ ft} \\ - 2 \text{ yd} \quad 2 \text{ ft} \\ \hline \end{array}$$

2. Subtract feet.

$$\begin{array}{r} \overset{5}{\cancel{6}} \text{ yd} \quad \overset{4}{\cancel{1}} \text{ ft} \\ - 2 \text{ yd} \quad 2 \text{ ft} \\ \hline 2 \text{ ft} \end{array}$$

3. Subtract yards.

$$\begin{array}{r} \overset{5}{\cancel{6}} \text{ yd} \quad \overset{4}{\cancel{1}} \text{ ft} \\ - 2 \text{ yd} \quad 2 \text{ ft} \\ \hline 3 \text{ yd} \quad 2 \text{ ft} \end{array}$$

Add.

10.

$$\begin{array}{r} 4 \text{ ft} \quad 7 \text{ in.} \\ + 3 \text{ ft} \quad 7 \text{ in.} \\ \hline \end{array}$$

$$\begin{array}{r} 6 \text{ ft} \quad 10 \text{ in.} \\ + 2 \text{ ft} \quad 4 \text{ in.} \\ \hline \end{array}$$

$$\begin{array}{r} 5 \text{ ft} \quad 9 \text{ in.} \\ + 3 \text{ ft} \quad 9 \text{ in.} \\ \hline \end{array}$$

$$\begin{array}{r} 7 \text{ ft} \quad 8 \text{ in.} \\ + 4 \text{ ft} \quad 9 \text{ in.} \\ \hline \end{array}$$

Subtract.

11.

$$\begin{array}{r} 3 \text{ yd} \quad 1 \text{ ft} \\ - 1 \text{ yd} \quad 2 \text{ ft} \\ \hline \end{array}$$

$$\begin{array}{r} 8 \text{ yd} \quad 1 \text{ ft} \\ - 2 \text{ yd} \quad 2 \text{ ft} \\ \hline \end{array}$$

$$\begin{array}{r} 5 \text{ yd} \\ - 2 \text{ yd} \quad 2 \text{ ft} \\ \hline \end{array}$$

$$\begin{array}{r} 6 \text{ yd} \\ - 3 \text{ yd} \quad 1 \text{ ft} \\ \hline \end{array}$$

Problem Solving
Reasoning

Solve.

12. Justin has a piece of wood 4 ft 3 in. long. If he uses 1 ft 5 in. for a project, will he have 1 yd left for another project? Explain.

_____

_____

13. Lindsey needs 3 ft 8 in. of ribbon for a project and 2 ft 7 in. of ribbon for another project. If she buys 2 yd of ribbon, will she have enough? Explain.

_____

_____

Test Prep ★ Mixed Review

14 Which measure will make this number sentence true? 0.009 km > ☐ ?

A 82.4 dm

B 8.24 m

C 8,240 cm

D 82,400 mm

15 The coach treated the team to pizza and punch. She bought 3 pizzas at $8.75 each and punch for $4.99. *About* what was her change from two $20 bills?

F more than $15

G between $10 and $15

H between $5 and $10

J less than $5

Name _____ **Measuring to the Nearest Inch**

To measure the length of small objects in the customary system,
you can use fractional parts of an inch.

This ruler measures
to the **nearest inch**.

This ruler measures
to the **nearest half-inch**.

This ruler measures
to the **nearest quarter-inch**.

This ruler measures
to the **nearest eighth-inch**.

The length of the crayon is: **4** inches to the nearest inch,

$3\frac{1}{2}$ inches to the nearest half-inch,

$3\frac{3}{4}$ inches to the nearest quarter-inch,

$3\frac{5}{8}$ inches to the nearest eighth-inch.

**Use a ruler to measure each to the nearest inch,
half-inch, quarter-inch, and eighth-inch.**

1. ────────────────────────

2. ──────────────────

3. ──────────────────────────────

4. ──────────────────────────

**A ruler is a kind of number line. Use the number line
to draw and label each point.**

5. Draw *A* at $\frac{3}{4}$.   Draw *B* at $1\frac{5}{8}$.   Draw *C* at $2\frac{3}{8}$.

For each figure, measure the length of each side to the nearest eighth-inch. Then write the total distance around the figure.

6.

_____

7.

_____

8.

_____

9.

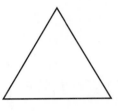

_____

Problem Solving
Reasoning

Use the picture to solve.

$1\frac{1}{2}$ ft

$\frac{1}{2}$ ft

10. If you make a ribbon border for this picture frame, how much ribbon would you need? _____

11. Suppose you already have a **1** yard piece of ribbon. How much more ribbon do you need? _____

Test Prep ★ Mixed Review

12 In a picture, the length of a pendant is 3.6 cm. The actual pendant is between 1.4 and 1.5 times longer. What is a reasonable estimate for the length of the actual pendant?

A 9 cm   C 5 cm

B 7 cm   D 3 cm

13 A lamb chop has 15.8 grams of protein, a frankfurter has 6.9 grams, and a piece of chicken has 21.2 grams. Which of these lists the foods from greatest to least grams of protein?

F chicken, lamb chop, frankfurter

G chicken, frankfurter, lamb chop

H lamb chop, frankfurter, chicken

J frankfurter, lamb chop, chicken

Customary Units of Weight and Capacity

In the customary system, weight is measured in **ounces**, **pounds**, or **tons**.

16 ounces (oz) = **1** pound (lb)
2,000 pounds = **1** ton (T)

Capacity is the amount of liquid a container can hold.

Capacity

8 fluid ounces = **1** cup (c)
2 cups = **1** pint (pt)
16 fluid ounces = **1** pint
2 pints = **1** quart (qt)
4 quarts = **1** gallon (gal)

4 quarts = **1** gallon

Complete.

1. 16 oz = 1 _____   _____ lb = **1** T   4 T = _____ lb

2. 5 T = _____ lb   _____ lb = 176 oz   2 T = _____ lb

3. _____ oz = 7 lb   10 lb = _____ oz   _____ oz = 9 lb

4. 9,000 lb = _____ T _____ lb   31 oz = _____ lb _____ oz

5. 15,000 lb = _____ T _____ lb   27 oz = _____ lb _____ oz

6. 2,003 lb = _____ T _____ lb   35 oz = _____ lb _____ oz

Complete.

7. 2 c = 1 _____   12 c = _____ pt   13 pt = _____ c

8. 2 pt = 1 _____   7 qt = _____ pt   25 qt = _____ pt

9. 4 qt = 1 _____   _____ gal = **52** qt   _____ gal = **48** pt

10. 2 qt = 1 half _____   _____ pt = **7** gal   28 c = _____ pt

11. 1 c = 1 half _____   40 pt = _____ gal   _____ c = **3** qt

12. 8 pt = 1 _____   76 qt = _____ gal   _____ c = **1** gal

Solve. Use the graph.

Hector's Weight

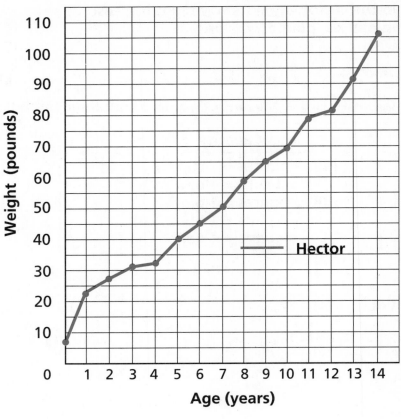

13. Was Hector's weight gain between **9** and **10** years old greater than, less than, or equal to his weight gain between **5** and **6** years old?

_____

14. How much did Hector weigh when he was **6** years old?

_____

15. Between which two years did Hector weigh **55** pounds?

_____

16. Between which two years did Hector gain the most weight?

_____

✓ Quick Check

Complete.

Work Space

17. 10,000 ft = _____ mi _____ ft

18. 90 in. = _____ yd _____ ft _____ in.

19. 3 ft 7 in. + 2 ft 8 in. = _____ ft _____ in.

20. 8 yd − (6 yd 2 ft) = _____ yd _____ ft

21. Use a ruler to measure the segment below to the nearest inch, half inch, quarter inch, and eighth inch.

_____

Complete.

22. 7,150 lb = _____ T _____ lb   **23.** 48 pt = _____ gal

24. 60 oz = _____ lb _____ oz   **25.** _____ pt = 80 fl oz

Name _____

Sometimes you need to draw a graph to solve a problem. First decide what type of graph to draw.

Line graph – shows changes over time

Bar graph – compares numbers

Pictograph – shows data expressed in multiples

Problem

Below are the highest monthly temperatures recorded in a town for nine months. How can you display the data to show the change from month to month?

September: 71°F   February: 27°F   October: 59°F
March: 39°F   November: 41°F   April: 57°F
December: 26°F   May: 69°F   January: 21°F

❶ Understand   **As you reread, ask yourself questions.**

What type of data is shown?   **What does the problem ask you to do?**

_____   _____

❷ Decide   Choose a method for solving.

Try the Draw a Graph strategy.

Since the data shows the change, what type of graph should you draw?

_____

❸ Solve   Label the horizontal scale with the months. You may abbreviate.

Look at the temperatures. What is the least value? _____

What is the greatest? _____

Use intervals of 10 for the vertical axis. Start at 0. Then draw a point on the graph for each temperature. Connect the points.

❹ Look back   Check your graph.

Does the graph show a trend?

Answer: _____

_____

Make a graph on another paper for problems 1–4. Use any other strategy for problems 5 and 6.

1. This is a table of Gail's height from age **1** to age **5**. How can you display the data to show the difference from year to year?

Age	Height in Inches
1	29
2	33
3	37
4	43
5	46

Think: What type of graph shows changes over time?

_____

Answer_____

2. How can you display this data in a graph so you can tell which lake is longest without comparing the numbers?

Great Lake	Length in Miles
Superior	350
Michigan	307
Huron	206
Erie	241
Ontario	193

Think: What type of graph allows you to compare length or distance?

_____

Answer_____

3. The table below shows the number of immigrants who came to the United States from 1930–1990.

Years	Number of Immigrants
1931-1940	528,431
1941-1950	1,035,039
1951-1960	2,515,479
1961-1970	3,321,677
1971-1980	4,493,314
1981-1990	7,338,062

a. How would you round the data so you can display it in a pictograph?

_____

_____

b. How many people would each symbol in the graph represent?

_____

4. A baseball fan made a graph showing how many players hit the most home runs in a single season. What did the graph look like?

Player	Number of Home Runs
Mark McGwire	70
Sammy Sosa	66
Roger Maris	61
Babe Ruth	60
Hank Greenberg	58
Jimmie Fox	58
Ken Griffey, Jr.	56

5. In degrees Fahrenheit, the freezing point of water is **32°F**. If the boiling point of water is **180°** higher, what is the boiling point of water?

_____

6. Each week Dan walks $\frac{1}{2}$ mile farther than the previous week. If he walks **2** miles the first week, how many miles does he walk the fifth week?

_____

Name _____

Use a ruler to measure the length of this segment to the nearest inch and to the nearest centimeter.

1. _____ in.

2. _____ cm

Complete each equation.

3. 8 m = _____ cm

4. 5 km = _____ m

5. 15 L = _____ mL

6. 50 mL = _____ L

7. 3.8 m = _____ dm

8. 0.4 kg = _____ g

9. 48 in. = _____ ft

10. 6 yd = _____ ft

11. 3 lb = _____ oz

12. 16,000 lb = _____ T

13. 3 pt = _____ c

14. 7 gal = _____ qt

This graph shows the Saturday and Sunday temperatures at different times of the day. Use the graph to help answer the questions that follow.

15. Was the temperature at **9** A.M. greater on Saturday or Sunday? By how many degrees was it greater? _____

16. At about what time was the temperature each day the same? _____

17. The temperature at **9** P.M. on Saturday was **70°F** and the temperature at **9** P.M. Sunday was **73°F**. Extend the graph and plot these times and temperatures.

Daytime Temperatures

°F

Key
_____ Saturday
_____ Sunday

Solve. Use the information in the table.

18. On the first day of a driving vacation, the Ramirez family drove from **7** A.M. to **11** A.M. at the rates shown in the table. How far from home were they when they stopped driving at **11** A.M.? _____

Time	Distance from Home
7 A.M.	0 mi
8 A.M.	40 mi
9 A.M.	90 mi
10 A.M.	150 mi
11 A.M.	

1

Which weighs the most?

A ⊖   C △

B ▯   D ☐

2 How many yards is it from the rock to the tree?

81 ft.

F 972   H 27

G 243   J $6\frac{3}{4}$

3

```
    A   B   C   D
◄─┼─●─┼─●─┼─●─┼─●─┼─►
  9     9.5     10
```

Which point on the number line is closest to $9\frac{15}{100}$?

A *A*

B *B*

C *C*

D *D*

4 A bag of oranges at a farm stand was on sale for $3.87. *About* how many bags did you buy if you spent about $50.00?

F 8

G 12

H 16

J 20

5 Which expression has the greatest value?

A $(2 \times 3^2) + 4^2$

B $2 \times (3^2 + 4^2)$

C $2 \times (3^2 \times 4^2)$

D $(2 + 3^2) + 4^2$

6 Nicky skied 0.35 second slower than his sister. If his time was 46.23 seconds, what was her time?

F 42.73 s

G 45.88 s

H 46.58 s

J 49.73 s

K Not here

7 A bag of dog food weighs 25 pounds. How much will 15 bags weigh?

A 40 lb

B 145 lb

C 275 lb

D 350 lb

E Not here

8 A pizza is cut into 12 slices. Four slices have mushrooms on them. Which number sentence could be used to show the fraction of slices that do not have mushrooms?

F $\frac{12}{12} - \frac{4}{12} = n$

G $\frac{12}{12} + \frac{4}{12} = n$

H $\frac{12}{12} - \frac{1}{12} = n$

J $\frac{12}{12} + \frac{1}{12} = n$

K $\frac{8}{12} + \frac{4}{12} = n$

UNIT 8 • TABLE OF CONTENTS

Geometry and Measurement

Dear Family,

During the next few weeks, our math class will be learning about geometry and measurement.

You can expect to see homework that provides practice in finding the areas of rectangles and right triangles. Here is a sample you may want to keep handy to give help if needed.

Areas of Rectangles and of Right Triangles

Area (**A**) is a measure in square units of a region or a surface.

The area of a rectangle is found by multiplying its length (**l**) by its width (**w**).

$$A = l \times w$$
$$A = 6 \times 3 \text{ or } \mathbf{18 \text{ in.}^2}$$

width (3 in.)

length (6 in.)

The area of a right triangle is $\frac{1}{2}$ the area of a rectangle. To find the area of a right triangle, first multiply its base by its height. Then multiply by $\frac{1}{2}$.

$$A = \frac{1}{2}(b \times h)$$

$$A = \frac{1}{2}(6 \times 3) \rightarrow \frac{1}{2} \times 18 \text{ or } \mathbf{9 \text{ in.}^2}$$

height (3 in.)

base (6 in.)

During this unit, students will need to continue practicing multiplication, addition, and subtraction facts.

Sincerely,

Name _____

Points, Lines, Line Segments, and Rays

A **point** is a location in space.

Read: point C

A **line** is a set of points in a straight path that extends in two directions without end.

Read: line CD or line DC

Write: $\overleftrightarrow{CD}$ or $\overleftrightarrow{DC}$

A **line segment** is part of a line that has two endpoints.

Read: line segment CD or line segment DC

Write: $\overline{CD}$ or $\overline{DC}$

Complete.

1. What is the name of this line? _____

2. Mark point *L* between points *E* and *F*. Is $\overleftrightarrow{EF}$ the same as $\overleftrightarrow{LF}$? _____

Use these two points to complete.

•   •

3. Label the two points *A* and *B*.

4. Use your ruler as a straightedge and connect the points.

5. You have drawn a line _____.

6. The endpoints of the figure are _____ and _____. Its name is _____.

Name all the line segments that are a part of each line.

7.

8.

_____   _____

A **ray** is a part of a line with only one endpoint. When you name a ray, always write its endpoint first.

Read: ray **AB**

Write: $\overrightarrow{AB}$

Lines that meet or cross each other are **intersecting lines.**

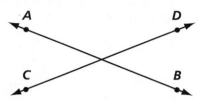

Read: $\overleftrightarrow{AB}$ intersects $\overleftrightarrow{CD}$

Lines that never intersect are **parallel lines.**

Read: $\overleftrightarrow{AB}$ is parallel to $\overleftrightarrow{CD}$.

Write: $\overleftrightarrow{AB} \parallel \overleftrightarrow{CD}$

Two intersecting lines that form right angles are **perpendicular lines.**

Read: $\overleftrightarrow{EF}$ is perpendicular to $\overleftrightarrow{GH}$.

Write: $\overleftrightarrow{EF} \perp \overleftrightarrow{GH}$

Name each ray.

9.

_____   _____   _____   _____

Write *intersecting, perpendicular,* or *parallel* to describe each pair of lines.

10.

_____   _____   _____

198   Unit 8 Lesson 1

Copyright © Houghton Mifflin Company. All rights reserved.

Name _____

Use a straightedge. Draw and label each figure.

11. line *PQ*

· · · · ·

· · · · ·

· · · · ·

12. point *R*

· · · · ·

· · · · ·

· · · · ·

13. line segment *ST*

· · · · ·

· · · · ·

· · · · ·

14. ray *GH*

· · · · ·

· · · · ·

· · · · ·

15. parallel lines *IJ* and *KL*

· · · · ·

· · · · ·

· · · · ·

· · · · ·

· · · · ·

16. intersecting lines *MN* and *RS*

· · · · ·

· · · · ·

· · · · ·

· · · · ·

· · · · ·

17. perpendicular lines *TU* and *VW*

· · · · ·

· · · · ·

· · · · ·

· · · · ·

· · · · ·

| Problem Solving |
| Reasoning |

How many line segments can you draw using the given points as endpoints?

18.

_____ line segments

19.

_____ line segments

Test Prep ★ Mixed Review

20 Dana bought a 19.8-pound turkey. What is its weight in ounces?

A 1.2

B 198

C 316.8

D 633.6

21 What number is equivalent to $2^3 \times 3^2$?

F 24

G 36

H 54

J 72

Name _____

An **angle** is formed by two rays that share a common endpoint. The common endpoint is called the **vertex**.

You name an angle using a point on each side and the vertex.

The name of the vertex is always in the *middle.* You can also name an angle by its vertex.

Read: angle **ABR**, angle **RBA**, or angle **B**
Write: ∠ABR, ∠RBA, or ∠B

....

You can use a **protractor** to measure an angle in **degrees**.

1. Place the center mark of the protractor on the vertex, **D**.

2. Align the **0°** mark of the scale of the protractor with $\overrightarrow{DF}$ of the angle.

3. To read the measure of the angle, find the place where $\overrightarrow{DE}$ passes through the scale on the protractor.
Read the inner scale if the angle opening is on the right.
Read the outer scale if the angle opening is on the left.

Read: ∠DEF measures 38°.

Name each angle in three ways.

1.

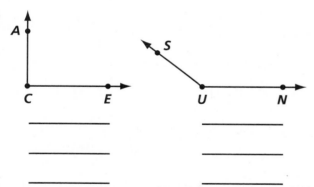

_____   _____   _____   _____

_____   _____   _____   _____

_____   _____   _____   _____

Measure each angle.

2.

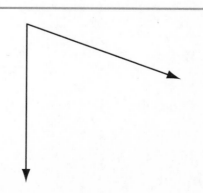

Name _____

You can classify angles by their measures.

right angle
measures **90°**

acute angle
measures less than **90°**

obtuse angle
measures greater than **90°**
but less than **180°**

Classify each angle as *right, acute,* or *obtuse.*
Then measure each angle with a protractor to check.

3.

_____

_____

4.

_____

_____

5.

_____

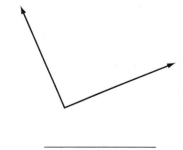

_____

You can use a protractor to draw an angle:

1. Draw a ray and label it.

2. Place the center mark of the protractor on the endpoint, or vertex. Align the **0°** mark with the ray.

3. Find **75°** on the scale. Mark a point.

4. Draw a ray from the vertex through the point you marked.

Draw ∠**XYZ** that measures **75°**.

← Mark this point.

Draw an angle with each measure. Classify the angle as right, acute, or obtuse.

6. 40°

7. 90°

_____

_____

| Problem Solving |
| Reasoning |

Solve.

8. Draw a kite having four straight sides. Measure each angle in your drawing. Classify each angle as right, acute, or obtuse.

Test Prep ★ Mixed Review

9 A clerk has $10\frac{1}{2}$ pounds of grapes. How many $\frac{1}{2}$-pound bags of grapes can she make?

A 21

B 11

C 10

D $5\frac{1}{4}$

10 A can of stew contains about $3\frac{1}{2}$ servings. If a serving is $6\frac{1}{4}$ ounces, about how many ounces of stew are in a can?

F 40

G 22

H 10

J 3

Name _____

A **polygon** is a closed figure made up of three or more line segments called **sides.** The sides meet only at their end points.

A **triangle** is a polygon made up of three line segments.

Read: triangle **ABC**
Write: △ **ABC**

You can classify triangles by the lengths of their sides.

3 in.   3 in.

3 in.

equilateral triangle
all sides of the
same length

5 cm   5 cm

4 cm

isosceles triangle
at least two sides of
the same length

2 ft   4 ft

5 ft

scalene triangle
no sides of the
same length

You can also classify triangles by their angle measures.

60°

90°   30°

right triangle
one right angle

70°

50°   60°

acute triangle
all acute angles

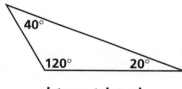

40°

120°   20°

obtuse triangle
one obtuse angle

Classify each triangle as equilateral, isosceles, or scalene.
Then classify each as right, acute, or obtuse.

1.

_____   _____   _____   _____

Use the information above about classifying triangles.

2. What is the sum of the measures of the

angles of each triangle?   right _____   acute _____   obtuse _____

3. What is the sum of the measures of the

angles of any triangle?   _____

Find the measure of each angle labeled with a question mark.

4.

_____   _____   _____

Solve.

Tear

5. Cut out a triangle. Then, tear off the three angles of the triangle as shown in the picture. Tape them side by side at one vertex.

   a. What do you observe?

   _____

Tape

   b. Another name for the figure you formed with the angles of a triangle is a **straight angle**. What is the measure of a straight angle? _____

✓ Quick Check

Draw and label each figure on a separate piece of paper.

  Work Space

   6. ray **PR** intersecting ray **ST** at point **V**

   7. line segment **BD** perpendicular to line **XY**

   8. 25° angle   **9.** 110° angle

 10. Classify the angles in exercise 8 and 9

      as acute, obtuse or right. _____

Complete.

 11. What are the measures of the acute angles in

      an isosceles right triangle? _____

 12. Two angles of a triangle are **15°** and **40°**. What

      is the measure of the third angle? What kind of

      triangle has these angle measures? _____

Name _____

Congruence

Congruent figures are figures that have the same size and shape.

These two triangles are congruent. If you trace figure *A* and put it on top of figure *B*, they will match.

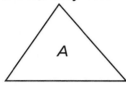

These two squares are not congruent. They are not the same size.

Sometimes a figure has sides or angles that are congruent to each other.

An equilateral triangle has three congruent sides and three congruent angles. The marks indicate congruent sides and congruent angles.

You measure the angles with a protractor to tell if they are congruent. They are congruent if their measures are equal.

This shows congruent sides.

This shows congruent angles.

Match each pair of congruent figures.

1.

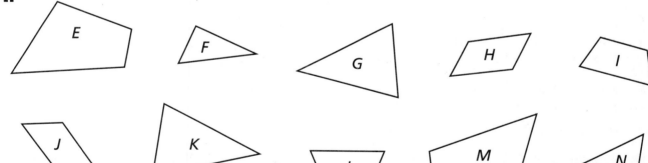

Mark the sides and angles that appear to be congruent.
Use a protractor to measure angles.

2.

  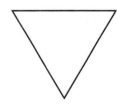

Name the angles and the sides that are congruent in each figure.

	Figure	Any Congruent Sides? Name them.	Any Congruent Angles? Name them.
3.			
4.			
5.			
6.			
7.			

Problem Solving Reasoning Use the figures in the table above to solve.

8. Look at the polygon in exercise 3. If the length of $\overline{AB}$ is **4** in. and the length of $\overline{BC}$ is **7** in., what is the total distance around polygon *ABCD?* _____

9. Look at the polygon in exercise 5. If the length of $\overline{PQ}$ is **6** cm, what is the total distance around polygon *PQRS?* _____

Test Prep ★ Mixed Review

10. Which two numbers have a difference of about 2,800?

   A 821 and 3,036

   B 3,036 and 7,385

   C 3,036 and 248

   D 7,385 and 9,162

11. A carpenter nailed two boards together. One board was $\frac{3}{4}$ in. thick and the other was $\frac{1}{8}$ in. thick. What is the total thickness of the boards?

   F $\frac{7}{8}$ in.   H $\frac{4}{12}$ in.

   G $\frac{7}{32}$ in.   J $\frac{5}{8}$ in.

Name _____

Quadrilaterals and Other Polygons

A quadrilateral is a four-sided polygon.

square
four congruent sides
four right angles

rectangle
opposite sides congruent
four right angles

parallelogram
opposite sides congruent
opposite sides parallel

rhombus
four congruent sides
opposite sides parallel

trapezoid
only one pair of
parallel sides

Write the name that best describes each quadritaleral.

1.

_____ _____ _____ _____

Use a straightedge. Draw each quadrilateral. Tell what kind of figure you have drawn.

2. A rectangle that is a rhombus

_____

3. A quadrilateral with opposite sides parallel and congruent

_____

4. A quadrilateral with all sides congruent but not all angles congruent

_____

Complete the chart.

5.

	Triangle △	Quadrilateral ⬠	Pentagon ⬠	Hexagon ⬡	Heptagon ⬡	Octagon ⬠
Sides	3	4				
Vertices	3					
Angles	3					

Write *true* or *false*.

6. All squares are rectangles. _____

7. It is possible to have a polygon with fewer sides than a triangle. _____

Name as many triangles, rectangles, and trapezoids as you can find in the figure at the right.

8. triangles _____

_____

9. rectangles _____

_____

10. trapezoids _____

_____

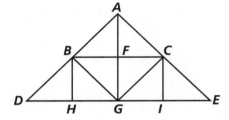

Problem Solving / Reasoning Use a straightedge. Solve.

11. Draw a quadrilateral. Divide it into two triangles. Use the figure to find the sum of the measures of the angles of the quadrilateral.

_____

Test Prep ★ Mixed Review

12. Which expression could you use to find the value in cents of *d* dimes?

A $d \div 10$

B $10 + d$

C $d - 10$

D $10 \times d$

13. Selma spent $.99 for 2 pencils and an eraser. Each pencil cost $.27. How much more than the pencil was the eraser?

F $2.25

G $.45

H $.18

J $.09

Name _____

Sometimes finding a pattern in a diagram or table helps you solve a problem.

Problem

Mr. Higgins arranges 3 pennies in the form of a triangle with 2 pennies in the bottom row and 1 on top. How many pennies will he need to make a triangle with 6 rows?

❶ Understand   As you reread, ask yourself questions.

- What do you know about the pennies that Mr. Higgins has?

  Mr. Higgins has 3 pennies.
  They are arranged in a triangle with 2 rows.

  What do you need to find?

  _____

❷ Decide   Choose a method for solving.

- Try the strategy Find a Pattern.

  First, draw a diagram of the 3 pennies.

     ← 1st row
  ← 2nd row

❸ Solve   Make a table to find the pattern.

Rows	2	3	4	5	6
Pennies	3				

❹ Look back   Describe the pattern. Draw a diagram if you wish.

_____

_____

_____

_____

_____

Copyright © Houghton Mifflin Company. All rights reserved.

Use the Find a Pattern strategy or any other strategy you have learned.

1. A diagonal of a polygon connects **2** opposite vertices. In a quadrilateral, a diagonal forms **2** triangles. How many triangles are formed by the diagonals from **1** vertex in a hexagon?

Think: Can you connect vertices next to one another and form a triangle?

_____

Answer: _____

2. A triangle has no diagonals. A quadrilateral has **2** diagonals. A pentagon has **5** diagonals. How many diagonals does a hexagon have?

Think: If you set up a table to solve the problem, what would the first entries be?

_____

Answer: _____

3. Look at this pattern.
angleangleangle
What letter will be in the thirty-eighth position?

_____

4. The first **4** square numbers are **1**, **4**, **9**, and **16**. What are the next four square numbers?

_____

5. Erin made this list of numbers.
2, 3, 5, 7, 11, 13, 17.
Jamal added the next three numbers to the list. What numbers did Jamal add to the list?

_____

6. On Sunday Andrew spent **$48**. On Monday he spent **$24**. On Tuesday he spent **$12**. If he continues the pattern, how much will he spend on Saturday?

_____

7. A bell rings in the Allen Middle School to signify the end of the class. The first three bells ring at **8:20**, **9:05**, and **9:50**. What time is the next bell?

_____

8. Caitlin practices the piano for **30** minutes every day after school and for **45** minutes on both Saturday and Sunday. How long does she practice each week?

_____

A **circle** is the set of all points that are the same distance from a given point called the **center.** The center of the circle at the right is point **O.**

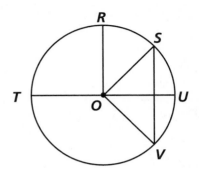

A **radius** is a line segment joining any point on the circle with its center. $\overline{OT}$ is one radius in this circle.

A **chord** is a line segment joining any two points on a circle. $\overline{SV}$ is a chord in this circle.

A **diameter** is a chord that passes through the center of a circle. $\overline{TU}$ is a diameter of this circle.

A **central angle** is an angle formed by two radii. ∠**ROU** is a central angle.

There are 360° in a circle. Use this information to write the measure of each central angle.

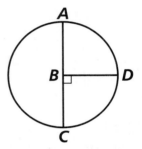

1. ∠**ABC** _____   ∠**ABD** _____

Use a compass.

2. Draw a circle.

    a. Draw a point for the center of the circle. Place the compass point on the center of the circle.

    b. Set the compass for a radius of **1** inch.

    c. Turn the compass completely around.

    d. Draw and label these parts of the circle:

        center **P**
        radius $\overline{AP}$
        chord $\overline{BC}$
        diameter $\overline{CD}$ through the center **P**
        central angle **EPF**

When a figure can be folded along a line, so that one half matches the other half, the figure has **line symmetry**.

one line of symmetry

four lines of symmetry

Does each figure have line symmetry? Write *Yes* or *No*. If it does, draw all the lines of symmetry.

3.

_____   _____   _____

Some figures have **rotational symmetry**. This means that you can turn a figure
     a quarter turn (or **90°**),
     a half turn (or **180°**), or
     a three-quarter turn (or **270°**),
and it will match the way it looked before the turn.

Figure *A* will match itself after a half turn, or **180°** turn.

- Try it. Trace Figure *A*. Align the point on the figure with the center point of the circle above.

- With one hand, hold the figure at the center point. With the other hand, slowly turn the figure **180°** to verify that it matches the original image.

original image

after 180° turn

Figure *A*   Figure *A*

Trace the figure. Turn it. Write *Yes* or *No* to tell if it has rotational symmetry. If it does, tell how many degrees it was turned.

4.

_____   _____   _____

Name _____

Use a compass to construct figures inside circles.

5. Construct a square inside a circle.
  a. Mark a point for the center of a circle. Use the compass to draw a circle.
  b. Draw a diameter. Use a protractor to draw a second diameter perpendicular to the first.
  c. Draw chords that connect the endpoints of the diameters to make a square.

6. Construct an equilateral triangle.
  a. Draw a circle with a radius of 2 cm.
  b. Use the same compass setting. Make 6 marks as shown. Connect the 6 marks with chords.
  c. Use the hexagon to make an equilateral triangle. Choose any vertex of the hexagon. Connect every second vertex.

✔ Quick Check

Name the angles and the sides that are congruent in each figure.

Work Space

7.

_____

_____

8.

_____

_____

9.

_____

_____

Complete.

10. Name the quadrilateral in exercise 9. _____

11. Name the polygon in exercise 8. _____

12. Which segments in circle *O* are congruent? Explain. _____

13. Name a central angle in the circle. _____

14. Which segment is a chord? _____

15. Does triangle *DOE* have a line of symmetry? Explain.

_____

Name _____

Perimeter and Area

The **perimeter** of a figure is the distance around it. The perimeter is measured in *linear units*.

The **area** of a figure is the amount of surface it covers. The area is measured in *square units*.

Formulas for Rectangle and Square

$P = 2(l + w)$ ← rectangle
$P = 4s$ ← square

$A = l \times w$ ← rectangle
$A = s^2$ ← square

This figure is made up of more than one geometric shape.

To find the perimeter of the figure, add the lengths of all its sides.

To find its area:
- Divide the figure into rectangles.
- Find any missing lengths.
- Find the area of each rectangle.
- Find the sum of the areas.

Think:
5 cm − 2 cm = 3 cm

Perimeter

$9 + 2 + 6 + 3 + 15 + 5 = 40$ cm

Area of rectangle A

$9 \times 5 = 45$ cm^2

Area of rectangle B

$6 \times 3 = 18$ cm^2

Total Area → $45 + 18 = 63$ cm^2

Find the perimeter and area of each figure.

1.

8 cm
5 cm

$P =$ _____ $A =$ _____

2.

7 mm
7 mm

$P =$ _____ $A =$ _____

3.

$10\frac{1}{2}$ in.
$12\frac{1}{2}$ in.

$P =$ _____ $A =$ _____

4.

10 cm
8 cm
←5 cm
12 cm

$P =$ _____ $A =$ _____

5.

1 in.
1 in.
7 in.
7 in.

$P =$ _____ $A =$ _____

6.

2 m
2 m
←2.6 m
4.4 m
6 m
8.4 m

$P =$ _____ $A =$ _____

Name _____

Find the perimeter and area of each figure.

7.

3 ft →
2 ft | 3 ft
6 ft   6 ft
6 ft

P = _____   A = _____

8.

5 cm
10 cm
2 cm   4 cm
3 cm

P = _____   A = _____

9.

8 ft
2 ft
4 ft →
1 ft   1 ft
2 ft

P = _____   A = _____

Find the rectangle with the greater perimeter. Write *a* or *b*.

10. a. length, **23** cm; width, **12** cm
b. length, **29** cm; width, **5** cm

_____

11. a. length, **8** in.; width, **16** in.
b. length, **10** in.; width, **15** in.

_____

| Problem Solving |
| Reasoning |

Solve.

12. Give the length and width in whole inches of three different rectangles that each have an area of **48 in.²**

_____

_____

_____

13. Melissa has **60** ft. of fencing for a garden. She wants a rectangular garden with the greatest possible area for planting. What is the length, width, and area of the garden she should make? (Use only whole units for the length and width.)

_____

Test Prep ★ Mixed Review

14 Which of these numbers is 7.5 when rounded to the nearest tenth and 7 when rounded to the nearest whole number?

A 7.499

B 7.39

C 7.2

D 7.009

15 A student's test grades were 86, 79, 83, and 72. What grade does she need to get on the fifth test so that her average is 83?

F 80

G 86

H 90

J 95

Name _____

Area of a Triangle and a Parallelogram

You can use what you know about the area of a rectangle to find the area of a triangle.

The length of the rectangle below and the **base** of the triangle below are the same.
The width of the rectangle and the **height** of the triangle are the same.

The triangle covers half the area that the rectangle covers.

So the area of a triangle is $\frac{1}{2}$ of the area of the rectangle.

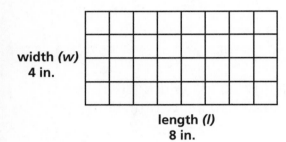

width *(w)*
4 in.

length *(l)*
8 in.

height *(h)*
4 in.

base *(b)*
8 in.

Area of rectangle $= l \times w$

$= 8 \times 4$

$= 32$ in.^{2}

Area of a triangle $= \frac{1}{2}(b \times h)$

$= \frac{1}{2}(8 \times 4)$

$= \frac{1}{2} \times 32$

$= 16$ in.^{2}

> Area of a triangle $= \frac{1}{2}(b \times h)$

Find the area of each triangle.

1.

7 cm

12 cm

A = _____

2.

10 ft

3 ft

A = _____

3.

5 m

11 m

A = _____

4.

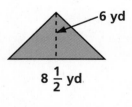

6 yd

$8\frac{1}{2}$ yd

A = _____

5.

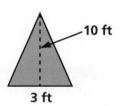

15 in.

5 in.

A = _____

6.

9 dm

8.4 dm

A = _____

Name _____

You can use what you know about the area of triangles to find the area of a **parallelogram**. Note that a diagonal divides the parallelogram into **2** congruent triangles.

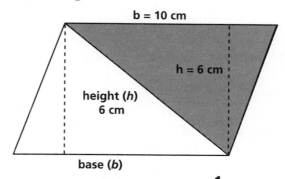

Area of a triangle $= \frac{1}{2}(b \times h)$

$$= \frac{1}{2}\,(10 \times 6)$$

$$= \frac{1}{2} \times 60$$

$$= 30 \text{ in.}^2$$

Area of a parallelogram $= \frac{1}{2}(b \times h) + \frac{1}{2}(b \times h)$

$$= 1\,(b \times h)$$

$$= 10 \times 6$$

$$= 60 \text{ cm}^2$$

> Area of a parallelogram $= b \times h$

Find the area of each parallelogram.

7.
1.3 cm
4.7 cm

$A =$ _____

8.
$5\frac{1}{4}$ yd
$4\frac{1}{2}$ yd

$A =$ _____

9.
7 in.
8 in.

$A =$ _____

| Problem Solving |
| Reasoning |

Solve.

10. Use what you know about area and dividing figures into other figures to find the area. _____

3 cm   6 cm
10 cm

Test Prep ★ Mixed Review

11 In the number 38,649,254 the 8 is in what place?

A billions

B millions

C hundred thousands

D thousands

12 On the average, between 25 and 30 people visit the museum each hour. What is a reasonable total number of people who will visit the museum in a 9-hour day?

F Less than 200

G Between 240 and 250

H About 300

J More than 300

Three-dimensional geometric figures are called
space figures or **solids**.

Prisms have two congruent bases.

bases

| cube | rectangular prism | triangular prism |

Pyramids have only one base.

base

| triangular pyramid | square pyramid | pentagonal pyramid |

Some other space figures or solids have curved surfaces.

2 bases   1 base   no base

| cylinder | cone | sphere |

Circle the kind of space figure you make if you fold each net.

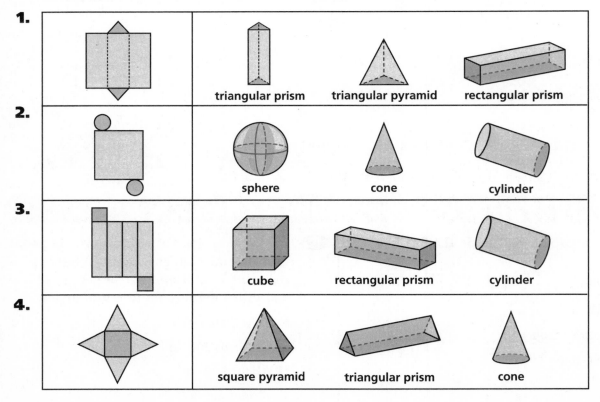

1.
triangular prism   triangular pyramid   rectangular prism

2.
sphere   cone   cylinder

3.
cube   rectangular prism   cylinder

4.
square pyramid   triangular prism   cone

Name _____

The flat surface of a space figure is a **face**. The line segment where two faces meet is an **edge**. The point where several edges meet is a **vertex**.

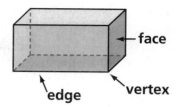

Complete this table.

	Figure	Number of faces	Number of edges	Number of vertices
5.	rectangular prism			
6.	triangular pyramid			
7.	triangular prism			
8.	square pyramid			

Write whether each statement is *always*, *sometimes*, or *never* true.

9. All the faces of a prism are congruent. _____

10. A pyramid can have two square faces. _____

11. A face of a triangular prism is a triangle or a rectangle. _____

12. A cone has two circular faces. _____

13. A space figure can have exactly one vertex. _____

Look at the space figures on page 218. Name the figure whose top and side views are shown.

A space figure looks different when you look at it from above or from a side.

Square pyramid

Front view

Top view

Side view

14.

Top view   Side view

_____

15.

Top view   Side view

_____

16.

Top view   Side view

_____

The space figures below are made from cubes.
Circle the figure whose views are shown.

17.

Top view   Side view   Front view

Problem Solving
Reasoning

Solve.

18. On grid paper, draw and label the front, side, and top views of the other figure above. (Hint: You may want to use cubes to model the figure first.)

☑ **Quick Check**

Find the area of these figures.

Work Space

19.
11 cm
5 cm
11 cm
5 cm
3 cm   3 cm

20.
6 cm   4 cm
7 cm

21.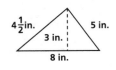
$4\frac{1}{2}$in.   5 in.
3 in.
8 in.

_____ _____ _____

22. Find the perimeter of the figure in exercise 19. _____

Complete.

23. Circle the kind of space figure you could make if you fold the net.

24. Name the space figure you could make. _____

25. How many faces, edges, and vertices does

the figure have? _____

26. Name the other figures in exercise 22. _____

Name _____

Many things are packed in cardboard cartons. What is the total area of the cardboard needed to form this box if no cardboard overlaps?

The total area of all the faces of a space figure is called its **surface area**. In a rectangular prism, the top and bottom are congruent, the two sides are congruent, and the front and back are congruent.

To find the surface area of a rectangular prism:
Find the areas of its top, one side, and front. Find the sum of those areas. Then multiply the sum by **2**.

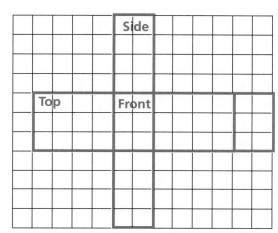

Top: $A = 3 \text{ ft} \times 4 \text{ ft} \longrightarrow 12 \text{ ft}^2$

Side: $A = 4 \text{ ft} \times 2 \text{ ft} \longrightarrow 8 \text{ ft}^2$

Front: $A = 3 \text{ ft} \times 2 \text{ ft} \longrightarrow 6 \text{ ft}^2$

Surface Area $= 2 \times (12 \text{ ft}^2 + 8 \text{ ft}^2 + 6 \text{ ft}^2)$

$= 2 \times 26 \text{ ft}^2$

$= 52 \text{ ft}^2$

So, **52 ft^2** of cardboard is needed for this box.

Find the surface area of each rectangular prism.

1.

4 cm
2 cm
4 cm

Surface Area = _____

2.

5 cm
4 cm
5 cm

Surface Area = _____

3.

2 in.
10 in.
1 in.

Surface Area = _____

4.

3 cm
3 cm
6.5 cm

Surface Area = _____

5.

9 cm
2 cm
4 cm

Surface Area = _____

6.

1.5 m
1.4 m
1.2 m

Surface Area = _____

Copyright © Houghton Mifflin Company. All rights reserved.

Unit 8 Lesson 11 **221**

Solve.

7. Find the surface area of each cube at the right. How can you find the surface area of a cube using multiplication?

3 cm

3 cm

3 cm

5 in.

5 in.

5 in.

_____

_____

8. Suppose you cut the block of wood at the right in half. You need to cover the pieces with adhesive paper. Did you need more or less paper before the block was cut? Explain.

8 in.

10 in.

20 in.

_____

_____

Each space figure is made up of centimeter cubes. Find each surface area by counting faces. Remember that some cubes cannot be seen.

9.

10.

11.

12.

Test Prep ★ Mixed Review

13 The speed of ships is measured in *knots*, or nautical miles per hour. A nautical mile is about $1\frac{1}{6}$ land miles. How many feet are in a nautical mile?

    A 4,526   **C** 6,160

    B 5,900   **D** 6,610

14 Marla's and Jolene's times in the 200-meter dash were 26.03 seconds and 29.58 seconds. Katy's time was 0.45 seconds slower than the winning time. What was Katy's time?

    F 25.58 s   **H** 29.13 s

    G 26.48 s   **J** 30.03 s

Name _____

Volume

You measure volume in **cubic units**.

Volume is the number of cubic units that a space figure can hold. To find how many cubic feet this cardboard box can hold, you can use a formula.

height (h)
2 ft

length (l)
4 ft

width (w)
3 ft

| Volume of a rectangular prism: $V = l \times w \times h$ |

$$V = l \times w \times h$$
$$= 4 \times 3 \times 2$$
$$= 24 \text{ ft}^3$$

To find the volume of a cube, you can also use a formula.

3 cm

3 cm

3 cm

| Think: s = length of a side |

| Volume of a cube: $V = s^3$ |

$$V = s^3$$
$$= 3^3$$
$$= 27 \text{ cm}^3$$

Find the volume of each prism.

1.

2 in.   8 in.
10 in.

$V =$ _____

2.

5 ft
5 ft
5 ft

$V =$ _____

3.

6 in.
9 in.
3 in.

$V =$ _____

4.

4 cm
3.2 cm
4 cm

$V =$ _____

5.

3 cm
2.8 cm
1.2 cm

$V =$ _____

6.

2.4 cm
2.4 cm
2.4 cm

$V =$ _____

Would you find perimeter, area, or volume to answer each question? Write *perimeter*, *area*, or *volume*.

7. How much wrapping paper is needed to cover a box? _____

8. How much ribbon is needed to go around a box? _____

9. How much packing material is needed to fill a box? _____

10. How much air can a room hold? _____

11. How much carpeting is needed to carpet a room? _____

12. How much wallpaper border is needed for a room? _____

Problem Solving Reasoning | Solve.

13. The surface area of a cube is **96 cm²**.
What is the volume of the cube?

_____

14. A rectangular prism is **4 in.** long and **2 in.** high.
Its volume is **40 in.³** What is its width?

_____

15. A rectangular prism is **6 cm** long and **3 cm** wide.
Its volume is **90 cm³**. What is its surface area?

_____

 Quick Check

Find the surface area.   **Work Space**

16.   **17.** $2\frac{1}{2}$ ft $2\frac{1}{2}$ ft $2\frac{1}{2}$ ft   **18.** 7.4 cm 5 cm 8 cm

4 cm
5 cm 3 cm

_____   _____   _____

Find the volume of each figure in exercises 16–18.

19. _____   **20.** _____   **21.** _____

Problem Solving Application:
Use Formulas

In order to solve some problems, you need to know and use formulas.

In this lesson, you will use perimeter, area, and volume formulas. Sometimes you will have to decide which formula is the correct one to use.

Tips to Remember

| 1. Understand | 2. Decide | 3. Solve | 4. Look back |

- Ask yourself whether you have solved a problem like this before.
- Make a rough sketch of the figure. Then write the correct formula.
- Think about what the problem is asking you to do. What information does the problem give you? What do you need to find out?

Solve.

1. Roger's garden is **9** ft long and **4** ft wide. He wants to put fencing around the entire garden to keep the rabbits out. How much fencing must he buy?

Think: Does Roger need to find the perimeter or the area of the garden? What formula will you use?

_____

_____

Answer_____

2. Judy covered a jewelry box with paper to match her wall decorations. The box measured **6** in. long, **2** in. wide, and **3** in. high. How much paper did she use?

Think: How many sides does the box have? Do you have to find the perimeter or area of each side of the box?

_____

_____

Answer_____

3. An aquarium measures **20** in. by **12** in. by **10** in. What is the volume of the aquarium?

_____

4. A bedroom measures **12** ft by **15** ft. How many square feet of carpeting are needed for this bedroom?

_____

Solve.

5. The cheerleaders used ribbon to form a rectangle. The rectangle was **15** feet long and **10** feet wide. How long was the piece of ribbon?

_____

6. Bethany's kitchen is **10** ft by **12** ft. She wants to tile half of its floor. Tiles are one square foot. How many tiles does she need?

_____

7. The Pentagon building in Arlington, Virginia is in the shape of a regular pentagon. Its perimeter is about **1,640** yd. What is the length of each side of the Pentagon?

_____

8. The Washington Monument in Washington, D.C. has a square base, **55** ft on each side. What is the area of the base of the monument?

_____

9. Coretta hit a home run during the schoolyard baseball game. How many yards did she run if one side of the baseball diamond measures **14** yd?

_____

10. One wall in Tony's bedroom measures **11.5** ft by **8** ft. Tony hung a poster measuring **2** ft by **3** ft on the wall. How much wall space is not covered?

_____

11. Mandy is wrapping a box **1** ft on each side. The wrapping paper is **26** in. by **60** in. What size piece should she cut to wrap the box?

_____

12. Leon is tiling part of the floor in his room. The room is **16** ft by **20** ft. He bought **80** tiles. Each tile is one square foot. What fractional part of the room is he tiling?

_____

Extend Your Thinking

13. Look back at problem 3. One cubic in. of water weighs **0.036** lb. If the aquarium is totally filled, what is the weight of the water in the aquarium?

_____

14. Look back at problem 4. Carpeting is sold by the square yard. Describe how you could find the number of square yards of carpeting needed.

_____

Name _____

Draw and label each figure.

1. line segment *RS*   **2.** point *H*   **3.** ray *AB*   **4.** line *PQ*

Classify each angle. Write *acute*, *obtuse*, **or** *right*.

5.

6.

7.

_____   _____   _____

Draw an angle with each measure.

8.   **9.**

45°   110°

Find the measure of ∠A.

10.

_____

11.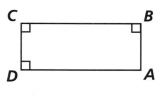

_____

Are each pair of figures congruent? Write *yes* **or** *no*.

12.

_____

13.

_____

14.

_____

Solve.

15. How many lines of symmetry does rectangle *WXYZ* have? _____ Draw the lines.

16. Draw a circle with center *D* and a diameter of **3** cm. Label the diameter $\overline{EF}$.

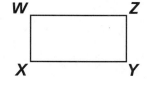

Find the perimeter or area of each figure. Use the formula if you need to.

17.

3 cm

5 cm

4 cm

$A = \frac{1}{2}(b \times h)$

$A =$ _____

18.

12 m

3 m

$P = 2\,(l+w)$

$P =$ _____

19.

$P =$ _____ units

$A =$ _____ sq. units

3

2

3

2

1

9

20. Name the space figure you could form if you folded this pattern.

_____

21. Find the volume (*V*) and surface area (*SA*) of this figure.

$V =$ _____ $SA =$ _____

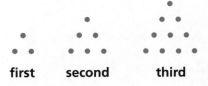

8 in.

1 in.

5 in.

Solve.

22. A sequence of dot figures is shown. The first figure is formed with **3** dots. The second figure is formed with **6** dots. The third figure is formed with **10** dots. How many dots would be needed to form the fifth figure? _____

first   second   third

23. A square has two different diagonals. A pentagon has **5**. A hexagon has **9**. How many different diagonals does an octagon, or eight-sided figure, have? (Hint: Draw a picture or find a pattern.) _____

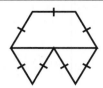

1 If the perimeter of the triangle on the left is 3 units and the area of the triangle is 1 unit^2 then what is the perimeter and area of the figure on the right?

A 9 units; 5 units^2

B 7 units; 5 units^2

C 5 units, 7 units^2

D 5 units, 9 units^2

2 What space figure will the pattern make when cut and folded?

F equilateral triangle

G cube

H triangular prism

J triangular pyramid

3 A compact car gets 27.28 miles per gallon. What is that number written as a mixed number?

F $\frac{27.28}{100}$

G $27\frac{2}{8}$

H $27\frac{28}{10}$

J $27\frac{28}{100}$

4 Use what you know about the properties of addition. What is the value of the variable n?

$$4 + (99 + 8) = n + (4 + 8)$$

F 8   H 99

G 12   J 107

5 One piece of ribbon is $3\frac{1}{2}$ feet. Another is about $\frac{5}{6}$ ft shorter. What is a reasonable length for the second piece of ribbon?

A Less than $2\frac{2}{3}$ ft

B More than 3 ft

C Exactly $2\frac{5}{6}$ ft

D Exactly $4\frac{1}{3}$ ft

6 Which rectangular prism has the same volume as this cube?

6 cm

6 cm   6 cm

A   4 cm
12 cm   3 cm

B   10 cm   2 cm
4.5 cm

C   4.5 cm
9 cm   4 cm

D   9 cm
8 cm   3 cm

Line *AB* intersects line *XY* at point *P*. The measure of angle *BPX* is 38°. Use this figure for questions 7–8.

7 Use a protractor. What kind of angle is angle *APB*?

A acute angle

B obtuse angle

C straight angle

D right angle

8 What is the measure of angle *BPY*?

F 38°

G 52°

H 142°

J 322°

9 A bag of oranges weighs 2.5 kilograms, a bag of onions weighs 11.1 kilograms, and a pineapple weighs 0.89 kg. How much do the oranges and pineapple weigh together?

A 13.6 kg

B 11.99 kg

C 11.189 kg

D 2.589 kg

E Not here

10 An inchworm crawled 1.68 m in one day. At this pace, which number sentence shows the number of meters the inchworm will travel in 100 days?

F $10^2 + 1.68 = \square$

G $10^2 \times 1.68 = \square$

H $10^3 \times 1.68 = \square$

J $1.68 \div \square = 10^2$

K $10^2 = 1.68 \times \square$

11 Ilie lives $\frac{3}{5}$ of a mile from school. She walks $\frac{1}{2}$ this distance to get to the bus stop. How far is the bus stop from her house?

A $\frac{1}{10}$ mi

B $\frac{3}{10}$ mi

C $\frac{6}{5}$ mi

D $\frac{11}{10}$ mi

E $1\frac{1}{6}$ mi

12 Every 3 months, a company gives its sales force money for gas based on the average number of miles driven on company business. Mr. Rosen estimates that he has driven 5,839 miles in 65 days. What is the average number of miles per day rounded to the nearest mile?

F 22

G 29

H 89

J 90

K Not here

UNIT 9 • TABLE OF CONTENTS

Ratio and Percent

Dear Family,

During the next few weeks, our math class will be learning about ratios and percents.

You can expect to see homework that provides practice with writing percents as fractions, and fractions as percents. Here is a sample you may want to keep handy to give help if needed.

Writing Percents as Fractions

Example Write **32** percent as a fraction.

1. Write the percent as a fraction with a denominator of **100**.

$$32\% = \frac{32}{100}$$

2. Write the fraction in simplest form.

$$\frac{32}{100} = \frac{32 \div 4}{100 \div 4} \rightarrow \frac{8}{25}$$

Writing Fractions as Percents

Example Write $\frac{3}{4}$ as a percent.

1. Write an equivalent fraction with a denominator of **100**.

$$\frac{3 \times 25}{4 \times 25} = \frac{75}{100}$$

2. Since percent means per hundred, you can think, **75** out of one hundred, then write **75%**.

$$\frac{75}{100} = 75\%$$

During this unit students will need to continue practicing addition, subtraction, multiplication, and division facts.

Sincerely,

Name _____

Ratios

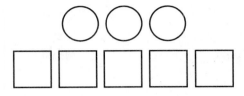

Ratios are used to compare two quantities.

The ratio of squares to circles is **5** to **3**.

The numbers in the ratio are called the **terms** of the ratio.

You can write the ratio of squares to circles

three ways: **5 to 3**, **5:3**, and $\frac{5}{3}$.

Each ratio is read in the same way: **5 to 3**.

Write each ratio three different ways.

1. **3** females to **2** males

_____

9 cats to **1** dog

_____

2. **6** cakes to **6** pies

_____

1 table to **4** chairs

_____

Write each ratio three different ways.

3. pentagons to triangles

_____

circles to pentagons

_____

4. circles to triangles

_____

pentagons to circles

_____

5. triangles to pentagons

_____

triangles to circles

_____

6. pentagons to all shapes

_____

all shapes to triangles

_____

You can write a ratio in simplest form the same way you write a fraction in simplest form.

Write the ratio **10** hammers to **5** saws in simplest form.

1. Find the GCF of both terms of the ratio. The GCF of **10** and **5** is **5**.

2. Divide each term by the GCF.

$$\frac{10 \div 5}{5 \div 5} = \frac{2}{1} \longleftarrow \text{simplest form}$$ You can also say the ratio is **2** hammers to **1** saw.

Write each ratio in simplest form three different ways.

7. circles to pentagons   squares to circles   hexagons to squares

_____   _____   _____

| Problem Solving |
| Reasoning |

Solve. Write each ratio in simplest form.

8. length of rectangle *A* to length of rectangle *B*

_____

9. width of rectangle *A* to width of rectangle *B*

_____

10. perimeter of rectangle *A* to perimeter of rectangle *B*

_____

11. area of rectangle *A* to area of rectangle *B*

_____

2 cm   [*A*]
3 cm

4 cm   [*B*]
6 cm

Test Prep ★ Mixed Review

12 You have four friends. The distances from your house to each of their houses are 3.1 miles, 1.7 miles, 2.6 miles, and 0.2 miles. What is the average distance between your house and your friends' houses?

A 1.9 mi

B 2 mi

C 2.1 mi

D 2.15 mi

13 A flower garden is 15 feet long and $2\frac{1}{2}$ feet wide. What is its perimeter?

F 6 feet

G $17\frac{1}{2}$ feet

H 35 ft

J $37\frac{1}{2}$ feet

Name _____

Rates and Unit Pricing

In **2** hours, Mrs. Carr drove **105** miles. If she continued driving at this rate, how far did she drive in **10** hours?

A rate is a special ratio that compares quantities that are in different units, such as miles and hours.

You can use a table to solve a rate problem.

The rate in this problem can be written as:

hours ➡ 2
miles ➡ 105

Hours	2	4	6	8	10
Miles	105	210	315	420	525

Mrs. Carr drove **525** miles in **10** hours.

Complete the table. Then use the table to answer the questions.

1. Lucas can read **3** pages in **5** minutes.

Pages	3	6						
Minutes	5	10						

How many pages can Lucas read in **15** minutes? _____

How long will it take Lucas to read **21** pages? _____

2. A 5-pound bag of oranges is on sale for **$2.95**.

Pounds	5					
Cost	$2.95					

What is the cost of **20** pounds of oranges? _____

A chef has **$15** to spend on oranges. How many pounds of oranges

can she buy? _____

3. A class completes **8** pages of math every **5** days of school.

Pages of Math	8									
Number of Days	5	10	15	20	25	30	35	40	45	50

How many pages will the class complete in **45** days? _____

How many pages will the class complete in a school year of **180** days? _____

Copyright © Houghton Mifflin Company. All rights reserved.

Unit 9 Lesson 2 **235**

The **unit price** of an item is the cost of that item *per unit,* such as the cost per pound or the cost per ounce.

Suppose a brand of ketchup you want to buy comes in two sizes:

16 ounces for **$1.59** or **12** ounces for **$1.29**.

To decide which is the **better buy,** you can compare their unit prices. The better buy is the one with the lower unit price.

Find the unit price of each size.

16-ounce bottle:

```
        $.099
16)$1.590
      −1 44
        150
      −144
          6
```

Round to
$.10

12-ounce bottle:

```
        $.107
12)$1.290
      − 1 2
        090
      − 84
          6
```

Round to
$.11

Since **$.10 per ounce** < **$.11 per ounce**, the **16**-ounce bottle is the better buy.

Circle the better buy in each pair.

4. sports drink

64 ounces for **$2.39** or

20 ounces for **$1.05**

5. frozen cheese pizza

21 ounces for **$4.59** or

10 ounces for **$1.59**

6. peanut butter

18 ounces for **$1.99** or

28 ounces for **$3.59**

Problem Solving
Reasoning

Solve.

7. Suppose you need **12** ounces of chocolate chips for a dessert you are making. A **10**-ounce bag of chips costs **$2.00**, and a **24**-ounce bag costs **$4.19**. What should you buy? Explain.

_____

_____

Test Prep ★ Mixed Review

8 What is the prime factorization of 45?

A 1×45

B 3×15

C 5×9

D $3^2 \times 5$

9 The diameter of a circle is between 8 cm and 10 cm. What might be the length of the radius?

F 4 cm

G 4.5 cm

H 8 cm

J 10 cm

Unit 9 Lesson 2

Copyright © Houghton Mifflin Company. All rights reserved.

Two ratios are equal if they name the same value.

To write equal ratios, multiply both terms by the same number or divide both terms by the same number.

Multiply to find the equal ratios.

$$\frac{6}{9} = \frac{?}{36}$$

$$\frac{6}{9} = \frac{6 \times 4}{9 \times 4} \rightarrow \frac{24}{36}$$

Think: $9 \times 4 = 36$, so multiply 6 by 4.

So, $\frac{6}{9} = \frac{24}{36}$.

Divide to find equal ratios.

$$\frac{6}{9} = \frac{2}{?}$$

$$\frac{6}{9} = \frac{6 \div 3}{9 \div 3} \rightarrow \frac{2}{3}$$

Think: $6 \div 3 = 2$, so divide 9 by 3.

So, $\frac{6}{9} = \frac{2}{3}$.

Jana's team scores an average of **3** runs in every **2** innings. Lisa's team scores an average of **6** runs in every **4** innings.

Are the ratios of runs to innings for both teams equal?

Jana's team $\rightarrow \frac{3}{2} = \frac{3 \times 2}{2 \times 2} \rightarrow \frac{6}{4}$ **Lisa's team**

Since $\frac{3}{2} = \frac{6}{4}$, the ratios are equal.

Determine whether each pair of ratios is equal. Write *yes* or *no*.

1. $\frac{3}{8}, \frac{6}{12}$ _____ $\frac{20}{15}, \frac{4}{3}$ _____ $\frac{1}{4}, \frac{8}{2}$ _____

2. 10:16, 5:4 _____   9:1, 18:2 _____   5:9, 15:27 _____

3. 12 to 16, 4 to 3 _____   7 to 5, 5 to 7 _____   9 to 3, 3 to 1 _____

Circle the ratio on the right that does *not* equal the ratio on the left.

4. $\frac{3}{4}$	$\frac{9}{12}$	$\frac{6}{8}$	$\frac{15}{16}$	$\frac{12}{16}$
5. 10:8	20:4	30:24	50:40	40:32
6. 24 to 30	12 to 15	10 to 8	48 to 60	4 to 5

Complete to form equal ratios.

7. $\frac{3}{7} = \frac{}{21}$ $\frac{10}{12} = \frac{5}{}$ $\frac{40}{15} = \frac{}{3}$ $\frac{18}{8} = \frac{}{4}$

8. $\frac{11}{9} = \frac{22}{}$ $\frac{1}{5} = \frac{}{30}$ $\frac{21}{18} = \frac{}{6}$ $\frac{9}{15} = \frac{3}{}$

9. $\frac{50}{70} = \frac{5}{}$ $\frac{7}{3} = \frac{}{12}$ $\frac{12}{6} = \frac{}{1}$ $\frac{8}{7} = \frac{}{21}$

10. $\frac{80}{90} = \frac{8}{}$ $\frac{28}{32} = \frac{}{8}$ $\frac{3}{2} = \frac{}{16}$ $\frac{7}{1} = \frac{}{6}$

Use the graph to solve each problem.

11. Write the ratio of bales of hay to horses.

     4 horses _____   **8** horses _____   **16** horses _____

12. What is the ratio of bales of hay to horses

     for **4, 8,** and **16** horses in simplest form? _____

13. If the graph continued, how many bales

     of hay would be needed for **48** horses? _____

Hay Needed Daily for Horses

Number of Bales of Hay (vertical axis: 0, 2, 4, 6, 8, 10, 12, 14, 16, 18)

Number of Horses (horizontal axis: 2, 4, 6, 8, 10, 12, 14, 16, 18)

✔ **Quick Check**

Write the ratio in simplest form in three different ways.

Work Space

14. **14** dogs to **20** cats _____

15. **24** cars to **16** vans _____

16. **95** miles to **40** miles _____

Write the unit price. Give the answer to the nearest cent.

17. **$1.69** for **8** ounces _____

18. **$5.99** for **3** notebooks _____

19. **$6.38** for **24** ounces _____

Complete the pair of equal ratios.

20. $\frac{3}{8} = \frac{}{40}$ **21.** $\frac{55}{66} = \frac{}{6}$ **22.** $\frac{7}{4} = \frac{}{48}$

Name _____

Scale Drawing

The picture of the flagpole is smaller than the actual flagpole. The ratio of the height in the picture to the height of the actual flagpole is called the **scale**. The picture is called a **scale drawing**.

Scale: 1 cm = 3 m

The scale is **1** cm = **3** m.

So, **1** cm in the scale drawing represents **3** m of the actual height.

To find the actual height of the flagpole:

1. Measure the flagpole's height in the drawing. The flagpole is **2** cm tall.

2. Write equal ratios of the height in the scale drawing to the actual height.

height in scale drawing → $\dfrac{1 \text{ cm}}{3 \text{ m}} = \dfrac{2 \text{ cm}}{?}$ ← height in scale drawing
actual height → ← actual height

$\dfrac{1 \text{ cm}}{3 \text{ m}} = \dfrac{2 \text{ cm}}{6 \text{ m}}$ **Think: 1** cm × **2** = **2** cm, so multiply **3** m by **2.**

The actual height of the flagpole is **6** m.

The scale of a map is 1 in. = 50 mi.
Complete each statement.

1. **3** in. represents _____ mi $\frac{1}{2}$ in. represents _____ mi

2. _____ in. represents **200** mi   _____ in. represents **350** mi

---

The scale of a blueprint is $\frac{1}{8}$ in. = 1 ft.

Complete each statement. Write your answer in simplest form.

3. _____ in. represents **5** ft   _____ in. represents **12** ft

4. $\frac{3}{8}$ in. represents _____ ft $\frac{5}{16}$ in. represents _____

Complete the table.

5.

Scale length	$\frac{1}{4}$ in.	1 in.	$\frac{1}{2}$ in.	2 in.		1$\frac{1}{2}$ in.		3$\frac{1}{4}$ in.	
Actual length	1 ft	4 ft			$\frac{1}{2}$ ft		11 ft		12 ft

Use the plans for building a bench to answer the questions. The grid lines are $\frac{1}{4}$ in. apart.

6. How long is the actual bench? _____

7. How tall is the actual bench?

_____

8. What is the area of the surface of the actual bench seat? _____

9. Make a scale drawing to show how the bench pieces could be cut from a **3**-feet by **6**-feet sheet of wood. Be sure to label what scale you use.

Seat

Scale: $\frac{1}{4}$ in. : 1 ft

Legs

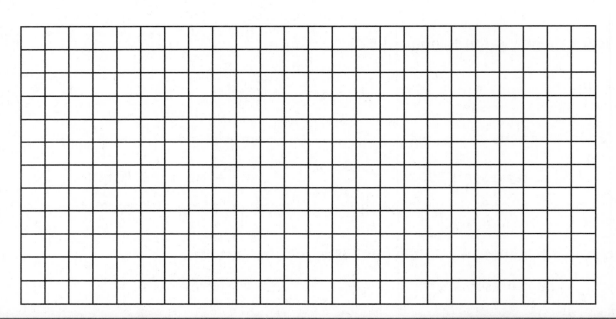

Test Prep ★ Mixed Review

10. Rosa baked two batches of cookies. One batch made $2\frac{2}{3}$ dozen cookies. The other made $3\frac{3}{4}$ dozen cookies. How many dozen cookies did she bake altogether?

A $5\frac{5}{7}$ C $6\frac{1}{13}$

B $5\frac{7}{12}$ D $6\frac{5}{12}$

11. Which number sentence shows the commutative property of addition using decimals?

F $1.2 + 3.7 = 2.1 + 7.3$

G $9.54 + 0 = 9.54$

H $6.45 + 2.35 = 2.35 + 6.45$

J $8.8 + (1.2 + 3.66) = (8.8 + 1.2) + 3.66$

Name _____

To solve some problems, you may need to make a table to see a pattern.

Problem

In the first week of the season, a soccer team won 2 out of 3 games. By the end of the second week their record of wins to played games was 4 out of 6 games. At the end of the third week it was 6 out of 9 games. At this rate, how many games should the team expect to win after 15 games?

---

1 **Understand**   As you reread the problem, ask yourself questions.

- What do you know about the record of wins to games played?

    Each week the record changed.
    1st week: 2 out of 3 won
    2nd week: 4 out of 6 won
    3rd week: 6 out of 9 won

    What do you need to find?

    _____

---

2 **Decide**   Choose a method for solving.

- Try the Make a Table strategy.

    What will you label the rows in the table?

    _____

    You should extend the table so you can find the pattern.

---

3 **Solve**   Make a table to solve.

- Complete the table.

Games Played	3	6			
Games Won	2	4			

---

4 **Look back**   Check your answer.

    Write your answer below.

    Answer: _____

Use the Make a Table Strategy or any other strategy you have learned.

1. On a trip of **150** miles, Mr. Gray's car used **5** gallons of gas. At this rate, how many gallons of gas will Mr. Gray need to go **270** miles?

   Think: How many miles can be traveled on one gallon?

   _____

   Answer _____

2. An architect wants to make a scale drawing of a room that is **12** ft by **20** ft. If the room is **3** in. wide in the scale drawing, find its length in the scale drawing.

   Think: How many feet are represented by one inch?

   _____

   Answer _____

3. The Camera Corner is having a sale on reprints. You can get **3** reprints for **72¢**. How much will you pay for **9** reprints?

   _____

4. Jerry paid **$2** sales tax on a coat that he bought for **$50**. How much will the sales tax be on the suit he is buying for **$200**?

   _____

5. For every half-hour TV show, there are **8** minutes of commercials. How many minutes of commercials are there in **2.5** hours of TV shows?

   _____

6. Shirley needed **9** rolls of wallpaper for her bedroom. Each roll covered **36** sq ft and cost **$12**. How much did the wallpaper for Shirley's bedroom cost?

   _____

7. Dana wants to enlarge a **3**-inch by **5**-inch photograph. If the new width will be **12** inches, what will be the new length?

   _____

8. Caryl used **2** pages in a photo album for **24** photos. She still has to put **60** more photos in the album. How many more pages does she need?

   _____

9. A punch recipe that serves **20** people calls for **5** cups of pineapple juice to be mixed with **4** cups of orange juice and **8** cups of ginger ale. How many cups of punch would serve **60** people?

   _____

10. In a survey of **400** people, it was found that **5** out of **8** people like Toasty Bread. How many people surveyed like Toasty Bread?

   _____

Percent is a special ratio that compares a number to **100**.

In the grid, **67** out of **100** squares are shaded. The ratio of shaded squares to all the squares is $\frac{67}{100}$, or **67**%. The symbol % stands for **percent**.

Percent means per hundred.

Write what percent of each grid is shaded.

1.

_____

_____

_____

2.

_____

_____

_____

Write each ratio as a percent.

3. $\frac{26}{100}$ _____ $\frac{80}{100}$ _____ $\frac{7}{100}$ _____ $\frac{55}{100}$ _____

4. $\frac{13}{100}$ _____ $\frac{71}{100}$ _____ $\frac{100}{100}$ _____ $\frac{3}{100}$ _____

Write each percent as a ratio.

5. 37% _____   85% _____   5% _____   29% _____

6. 15% _____   91% _____   10% _____   50% _____

Shade each grid to show the percent.

7.

73%

8%

30%

8.

59%

100%

17%

Problem Solving
Reasoning **Use the table to solve.**

9. What percent of the students chose pepperoni pizza? _____

10. What percent of the students chose cheese or sausage pizza? _____

11. What percent of the students did **not** choose vegetable pizza? _____

12. Would it have been possible for the table to show **110%** of the students surveyed? Explain. _____

_____

Favorite Pizza of 100 Students	
Kind	**Number of Students**
Cheese	14
Pepperoni	38
Sausage	27
Vegetable	6
Deluxe	15

Test Prep ★ Mixed Review

13 Halley is making scarves for a craft fair. Each scarf uses $1\frac{3}{8}$ yards of fabric. How much fabric does she need to make 12 scarves?

   A 16 yards   **C** 17 yards

   B $16\frac{1}{2}$ yards   **D** $17\frac{1}{2}$ yards

14 A 25-pound bag of potatoes costs $9.75. What is the cost of 1 pound of potatoes?

   F $.39

   G $.49

   H $.59

   J $.69

Name _____   **Fractions and Percent**

You can write a **percent** as a **fraction**.

1. Write the percent as a fraction with a denominator of **100**.

2. Write the fraction in simplest form.

$$28\% = \frac{28}{100}$$

$$= \frac{28}{100} = \frac{7}{25}$$

28 out of **100** shaded

You can also write a **fraction** as a **percent**.

1. Write an equivalent fraction with a denominator of **100**.

2. Since percent means per hundred, you can think, **45** out of **100** and write **45%**.

$$\frac{9 \times 5}{20 \times 5} = \frac{45}{100}$$

$$\frac{45}{100} = 45\%$$

What part of each grid is shaded? Write a percent and a fraction in simplest form.

1.

_____   _____   _____

What part of each shape is shaded? Write a fraction in simplest form and a percent.

2.

_____   _____

3.

_____   _____   _____

Write each percent as a fraction in simplest form.

4. 65% _____   68% _____   17% _____   100% _____   6% _____

Write each fraction as a percent.

5. $\frac{9}{100}$ _____ $\frac{23}{25}$ _____ $\frac{1}{10}$ _____ $\frac{1}{50}$ _____ $\frac{7}{10}$ _____

Complete the table.

6.

Fraction	$\frac{1}{2}$		$\frac{9}{10}$		$\frac{3}{4}$		$\frac{4}{5}$		$\frac{2}{5}$
Percent		60%		30%		20%		25%	

Problem Solving Reasoning Solve.

7. On a 20-question test, Molly answered 18 questions correctly. What percent of the questions did Molly answer correctly? _____

8. On a 25-question test, Paul answered 19 questions correctly. What percent of the questions did Paul answer **incorrectly?** _____

 Quick Check

The scale on a map is 1 in. = 30 mi. Complete the statement.

Work Space

9. 6 in. represents _____ mi.

10. _____ in. represents **75 mi.**

Write the ratio as a percent.

11. $\frac{32}{100}$ **12.** $\frac{9}{100}$ **13.** $\frac{2}{100}$

_____   _____   _____

Write the percent as a fraction in simplest form.

14. 60%   **15.** 8%   **16.** 59%

_____   _____   _____

Write the fraction as a percent.

17. $\frac{3}{4}$ **18.** $\frac{7}{10}$ **19.** $\frac{19}{25}$

_____   _____   _____

Name _____

You can write a percent as a decimal.

1. Write the percent as a fraction with a denominator of **100**.

2. Write the fraction as a decimal.

$$49\% = \frac{49}{100} = 0.49$$

49 out of **100** shaded

You can also write a decimal as a percent.

1. Write the decimal as a fraction with a denominator of **100**.

$$0.64 = \frac{64}{100}$$

2. Write the fraction as a percent.

$$\frac{64}{100} = 64\%$$

What part of each grid is shaded?
Write a percent and a decimal.

1.

_____   _____   _____   _____

_____   _____   _____   _____

Write each percent as a decimal.

2. 62% _____   5% _____   30% _____   99% _____

3. 1% _____   40% _____   33% _____   58% _____

4. 6% _____   21% _____   100% _____   60% _____

5. 33% _____   68% _____   8% _____   87% _____

6. 17% _____   9% _____   10% _____   5% _____

Write each decimal as a percent.

7. 0.76 _____   0.9 _____   0.02 _____   0.11 _____

8. 0.6 _____   0.39 _____   0.65 _____   0.01 _____

9. 0.27 _____   0.08 _____   0.84 _____   0.4 _____

10. 0.8 _____   0.4 _____   1.00 _____   0.95 _____

Complete the table.

11.

Decimal			0.3		0.25	0.6		0.2	
Percent	75%	40%		50%			10%		80%

Problem Solving Reasoning   Solve.

12. A race was held last weekend. Nine tenths of the cars finished the race. What percent of the cars did **not** finish the race?

_____

13. A car still had **87** hundredths of the race to finish when it developed engine trouble. What percent of the race had it completed?

_____

14. Marcus got **45** out of **50** questions correct on a math test. What percent did he get correct?

_____

15. A 1-liter juice drink contains **0.10** liter of juice. What percent of the drink is juice?

_____

Test Prep ★ Mixed Review

16 The ABC Bottling Company measured the diameter of several bottle caps. Which four of these measurements are listed from least to greatest?

A 2.72 cm, 2.702 cm, 2.707 cm, 2.722 cm

B 2.7 cm, 2.722 cm, 2.702 cm, 2.707 cm

C 2.702 cm, 2.707 cm, 2.72 cm, 2.722 cm

D 2.702 cm, 2.707 cm, 2.722 cm, 2.72 cm

17 A company makes bars of soap. The soap is mixed in large vats, then poured into molds to make 560 bars of soap. The mixture weighs 1,792 ounces. How much does each bar of soap weigh?

F 3 oz

G 3.2 oz

H 30 oz

J 32 oz

Name _____

Fractions, decimals and percents are all related. You know that a number that can be written as a fraction can also be written as a decimal or percent.

Complete the table. Write each fraction in simplest form.

	Fraction	Decimal	Percent
1.		0.37	
2.			48%
3.	$\frac{2}{5}$		
4.			8%
5.	$\frac{1}{10}$		
6.		0.85	
7.			100%
8.	$\frac{11}{20}$		

Write the fraction, decimal, and percent for the point on the number line.

9.

_____   _____   _____

10.

_____   _____   _____

11.

_____   _____   _____

You can compare and order fractions, decimals, and percents.
First rewrite them in the same form.

Compare 0.3 ◯ 25%. Write >, <, or =.

| Think: 0.3 = 0.30 = 30% | **or** | Think: 25% = 0.25 |

30% (>) 25%   0.3 (>) 0.25

0.3 (>) 25%   0.3 (>) 25%

Compare. Write >, <, or =.

12. $\frac{1}{10}$ ◯ 0.11 $\frac{3}{5}$ ◯ 53%   90% ◯ 0.9 $\frac{18}{25}$ ◯ 72%

13. 0.8 ◯ 88%   50% ◯ 0.06   0.2 ◯ $\frac{1}{5}$ 70% ◯ $\frac{3}{4}$

Order each set of numbers from least to greatest.

14. 56%, $\frac{1}{2}$, 0.6   0.7, $\frac{17}{25}$, 8% $\frac{3}{4}$, 72%, 0.5

_____   _____   _____

| Problem Solving |
| Reasoning |

Solve.

15. In one class, **0.8** of the students like to play baseball and $\frac{5}{8}$ like to play basketball. Do more students like to play baseball or basketball?

Explain._____

_____

16. In another class, **60%** of the students have a dog and $\frac{2}{3}$ have a cat. Do more students have a dog or a cat?

Explain._____

_____

Test Prep ★ Mixed Review

17 Which mixed number is equivalent to **2.125**?

  A $2\frac{1}{8}$ **C** $2\frac{1}{80}$

  B $2\frac{3}{25}$ **D** $2\frac{125}{100}$

18 At birth, Rita's baby sister weighed $7\frac{1}{4}$ pounds. How many ounces is this?

  F 58 ounces   **H** $72\frac{1}{2}$ ounces

  G 87 ounces   **J** 116 ounces

A pair of inline skates regularly costs **$120.**
They are now on sale for **25%** off.
How much would you save if you bought the skates on sale?

> **Think:** Find **25%** of **$120.**

You can find a percent of a number in different ways.

1. Write the percent as a fraction.

$$25\% = \frac{25}{100}$$
$$= \frac{1}{4}$$

2. Multiply **120** by the fraction.

$$120 \times \frac{1}{4} = \frac{120}{4}$$
$$= 30$$

1. Write the percent as a decimal.

$$25\% = \frac{25}{100}$$
$$= 0.25$$

2. Multiply **$120** by the decimal.

$$\begin{array}{r} \$120 \\ \times\ 0.25 \\ \hline 600 \\ +\ 2400 \\ \hline \$30.00 \end{array}$$

You would save **$30.**

Find each percent.

1. 20% of 75

_____

2. 50% of 64

_____

3. 30% of 270

_____

4. 75% of 60

_____

5. 80% of 45

_____

6. 70% of 700

_____

7. 25% of 3,600

_____

8. 90% of 2,000

_____

9. 40% of 1,500

_____

When an exact amount is not needed, you can estimate the percent of a number.

Think of compatible numbers when you estimate.

52% of 609	13% of 78	21% of 115	74% of 62
Think: 50% of 600 $\frac{1}{2} \times 600 = 300.$	Think: 10% of 80 $\frac{1}{10} \times 80 = 8.$	Think: 20% of 100 $\frac{1}{5} \times 100 = 20.$	Think: 70% of 60 $\frac{7}{10} \times 60 = 42.$

Estimate the percent.

10. 9% of 28 _____   77% of 16 _____   48% of 98 _____

11. 59% of 206 _____   51% of 3,956 _____   42% of 1,017 _____

Problem Solving
Reasoning

Solve.

12. A store just received **20** jackets. Of these, **15%** were damaged. How many jackets are **not** damaged?

_____

13. A jacket regularly sells for **$78.95**. It is now on sale for **20%** off. Carlos has saved **$55**. Does he have enough money to buy the jacket? Explain.

_____

 Quick Check

Write the percent as a decimal.

14. 86% _____   **15.** 4% _____   **16.** 30% _____

Write the decimal as a percent.

17. 0.83 _____   **18.** 0.1 _____   **19.** 0.09 _____

Write the numbers in order from least to greatest.

20. 45%, $\frac{2}{5}$, 0.48   **21.** $\frac{2}{3}$, 0.65, 6%

_____   _____

Write the percent of the number.

22. 80% of 35   **23.** 30% of 90   **24.** 75% of 56

_____   _____   _____

Work Space

Name _____

This circle graph shows the results of a survey of how often people correspond with family and friends by e-mail. There were 800 people in the survey.

In this lesson, you will use the graph to compare or draw conclusions about data in the graph.

Survey: How often do you use e-mail to correspond with friends and family?

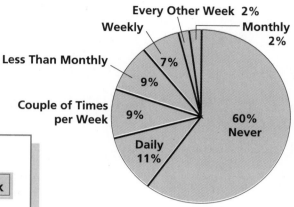

Tips to Remember

| 1. Understand   2. Decide   3. Solve   4. Look back |

• Read the problem carefully. Ask yourself questions about any part that does not make sense. Reread to find answers.

• Compare the labels on the graph with the words and numbers in the problem. Find the facts you need from the graph.

• Ask yourself whether you have solved a problem like this before.

Solve.

1. Is it true that more than half the people have never used e-mail?

   Think: What percent is the same as half?

   _____

   Answer_____

2. How many people use e-mail at least once a week?

   Think: What operations do you need to do to solve this problem?

   _____

   Answer_____

3. How many people never use e-mail?

   _____

4. How many more people use e-mail weekly than monthly?

   _____

This circle graph shows how the students of the Hancock School raised money to buy a new computer. The total amount raised was **$1,200**.

How Money Was Raised by Students of Hancock School

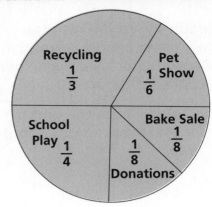

Solve.

5. How was the greatest amount of money raised? How much was raised this way?

_____

_____

6. Which three ways of raising money for the new computer are together equivalent to **75%** of the money raised?

_____

_____

7. How much more money was raised from the school play than from the bake sale?

_____

8. How much money was raised from the pet show and donations?

_____

9. How much money was raised without donations?

_____

10. Which single event represents **25%** of the money raised?

_____

Extend Your Thinking

11. A circle has **360°**. How many degrees are in the Pet Show part of the circle graph?

_____

12. Look back at problem 6. Explain the method you used to solve the problem.

_____

_____

Name _____

Write each unit cost. Round your answer to the nearest cent when necessary.

1. 42 oz for $12.18 _____

2. 6 cans for $1.49 _____

Use the scale drawing.

3. What is the actual distance between the library and the school? Use a ruler to help decide._____

4. If two places are actually **15** miles apart, how far apart would they be on this scale drawing? _____

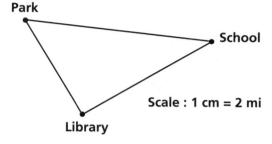

Scale : 1 cm = 2 mi

5. What percent of this grid is shaded? _____

6. What percent is **not** shaded? _____

Write each percent as a decimal and fraction in simplest form.
Write each fraction as a decimal and percent.

7. 16% _____

8. 40% _____

9. $\frac{3}{8}$ _____

10. What is **75%** of **120**? _____

11. What is **60%** of **25**? _____

Solve. Use the circle graph.

12. How many students said they would **not** vote for Candidate C?

_____

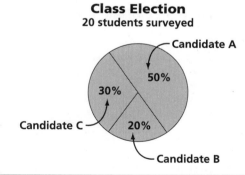

Class Election
20 students surveyed

Candidate A

50%

30%

Candidate C

20%

Candidate B

Solve. Make a table or use another strategy.

13. During a **256** mile trip, an automobile used **8** gallons of gasoline. At that rate, how far can the automobile travel using **12** gallons of gasoline? _____

Name _____

Cumulative Review
★ Test Prep

Ms. Li's class recorded the temperature at 11 A.M. every day for two weeks. Use the graph of their data for exercises 1 and 2.

1 What was the difference in temperature between the two Thursdays?

A 5°F   C 7°F

B 6°F   D 8°F

2 Between which two days did the temperature have the greatest decrease?

F Monday and Tuesday, Week 1

G Monday and Tuesday, Week 2

H Tuesday and Wednesday, Week 1

J Tuesday and Wednesday, Week 2

3 What is the surface area of the prism?

A 200 cm²   C 499.2 cm²

B 400 cm²   D 500 cm²

4 The sixth grade students at River City are planning a field trip. Of the 150 sixth graders, 68% have decided to go. How many students is this?

F 48   H 100

G 68   J 102   K Not here

Use the figure below for exercises 5–7.

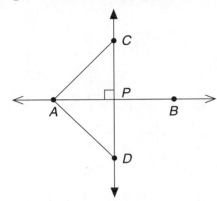

5 Use your centimeter ruler. How long is $\overline{AB}$?

A 3 cm   C 3.4 cm

B 3.2 cm   D 3.6 cm

6 Which two lines are perpendicular?

F $\overline{AD}$ and $\overline{CD}$

G $\overline{AB}$ and $\overline{CD}$

H $\overline{AC}$ and $\overline{CD}$

J $\overline{AB}$ and $\overline{AD}$

7 Which angle is a right angle?

A ∠CAB   C ∠CPB

B ∠CAP   D ∠CPD

8 What percent of the square is shaded?

F 9%   H 82%

G 18%   J 91%

UNIT 10 • TABLE OF CONTENTS

Data, Statistics, and Probability

Dear Family,

During the next few weeks, our math class will be learning about data, statistics, and probability.

You can expect to see homework that provides practice with finding the mean and the median. Here is a sample you may want to keep handy to give help if needed.

We will be using this vocabulary:

average the sum of the numbers in a set of data divided by the number of addends in the set; an average is also called a **mean**

median the middle number in a set of data after the data set has been arranged in order from least to greatest or from greatest to least

mode the number(s) that appear(s) most often in a set of data

range the difference between the greatest and the least number in a set of data

probability the chance that an event will occur

Mean and Median

Example Find the mean of this set of data: 41, 37, 27, 21, 34.

1. To find the mean of a set of numbers, first add the numbers.

$$41 + 37 + 27 + 21 + 34 = 160$$

2. Then divide the sum by the number of addends (or numbers that were added). The quotient or answer is the mean.

mean
↓
$$160 \div 5 = 32$$
↑
number of addends

Example Find the median of this set of data: 41, 37, 27, 21, 34.

1. To find the median of a set of numbers, first order the numbers from least to greatest.

21 27 34 37 41

2. Then find the middle number. In this set, 34 is the middle number or median.

21 27 **34** 37 41

If a set of data has two middle numbers, the median is the mean or average of those two numbers.

During this unit, students will need to continue practicing addition and division facts.

Sincerely,

The speed limit near Kim's school is **20** miles per hour. A police officer recorded the speeds at the right for **14** cars.

You can organize this data in a **stem-and-leaf plot**. To understand stem-and-leaf plots, think how the leaves of a plant are connected to the stem. In a stem-and-leaf plot for 2-digit numbers:
  • the tens' digits form the stem,
  • the ones' digits form the leaves.

Speeds of cars (miles per hour)				
18	20	25	25	45
18	32	15	21	10
12	19	30	9	

Use these steps to make a stem-and-leaf plot of the data.

1. Write the tens' digits in the stem

Stem	
0	
1	
2	
3	
4	

2. Write each ones digit to form the leaves.

Stem	Leaves
0	9
1	8 8 5 0 2 9
2	0 5 5 1
3	2 0
4	5

3. Order the leaves from least to greatest.

Stem	Leaves
0	9
1	0 2 5 8 8 9
2	0 1 5 5
3	0 2
4	5

Key:
0 | 9 means
9 miles per hour

A stem of **0** and a leaf of **9** means that the slowest speed was **9** mph.

A stem of **4** and a leaf of **5** means that the fastest speed was **45** mph.

Use the stem-and-leaf plot to answer each question.

1. What was the greatest score on the history test? _____

2. What was the least test score? _____

3. How many test scores are shown in the plot? _____

4. How many scores were less than **80**? _____

History Test Scores

Stem	Leaves
9	0 1 2 8
8	0 3 3 8 9
7	0 5 5 9
6	3 8

Key: 9|0 means a score of 90

Refer to the height data in the table.

5. How many heights are shown? _____

6. Complete the stem-and-leaf plot of the data.

Teachers' Height in Inches

Stems	Leaves
____	____ ____ ____ ____ ____
____	____ ____ ____ ____

Height in Inches of West Middle School Teachers
66, 72, 73, 65, 60,
62, 70, 75, 66, 64

7. Order the heights from least to greatest.

_____

A **histogram** is a special bar graph. Look at the histogram for Speed of Cars. The **horizontal scale** shows numbers that represent miles per hour. The **vertical scale** shows the number of cars. There are no spaces between the bars in a histogram.

You can use a stem-and-leaf plot to make a histogram.
1. Draw rectangles around each row of leaves to make bars.
2. Turn the plot so that the bars you drew are vertical.
3. Use the stem as a guide for dividing the data into sets of numbers on the horizontal scale. Each set is called an interval.

Speed in Miles Per Hour

no tens	Stem	Interval
	0	0–9
	1	10–19
all numbers from 20–29	2	20–29
	3	30–39
	4	40–49

Ten numbers are in each interval.

Label the horizontal scale.
4. Since the greatest number of leaves on the plot is 6, make six equal sections on the vertical scale. Label the sections **0–6.** Label the vertical scale.
5. Choose a title. Then shade the bars.

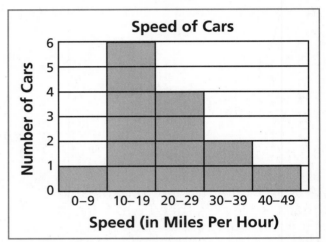

Use the histogram above to answer each question.

8. How many cars had speeds from **20** mph to **29** mph? _____

9. How many cars had speeds from **40** mph to **49** mph? _____

10. Which interval has the least number of speeds? _____

11. How many speeds were greater than or equal to the speed limit of **20** mph? _____

Test Prep ★ Mixed Review

12 Lena shaded 25 out of 100 squares. What percent of the squares did she shade?

A 25

B $\frac{1}{4}$

C 0.25%

D 25%

13 A gift box is in the shape of a cube 8 in. on each side. How much wrapping paper would you need to wrap the box?

F less than 300 in.^{2}

G less than 384 in.^{2}

H more than 384 in.^{2}

J more than 512 in.^{3}

Name _____

These data show the number of students in each after-school activity.

Students' After-School Activities

Activity	Students
Tennis	40
Softball	45
Basketball	55
Swimming	60
Language Club	33
Baseball	55
Glee Club	28
Chess Club	22

You can make a graph to see the relationships among the data.
First, you need to choose the appropriate graph to make.

A bar graph is a good choice when the data can be counted.

A line graph is appropriate when you want to show changes over time.

A pictograph is a good choice when the data are in multiples.

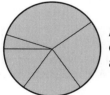

A circle graph is a good choice when the data are part of a whole.

A histogram is a good choice to show how often something happens within a given set of numbers.

Use the data to answer the questions.

1. Which kinds of graphs could represent the data in the table?

_____

2. Which kind of graph would **best** represent the after-school data? Explain.

_____

3. Which type of graph would you use to show how the number of students in the Chess Club changes throughout the year? Explain.

_____

4. Which type of graph would you use to show how many of the Glee Club members are sopranos, altos, tenors, or basses? Explain.

_____

Graphs also can be used to show patterns in data.
These two graphs show the weather conditions for a month.

Weather Conditions					
Sunny	◯	◯	◯	◯	◯
Cloudy	◯	◯			
Partly Cloudy	◯	◯			
Rainy	◯				
Key	Each ◯ = 3 days				

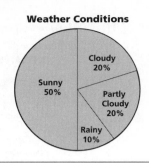

Weather Conditions

Complete. Tell which graph you used to answer the question.

5. Which months could this data represent? Explain.

_____

_____

6. True, false, or can't tell? Most days of the month had some sunshine.

_____

_____

7. By looking at the graphs can you tell that half the days were not sunny? Explain.

_____

_____

8. Which graph clearly shows the large difference between rainy and sunny days?

_____

_____

Problem Solving
Reasoning

Solve. Use the bar graph to answer the question.

9. What might make you think that Kyle sold more buttons than the others?

_____

10. How could you change the graph to correctly display the data?

_____

Number of School Campaign Buttons

Test Prep ★ Mixed Review

11 What are the next two decimals in the number pattern?

5.028, 5.018, _____?, _____?

A 5.0008, 5.008

B 5.008, 4.998

C 5.038, 5.048

D 5.08, 4.98

12 A 4-sided kite has 2 acute angles, 1 right angle, and 1 obtuse angle. What is the sum of all the angles of the kite?

F 360°

G 270°

H 180°

J 90°

Name_____

"How many uses for string can you name?" This survey question was asked of **15** students. Their answers are listed below.

The **range**, **mean**, **mode**, and **median** are different ways of describing this data.

The **range** is the difference between the greatest and least numbers. **10 − 1 = 9**, so the range is **9**.

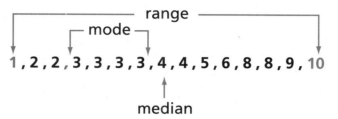

The **mean,** or average, is the sum of the items divided by the number of items. The mean rounded to the nearest tenth is **4.7.**

$1 + 2 + 2 + 3 + 3 + 3 + 3 + 4 + 4 + 5 + 6 + 8 + 8 + 9 + 10 = 71$

$71 ÷ 15 = 4.73$

↑

number of students

The **mode** is the number that occurs most often. The mode is **3.** Data may have more than one mode or no mode at all.

The **median** is the middle number when the items are arranged in order. The median for the data above is **4.** In the data below, the median is the mean of the two middle numbers.

3, 7, 8, 9, 11, 14 ➝ **8 + 9 = 17** ➝ **17 ÷ 2 = 8.5** | The median is **8.5** |

Find the mean, median, range, and mode for each set of data. Round the mean to the nearest tenth. Remember to order the numbers.

1. 10, 12, 15, 15, 10, 9

mean: _____

median: _____

range: _____

mode: _____

72, 62, 75, 76, 72, 66, 72

mean: _____

median: _____

range: _____

mode: _____

22, 22, 11, 21, 20, 21, 23

mean: _____

median: _____

range: _____

mode: _____

2. 4, 1, 1, 5, 8, 9, 8, 4, 8, 2

mean: _____

median: _____

range: _____

mode: _____

11, 12, 11, 5, 13, 8, 8, 11

mean: _____

median: _____

range: _____

mode: _____

100, 120, 117, 116, 100

mean: _____

median: _____

range: _____

mode: _____

Solve. Use the table to answer the questions.

Skateboards	
Style	**Price**
Red	$20
Metallic Blue	$22
Metallic Green	$22
Glow-in-the-Dark	$48
Special Wheels	$52
Extra Features	$75
Deluxe	$98

3. What is the median price? _____

4. What is the range of prices? _____

5. Will adding a $25 skateboard to the list increase, decrease, or leave the median unchanged? Explain.

_____

_____

6. Melissa wants to know how much she should save to buy a skateboard. Wilma said, "The price most often seen for a skateboard is $22." Tommy said, "The average cost of a skateboard is about $48." To whom should Melissa listen? Explain.

_____

_____

 Quick Check

The stem-and-leaf plot shows the fat grams of a cup of nuts. Use the stem-and-leaf plot to answer the questions.

Fat Grams per Cup of Nuts

Stems	Leaves
6	4 7 9
7	2 5 7 7
8	7
9	6

Work Space

7. Peanuts have **72** grams of fat per cup. How many nuts have less than **72** grams of fat? _____

8. In a histogram of the data, which interval would have the highest bar? _____

9. Suppose you want to find the differences between fat grams. Could a line graph of the data help you do this? Explain. _____

10. Suppose that a cup of peanuts has **38** grams of protein and **27** grams of carbohydrate. What kind of graph would you use to compare fat, carbohydrate, and protein grams as part of the total number of grams?

Explain. _____

11. Find the mean, median, mode, and range for the fat data in the completed stem-and-leaf plot.

_____

Name _____

According to the Constitution, the President of the United States must be at least 35 years old. This list shows the inaugural ages of all U.S. presidents since **1901.**

Ages: **42, 51, 56, 55, 51, 60, 62, 43, 55, 56, 61, 52, 64, 46, 69, 54, 51**

A **line plot** can be used to order lists of data. To make a line plot, first make a number line. Then put an X above each number as many times as the number appears in the list.

Use the line plot to answer these questions about the data.

1. Explain how to find the range of the data. What is the range?

   _____

2. Vice President Theodore Roosevelt became president

   upon the death of William McKinley in 1901. He was the youngest president

   inaugurated. How old was he then? _____

3. The next-youngest president was John F. Kennedy.

   How old was he at his inauguration in 1961? _____

4. Ronald Reagan was the oldest president at his

   inauguration in 1981. How old was he then? _____

5. The greatest number of presidents were inaugurated

   at what age? _____

6. What is the median of these presidents' ages

   at inauguration? _____

7. What is the mean of these presidents' ages

   at inauguration? Round your answer to the nearest tenth. _____

8. What is the mode of the ages? _____

9. If **42, 43,** and **69** are removed from this list of data, how

   does the mean change? Explain. _____

A line plot also allows you to see the *shape* of the data. If you draw a line above the Xs, you can see that the data curve up and down.

A **cluster** is a group of data on a line plot that are close together.

A **gap** is a space between data on a line plot.

An **outlier** is a data point on either end of a line plot that is very far away from the other values.

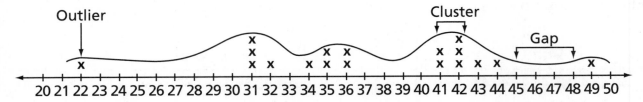

Use the line plot to answer each question.

10. There are **3** clusters in this line plot. Between which numbers are the clusters? _____ and _____

11. Name **2** outliers in this line plot. _____ and _____

12. Name the **4** gaps in this line plot. _____ to _____;

at _____; _____ to _____; _____ to _____

13. What is the mode of the data? _____ and _____

14. What is the range of the data? _____

| Problem Solving |
| Reasoning |

Solve.

15. Could eliminating outliers from a set of data affect the range, median, mode, or mean? Explain.

_____

_____

Test Prep ★ Mixed Review

16 At what time do the hands of a clock form a right angle?

   A 8:00   **C** 9:00

   B 8:30   **D** 9:30

17 On a number line, which point would be to the right of 0.7?

   F $\frac{70}{1,000}$ **H** $\frac{700}{1,000}$

   G $\frac{699}{1,000}$ **J** $\frac{770}{1,000}$

Problem Solving Application: Too Much Information

Some problems give more facts than you need. In a problem with too many facts, you have to select only the information you need.

> **Tips to Remember**
>
> | 1. Understand | 2. Decide | 3. Solve | 4. Look back |
> |---|---|---|---|
>
> - Write down the facts in the problem. Decide whether there are extra facts.
> - Read each problem more than once. Circle the important words and numbers. Cross out the words and numbers that you don't need.
> - Think about each fact in the problem. Ask yourself: Is this an extra fact? Or do I need it to find a solution?

Cross out the extra information. Then solve the problem.

1. The girls basketball team scored the following points in their games: **65, 52, 59, 48,** and **66**. The boys basketball team scored these points in their games: **47, 71, 69, 55,** and **53**. What was the average number of points scored by the boys basketball team?

Think: What information do you need to solve the problem? What information is extra?

_____

_____

_____

_____

_____

Answer _____

2. On a math quiz, **11** students scored **100**, **7** students scored **90**, **6** students scored **80**, and **4** students scored **70**. Two students were absent from math class and didn't take the quiz. What was the range of the scores on the quiz?

Think: What information do you need to find the range? What information is not necessary?

_____

_____

_____

_____

_____

Answer _____

Cross out the extra information. Then solve the problem.

3. On her science tests, Ana scored **80, 93, 87** and **96**. On her math tests, Ana scored **100, 84, 89,** and **79**. Ana's English average was **95**. What was Ana's science average?

_____

4. There are **6** people in the Jones family. There are **2** sons and **2** daughters, who are twins. Their ages are **32, 34, 3, 7, 10,** and **3**. What is the median age in this family?

_____

5. Brian bought some CDs for **$14.00** each. He counted the number of tracks on each and found them to be **12, 13, 18, 15, 11, 16,** and **13**. What was the mode of the number of tracks on the CDs?

_____

6. A class made a line plot of the number of books read by each student. The teacher read 10 books. Five students read **8** books each. Three students read **5** books each. Ten students read **9** books each. What was the mode?

_____

7. Sandy made a stem-and-leaf plot of the prime numbers between **1** and **32**. The numbers in the stem-and-leaf plot were **2, 3, 5, 7, 11, 13, 17, 19, 23, 29,** and **31**. What was the median of the numbers?

_____

8. Mr. Green keeps a log of how many miles he can go on a tank of gas. He averages **23** miles per gallon. The entries in his log are **325, 336, 320, 308,** and **297**. What is the range of the mileage?

_____

Extend Your Thinking

9. Look back at problem 3. What was the difference between Ana's science average and her math average?

_____

10. Look back at problem 5. What was the average price per track on the CDs that Brian bought?

_____

11. Explain how you decided what was extra information in problem 7.

_____

_____

12. Explain how you formed the answer to problem 4.

_____

_____

The measure of the possibility that something may or may not happen is called **probability**.

A probability of 0 means that it is *impossible* for an event to happen.

A probability of 1 means that an event is *certain* to happen.

A probability between **0** and **1** means an event may or may not happen.

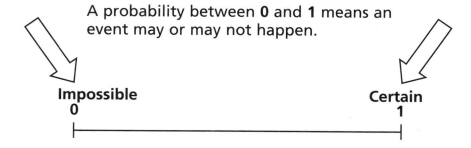

Impossible
0

Certain
1

Choose *0, 1,* or *between 0 and 1* to describe each probability.

1. A person's name contains the letter *a*. _____

2. You will sleep sometime during your lifetime. _____

3. Tomorrow's date is October 14, 1925. _____

4. On your next birthday you will be **34** years old. _____

5. You will toss a **6** if you toss a cube numbered **1, 2, 3, 4, 5, 6.** _____

6. You will toss a **1, 2, 3, 4, 5,** or **6** if you toss a cube numbered **1, 2, 3, 4, 5, 6.** _____

Circle the letter of the event that has the greater chance of happening.

7. a. You will attend school next year.

    b. You will graduate from high school next year.

8. a. Tossing a **4** on a cube numbered **1, 2, 3, 4, 5, 6.**

    b. Tossing a **4** on a cube numbered **2, 2, 4, 4, 6, 6.**

9. a. Tossing a coin and getting tails.

    b. Tossing a coin and getting heads or tails.

Change each sentence so that the probability of each event happening is 1.

10. You can find a herd of sheep in your classroom. _____

_____

11. You can toss a **2** on a cube numbered **3, 4, 5, 6, 7, 8.** _____

_____

12. It will be exactly three o'clock four different times today. _____

_____

Suppose these squares were placed inside the bag.

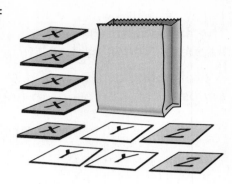

13. Name a letter of the alphabet that has a probability of **0** of being drawn from the bag. _____

14. Name a letter that has a greater chance of being drawn than **Y**. _____

15. Of the letters **X**, **Y**, and **Z**, which letter has the least chance of being drawn? _____

Solve.

16. Conduct an experiment. Follow these steps.

    1. Make **10** two-inch-squares of paper. Label **5** squares **X**, **3** squares **Y**, and **2** squares **Z**. Place them in a paper bag.

    2. Without looking, draw a square from the bag and record the result on the tally chart. Put the square back into the bag.

    3. Repeat Step 2 forty-nine times more.

Paper Squares		
Letter	Tally	Total
X		
Y		
Z		

17. Which result(s) occurred most often? _____

 Quick Check

Use the line plot about class quiz scores to complete.

18. What are the mean and median scores? Round the mean to the nearest tenth.

_____

19. Suppose a student got a score of **15**. Would this score be considered a cluster, a gap, or an outlier? Explain.

_____

Suppose you have cards numbered 0–9.
Choose *0, 1,* or *between 0 and 1* to describe the probability.

20. Picking a 5. _____

21. Picking a 10. _____

Work Space

Name _____

Problem Solving Strategy: Make a List

An organized list can sometimes help you find the answer to a problem.

Problem

Alex, Barika, and Clara sit in the front row. Make a list to find how many different ways they can be seated.

❶ Understand As you reread the problem, ask yourself questions.

- What do you know about Alex, Barika, and Clara?

    They all sit in the front row.

    What do you need to find out?

    _____

❷ Decide Choose a method for solving the problem. Try the strategy Make a List.

- If Alex is in the first seat, who can be in the seat next

    to him? _____

❸ Solve Make a list to show the possible ways they can sit.

    Alex in first seat: ABC or _____.

    Barika in first seat: BAC or _____.

    Clara in first seat: CAB or _____.

❹ Look back Check your answer.
Write your answer below.

- Are there any other possible seating arrangements?

    _____

    List all the possibilities.

    Answer: _____

    _____

Solve. Use the Make a List strategy or any other strategy you have learned.

1. A deli offers lunch specials. For **$3.79**, you can choose a cheese, tuna, or bologna sandwich and a macaroni or potato salad. What lunch specials are available?

Think: Could you order macaroni salad with each sandwich?

_____

Answer _____

2. I have a number cube with the numbers **1, 2, 3, 4, 5,** and **6** on it. If I toss a nickel and toss the number cube, what are all the possible outcomes?

Think: How many outcomes are possible with a nickel?

_____

Answer _____

_____

3. A hamburger can be ordered with or without cheese, with or without ketchup, and with or without pickles. How many different ways can you order the hamburger?

_____

4. A bag contains **56** marbles. Ten are red, **18** are blue, **15** are yellow, and the rest are green. How many green marbles are in the bag?

_____

5. A rectangle has a perimeter of **30** in. Its length is twice its width. What are the dimensions of the rectangle?

_____

6. A rectangular garden measured in whole feet has an area of **24** ft^2. What is the greatest length of fencing needed to put a fence around the garden?

_____

7. A family room in the shape of a square measures **15** ft on each side. How much will it cost to carpet the family room if carpeting sells for **$19** per square yard?

_____

8. The results of a skating survey showed that **15** students like to use in-line skates, **12** students like to ice skate, and **4** like to do both. How many students were surveyed?

_____

9. How many different ways can Kate, Leo, Mike, and Nan be standing in line for the movies?

_____

10. Emma scored **88** and **85** on two quizzes. How many points does she need to score on the next quiz to have an average quiz score of **90**?

_____

A result of a probability experiment is an **outcome.**

To find the *probability* of an event, or how likely it is to occur, use this ratio:

Probability (P) = $\dfrac{\text{number of favorable outcomes}}{\text{total number of possible outcomes}}$

- The probability that this spinner will point to white is $\dfrac{1}{6}$. There is one white section on the spinner, or **1** favorable outcome. There are six sections on the spinner altogether, or **6** possible outcomes.

- The probability that the spinner will point to gray is $\dfrac{3}{6}$. Out of **6** possible outcomes, **3** sections are gray, or favorable.

It is **more likely** that the spinner will point to gray than to white because $\dfrac{3}{6} > \dfrac{1}{6}$

Use the spinner below to answer questions 1–6.

1. What is the total number of possible outcomes on the spinner? _____

2. How many sections are labeled **A**? _____
T? _____ S? _____

Suppose the spinner is spun once.
Write each ratio in simplest form.

3. What is the probability of the spinner pointing
to **A**? _____ out of _____ or _____

4. What is the probability of the spinner pointing
to **S**? _____ out of _____ or _____

5. Is it *more likely* or *less likely* that the spinner will
point to **A** than to **S**? Explain. _____

6. Describe the probability of the spinner pointing
to **A, T,** or **S**. _____

Suppose a number cube is tossed once. The cube is
numbered 1, 2, 3, 4, 5, 6. Write each ratio in simplest form.

7. What is the probability of tossing a **6**? _____ out of _____ or _____

8. What is the probability of tossing a **3** or a **6**? _____ out of _____ or _____

9. What is the probability of tossing an even number? _____ out of _____ or _____

When each player in a game has an equal probability
of winning, the game is said to be *fair*. Write *fair* or *unfair*.

10. The player with the greatest number of **2**'s wins the game.
Isabella tossed a 6-sided cube numbered **1, 2, 3, 4, 5, 6**.
Roman tossed a 6-sided cube numbered **1, 2, 3, 4, 5, 6**. _____

11. The player with the greatest number of **3**'s wins the game.
Hanna tossed a 6-sided cube numbered **1, 2, 3, 4, 5, 6**.
Noah tossed a 6-sided cube numbered **3, 4, 5, 3, 7, 3**. _____

Problem Solving
Reasoning

Solve.

A   **B**

12. On which spinner is **w** an impossible

outcome? Explain. _____

_____

13. Which spinner has a $\frac{1}{3}$ probability of

pointing to **y**? _____

14. Which spinner is least likely to point to **x**? Explain. _____

15. On a separate piece of paper, draw a spinner with
2 possible outcomes: **P** and **R**. Arrange the sections,
P and **R**, so that the spinner is more likely to
point to **P** than to **R**.

Test Prep ★ Mixed Review

16 What kind of graph is appropriate to use
to compare the price differences for
lettuce over a 6 month period?

   A line graph   **C** circle graph

   B bar graph   **D** line plot

17 A class made a circle graph to show how
they spent a $55.00 budget for a party.
The section for decorations was 8% of the
circle. About how much money does that
section stand for?

   F Less than $4.00   **H** Between $6.00
                            and $8.00

   G Between $4.00   **J** More than $8.00
          and $6.00

You can use a small part of a large group of data to represent the whole group. The small part is called a **sample**. Then you can use the sample to make predictions about the large group.

Suppose there are **100** cookies in a box. There are chocolate chip, sugar, and raisin cookies. You can predict how many of each type are in the box by studying a sample.

Without looking, you take a sample of **10** cookies out of the box and use the table at the right to record the number of each type of cookie.

You can use the data in the table to make a prediction about all of the cookies in the box.

Cookies		
Cookie	**Tally**	**Total**
Chocolate chip	|||	3
Sugar	||	2
Raisin	༔	5

Number of chocolate chip cookies in the sample → $\dfrac{3}{10}$ = $\dfrac{?}{100}$ ← Number of chocolate chip cookies in the box

Number of cookies sampled → $\dfrac{3}{10}$ = $\dfrac{?}{100}$ ← Number of cookies in the box

Multiply by **10** to find an equal ratio.

$$\frac{3 \times 10}{10 \times 10} = \frac{30}{100}$$

You can predict that there are **30** chocolate chip cookies out of **100** cookies in the box.

Based on the sample, the probability of getting a chocolate chip cookie is $\dfrac{3}{10}$.

Use the sample data above to answer each question.

1. What is the number of sugar cookies in the sample? _____

2. What ratio can you write to compare the number of sugar cookies in the sample with the total number of cookies in the sample? _____

3. How many sugar cookies do you predict are in the box? Explain.

_____

4. How many raisin cookies would you predict are in the box? Explain.

_____

5. Suppose the box contained **200** cookies. In an experiment the same sample as above was the outcome. Predict how many chocolate chip cookies would be in the box. _____

Perform each probability experiment. Then answer each question.

6. Toss a coin fifty times. Record each outcome. Based on your sample, what is the probability of the coin landing heads up? Tails up?

_____

7. Use a cube numbered **1, 2, 3, 4, 5,** and **6**. Toss it fifty times. Record each outcome. Based on your sample, what is the probability of tossing an odd number?

_____

Problem Solving
Reasoning

Solve.

8. A class is divided into **8** study groups, numbered **1–8**. Every student is randomly assigned to one of the **8** groups. You want to be assigned to a group whose number is less than **6**.

Name the favorable outcomes: _____

What is the total number of possible outcomes? _____

What is the probability of being assigned to a group whose

number is less than **6**? _____

✔ Quick Check

A number cube is numbered 1, 2, 3, 4, 5, 6. Write each probability in simplest form.

Work Space

9. The probability of tossing a **2**. _____

10. The probability of tossing a number greater than **2**. _____

11. The probability of tossing an odd number that is greater than **2**. _____

A spinner has 3 colors (red, blue, and yellow) and 6 sections. You spin the spinner 9 times and make this tally:

Red	Blue	Yellow
IIII	III	II

12. What ratio can you write to describe the number of times you spun blue in the sample? _____

13. Based on the sample, how many sections of the spinner would you predict are blue? _____

14. Based on the sample, how many sections of the spinner would you predict are red? Yellow? _____

Name _____

Use the data about ages of teachers at West Middle School to answer the questions.

Ages of West School Teachers
36, 32, 41, 25, 25, 48, 40, 42, 22, 27,
30, 32, 40, 46, 44, 28, 28, 25, 39, 42,

Stem	Leaves
2	
3	
4	

1. Use the data to complete the stem-and-leaf plot.

2. Use the stem-and-leaf plot to help you draw a histogram.

3. What is the mean age of the teachers? _____

4. What is the mode of the age of teachers? _____

5. What is the range of ages for the teachers? _____

6. What is the median age of all the teachers? _____

Use the spinner to answer the question.

7. If you spun this spinner **100** times, how many times would you predict it would point to **M**? Explain.

_____

_____

8. A penny, a nickel, and a dime are tossed at the same time. On another sheet of paper, show all of the possible outcomes that can occur. What is the probability of the outcome (Heads, Heads, Heads)?

_____

A book mark is in the shape of a parallelogram. Use your centimeter ruler to help you answer questions 1 and 2.

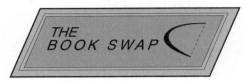

1 Measure the parallelogram to the nearest millimeter. What is the perimeter of the book mark to the nearest mm?

A 12.6　　　　　C 162

B 18　　　　　　D 180

2 What is the area of the book mark rounded to the nearest cm²?

F 1,944　　　　H 15

G 145.8　　　　J 14.6

3 The science club found the average monthly temperature from October through May and made a line graph. The temperatures, in order from October through May, are 18°C, 13°C, 10°C, 3°C, 5°C, 13°C, 19°C, and 26°C. What two months on the graph would show the same temperature?

A October, February

B November, March

C December, April

D January, May

4 Sandro has 12 blue pencils and 8 red pencils. He wants to divide the pencils into boxes so that each box has the same number of red and the same number of blue pencils. What is the greatest number of boxes he can make?

F 2　　　　　H 6

G 4　　　　　J 8　　　　K NH

5 Amber caught a $3\frac{1}{2}$ lb. fish. The record for the day was a $10\frac{1}{4}$ lb. fish. How much more did the record fish weigh?

A $13\frac{3}{4}$ lb　　C $7\frac{1}{4}$ lb　　E $6\frac{1}{8}$ lb

B $6\frac{3}{4}$ lb　　D $6\frac{5}{8}$ lb

6 A baby was 3.5 kilograms at birth. While the baby was in the hospital, he lost 0.2 kilogram. Before going home, he gained 0.3 kilogram. How many kilograms was the baby when he went home?

F 2.5　　　　H 6.3　　　　K Not here

G 4　　　　　J 8.5

7 Tajma's mother is a travel agent and she brings extra posters home. Of the 72 posters Tajma has, 25% of the posters are sites in Asia while $\frac{1}{3}$ of the posters are of sites in the United States. How many more posters of the United States does she have than posters of Asia?

A $\frac{7}{12}$　　　　C 6　　　　E 42

B $\frac{1}{12}$　　　　D 36

8 Ravi worked $2\frac{1}{2}$ h on his scout project on Friday, $4\frac{1}{2}$ h on Saturday, and $3\frac{3}{4}$ h on Sunday. What are the mean and median times he worked?

F $2\frac{1}{2}$ h, $3\frac{1}{2}$ h

G 3 h, $3\frac{1}{2}$ h

H $3\frac{1}{6}$ h, $3\frac{5}{6}$ h

J $3\frac{1}{2}$ h, $3\frac{3}{4}$ h

K NH

UNIT 11 • TABLE OF CONTENTS

Algebra: Integers, and the Coordinate Plane

Dear Family,

During the next few weeks, our math class will be learning about integers and the coordinate plane.

You can expect to see homework that provides practice in ordering integers. Here is a sample you may want to keep handy to give help if needed.

Ordering Integers

Integers are the set of numbers that include positive whole numbers, negative whole numbers, and zero, for example: ⁻2, ⁻1, 0, 1, 2.

Example Here are steps for ordering the set of integers ⁻1, 5, and ⁻4 from greatest to least.

1. One way to order integers is to use a number line.

2. Locate the integers on the number line.

3. Compare and order the integers. On a number line, the integer farthest to the right is greatest and the integer farthest to the left is least. So the integers from greatest to least are: **5, ⁻1, ⁻4.**

During this unit, students will need to practice comparing and ordering integers as well as add, subtract, multiply, and divide with integers.

Sincerely,

Name _____

Words have opposites. Some examples are: *enter* a room and *leave* a room, *stand up* and *sit down*, and *in* and *out*. In mathematics, numbers have opposites too.

Whole numbers greater than **0** are **positive numbers.** Their opposites are whole numbers less than **0**, called **negative numbers.**

Positive numbers, negative numbers, and **0** make up a set of numbers called integers.

... ⁻7, ⁻6, ⁻5, ⁻4, ⁻3, ⁻2, ⁻1, 0, 1, 2, 3, 4, 5, 6, 7 ...

negative integers   positive integers

0 is neither positive nor negative.

A positive number may or may not have a positive sign (+) in front of it. A negative sign (−) must always be placed in front of a negative number.

The number ⁺**5** is read "positive 5." Its opposite, ⁻**5**, is read "negative 5."

Write the opposite.

1. 50 feet up _____   lose **5** lb _____

2. 6 m below sea level _____   add **9** cups _____

3. move back **2** units _____   **20** years ago _____

4. 60 km south _____   5 miles east _____

5. to the right **6** in. _____   multiply by **8** _____

Write *yes* if the number is an integer. Write *no* if it is not.

6. 50 _____   ⁻1,000 _____ $\frac{1}{2}$ _____   0 _____

7. 2 _____   3.2 _____   ⁻6.58 _____   ⁻402 _____

Write the opposite of each integer.

8. 7 _____   ⁻9 _____   250 _____   ⁻1 _____

9. 15 _____   ⁻101 _____   64 _____   0 _____

10. ⁻91 _____   4,678 _____   2 _____   13 _____

Represent each situation with an integer.

11. 14 degrees below zero _____   Rita owes $15. _____

12. Sam grew **3** inches. _____   Myron lost **2** books. _____

13. water level **4** m below normal _____   **10** pennies saved _____

14. gain of **15** feet _____   loss of **5** gallons _____

| Problem Solving |
| Reasoning |

Solve.

15. The fifth grade class held a bake sale. Their expenses were **$24**. They earned **$48**. Write each money amount as an integer.

_____

16. A football player ran with the football two times. The first time he gained **8** yards. The second time he lost **3** yards. Write the gain and loss as integers.

_____

17. One night the temperature fell **14** degrees from midnight to **5** A.M. Then it rose **21** degrees from **5** A.M. to noon. Write the rise and fall of the temperature as integers.

_____

18. On Monday the stock of Zip Company rose **12** points, then it fell **8** points on Tuesday. Write the rise and fall of the stock prices as integers.

_____

19. Look at your answers to rows **6** and **7** on page 281. Which numbers are not integers? Explain.

_____

_____

20. Use the number line on page 281. Find **6** and ⁻**6**. How many units from zero is each integer? Write a rule that describes the location of opposites on the number line.

_____

_____

Test Prep ★ Mixed Review

21 Which number sentence is true?

  A 957 mL > 9.2 L

  B 1.94 m < 20.2 cm

  C 0.15 kL < 110 L

  D 9.14 g > 892 mg

22 A test had 50 items and Hakim got 48 correct. What percent did he get correct?

  F 98%

  G 96%

  H 90%

  J 48%

Name _____

You can use a thermometer to help you understand integers.

1. The temperatures that are above zero are written with positive numbers. →

5° above zero is written: 5°. You can read it as "positive five degrees."

2. The temperatures that are below zero are written with negative numbers. →

5° below zero is written: ⁻5°. You can read it as "negative five degrees."

A number line can also help you understand integers.

Negative integers are less than 0.

Zero is neither positive nor negative.

Positive integers are greater than 0.

Write the integer that represents each temperature.

1. 8 degrees below zero _____   3 degrees above zero _____

2. 2 degrees above zero _____   9 degrees below zero _____

Compare the temperatures. Write the colder temperature.

3. ⁻8° or 3° _____   ⁻10° or 0° _____   8° or 3° _____

4. ⁻8° or ⁻3° _____   ⁻1° or ⁻5° _____   ⁻10° or 2° _____

How many integers are *between* these integers?

5. ⁻3 and 3 _____   ⁻1 and ⁻9 _____   ⁻6 and 5 _____

The **coordinate** of a point on a number line is the number that identifies the location of the point.

The coordinate or location of point **A** is ⁻**8**, of point **B** is ⁻**3**, and of point **C** is **3**.

Name the coordinate of each point on the number line.

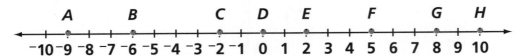

6. A _____   B _____   C _____   D _____

7. E _____   F _____   G _____   H _____

Locate and label each point on the number line.

8. *A* at ⁻**8**   *B* at **7**   *C* at **4**   *D* at ⁻**5**

9. *E* at **1**   *G* at ⁻**3**   *H* at **0**   *I* at ⁻**10**

| Problem Solving |
| Reasoning |

Solve.

10. How many negative integers are greater than ⁻**6**?

_____

11. How many integers are both greater than ⁻**3** and less than **3**?

_____

12. On the number line for rows **8** and **9** above, what are the next **4** negative integers?

_____

Test Prep ★ Mixed Review

13 What is the value of this expression?
$\left(\frac{8}{15} \times \frac{2}{9}\right) \div \frac{8}{9}$

A $\frac{64}{81}$ C $\frac{2}{15}$

B $\frac{8}{9}$ D $\frac{2}{9}$

14 6.8 in.³ could represent the dimension of what?

F the perimeter of a box top

G the size of the picture on the front of the box

H the sum of the areas of all the faces of the box

J how much cereal the box will hold

Comparing and Ordering Integers

The numbers on a number line *increase* as you move *to the right.* The numbers ⁻8 and **4** are labeled on the number line below. You can see **4** is to the right of ⁻**8**.

Words: four is greater than negative eight

Symbols: **4 > ⁻8**

The numbers on a number line *decrease* as you move *to the left.* You can see ⁻**8** is to the left of **4**.

Words: negative eight is less than four

Symbols: **⁻8 < 4**

Use > or < to compare the integers.

1. 8 ◯ 7   ⁻1 ◯ ⁻2   ⁻3 ◯ 5   9 ◯ ⁻10

2. ⁻6 ◯ 0   5 ◯ ⁻5   ⁻2 ◯ ⁻8   5 ◯ 9

Graph the numbers on the number line.
Then order the numbers from *greatest* to *least.*

3. 6, 0, ⁻3, 1

_____

4. 4, ⁻1, ⁻6, ⁻5

_____

5. ⁻10, 5, 3, ⁻9, ⁻3

_____

6. 0, ⁻2, ⁻1, 1

_____

7. 8, ⁻7, 6, ⁻5

_____

Any number that can be shown as the quotient of two integers is called a **rational number**. Rational numbers include fractions, mixed numbers, and *some* decimals.

Remember: A fraction is another way to show division.

Examples: **2** Think: $\frac{2}{1}$ or $2 \div 1 = 2$ **0.25** Think: $\frac{25}{100}$ or $25 \div 100 = 0.25$

You can use a number line to compare and order rational numbers.

$\frac{-8}{3}$ is to the left of ⁻1.75.	⁻1 is to the right of ⁻1.75.	So, the numbers ordered from least to greatest are:
$\frac{-8}{3} <$ ⁻1.75	⁻1 > ⁻1.75	$\frac{-8}{3}$, ⁻1.75, ⁻1.

Graph the numbers. Then order them from *greatest* to *least*.

8. ⁻1 2 $\frac{3}{4}$ $\frac{-3}{4}$ 0

_____

9. 2 ⁻1 ⁻0.5 0.75 ⁻1.75

_____

✓ Quick Check

Write each number as an integer. Then write the opposite.

Work Space

10. down **3** floors   _____   _____

11. loss of **7** gallons   _____   _____

12. the opposite of ⁻4   _____   _____

Locate and label each point on the number line.

13. *C* at ⁻4   **14.** *A* at ⁻1   **15.** *B* at 2

Use > or < to compare. Draw a number line if you need to.

16. ⁻4 ◯ 4   **17.** ⁻9 ◯ ⁻10   **18.** $\frac{-3}{4}$ ◯ $\frac{2}{5}$

19. Write the numbers $\frac{8}{10}$, ⁻1$\frac{3}{4}$, ⁻3, 9, ⁻10, 6, 0.7 in order from least to greatest. _____

Name _____

The Coordinate Plane

Two number lines form the **coordinate plane.**

The horizontal number line is called the **x-axis.** The vertical number line is called the **y-axis.**

The axes cross at the **origin** and divide the plane into 4 **quadrants,** numbered I, II, III, and IV.

An **ordered pair** represents a **coordinate** or location on a coordinate plane.

To locate a point on the grid, follow these steps.

1. Start at the origin.

2. Look at the first number of the ordered pair, **x**. If it is *positive* move *right* that number of units. If it is *negative* move *left*.

3. Look at the second number of the ordered pair, **y**. If it is *positive* move *up* that number of units. If it is *negative* move *down*.

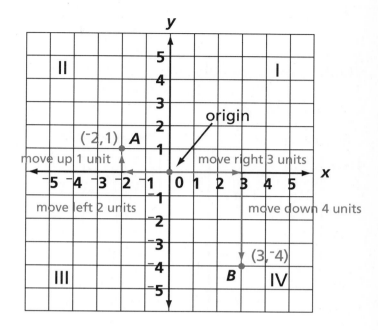

move left **2** ↘   ↙ move up **1**
          x, y
       (⁻2, 1)

The point located at (⁻2, 1) is **A**.

move right **3** ↘   ↙ move down **4**
            x, y
         (3, ⁻4)

The point located at (3, ⁻4) is **B**.

Circle the set of directions that best describes the location of the ordered pair.

1. (⁻2, 5)   right **2**, down **5**   left **2**, up **5**   right **5**, down **2**

2. (⁻3, ⁻2)   right **3**, left **2**   right **3**, right **2**   left **3**, down **2**

3. (4, ⁻1)   right **4**, down **1**   left **1**, up **4**   left **4**, down **1**

4. (3, 2)   right **3**, left **2**   right **3**, up **2**   left **3**, down **2**

Write the letter of the point at each location.

5. (⁻2, 6) _____   (⁻1, ⁻2) _____

6. (0, 5) _____   (5, ⁻1) _____

7. (⁻1, 5) _____   (6, ⁻2) _____

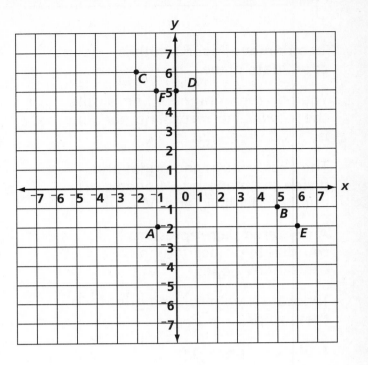

Look at the table for the equation $x + y = 4$.
Think: What 2 numbers equal 4?
Then complete the table and write the
ordered pairs (x, y).

8. $x + y = 4$

x	y
0	4
1	
2	

Ordered Pairs

(x, y)
(0, 4)
(1,)
(,)
(,)
(,)

9. Graph the ordered pairs from exercise 8 on the coordinate plane.
   a. Connect the points to form a line segment.

   b. Extend the line segment in both directions.
      What other ordered pairs are on this line segment?

   _____

Problem Solving
Reasoning   Solve.

10. Give an ordered pair for another point that is on a line segment
    that connects (0, 3), (1, 2), and (2, 1) but extends in both directions.

    _____

Test Prep ★ Mixed Review

⓫ Some students measured a segment as
6.71 cm, 6 cm, and 5.9 cm. What is the
mean length to the nearest mm?

   A 62 mm

   B 62 cm

   C 6 cm

   D 6 mm

⓬ Which number in this list has the greatest
value? $\frac{5}{4}$ 75%   1.54 $\frac{72}{100}$

   F $\frac{5}{4}$

   G 75%

   H 1.54

   J $\frac{72}{100}$

Name _____   **Adding Integers**

You can use a number line to add integers.

Follow these steps when adding integers on a number line.

1. Start at the location of the first addend.

2. To add a positive number, move that number of units to the *right*.
To add a negative number, move that number of units to the *left*.

3. The answer is where you stop on the number line.

$^-2 + 3 = ?$

Begin at $^-$**2.**
Move **3** units right.   So, $^-$**2** + **3** = **1.**

$^-3 + {}^-1 = ?$

Begin at $^-$**3.**
Move **1** unit left.   So, $^-$**3** + $^-$**1** = $^-$**4.**

Use the number line to find the sum of the integers.

1. $^-1 + 4$ Begin at _____, move 4 units _____. The sum is _____.

2. $3 + {}^-5$ Begin at _____, move _____ units left. The sum is _____.

3. $^-1 + {}^-4$ Begin at _____, move _____ units _____. The sum is _____.

4. $2 + 3$ Begin at _____, move _____ units _____. The sum is _____.

5. $^-2 + {}^-4$ Begin at _____, move _____ units _____. The sum is _____.

6. $^-6 + 6$ Begin at _____, move _____ units _____. The sum is _____.

Find the sum. Use the number line when necessary.

7. $3 + 7 =$ _____ $3 + {}^-7 =$ _____ $^-3 + 7 =$_____ $^-3 + {}^-7 =$ _____

8. $8 + {}^-8 =$ _____ $2 + {}^-5 =$ _____ $1 + {}^-1 =$ _____ $8 + {}^-3 =$ _____

9. $10 + {}^-7 =$ _____ $^-10 + 7 =$ _____ $6 + {}^-8 =$ _____ $^-4 + {}^-4 =$ _____

Find the sum.

10. $^-3 + {}^-3 =$ _____ $6 + 2 =$ _____ $4 + {}^-4 =$ _____ $0 + {}^-5 =$ _____

11. $^-3 + 21 =$ _____ $^-9 + {}^-5 =$ _____ $17 + {}^-9 =$ _____ $^-17 + {}^-5 =$ _____

12. $^-15 + {}^-3 =$ _____ $^-5 + 2 =$ _____ $^-4 + {}^-4 =$ _____ $7 + {}^-5 =$ _____

13. $28 + {}^-2 =$ _____ $45 + {}^-2 =$ _____ $^-39 + {}^-4 =$ _____ $10 + {}^-35 =$ _____

14. $^-43 + {}^-21 =$ _____ $^-16 + 2 =$ _____ $4 + {}^-24 =$ _____ $^-25 + 25 =$ _____

15. $^-23 + {}^-3 =$ _____ $16 + 22 =$ _____ $14 + {}^-4 =$ _____ $50 + {}^-45 =$ _____

16. $^-1 + 2 + 3 =$ _____ $3 + {}^-7 + {}^-2 =$ _____ $^-1 + {}^-3 + {}^-4 =$ _____

17. $3 + 5 + 1 =$ _____ $^-1 + {}^-7 + 9 =$ _____ $6 + {}^-6 + 5 =$ _____

| Problem Solving |
| Reasoning |

Solve.

18. Is the sum of two negative numbers positive or negative? _____

19. When adding a positive number and a negative number, is the sum greater than or less than the positive number? _____

20. What is the sum of two opposites? _____

21. When $x = 2$ and $y = 0$, then $x + y$ equals **2**. Name **3** other pairs of numbers for x and y that will also equal **2** when added.

_____

Test Prep ★ Mixed Review

22 Which figure is a parallelogram that has all its sides congruent but not all its angles congruent?

A equilateral triangle *ABC*

B square *WXYZ*

C rhombus *JKLM*

D pentagon *QRSTU*

23 There are 192 seats set up for a 2:30 p.m. meeting. As of 2:00 p.m., only 75% of the seats were filled. How many empty seats are there?

F $38\frac{2}{5}$

G 48

H 144

J 768

Subtracting Integers

Follow these steps when subtracting integers on a number line.

1. Rewrite the subtraction equation as an addition equation:

   a. Do *not* change the first number.

   b. Change the subtraction sign to an addition sign.

   c. Change the second number to its opposite.

2. Start at the location of the first addend.

3. To add a *positive* number, move that number of units to the *right*.
To add a *negative* number, move that number of units to the *left*.

4. The answer is where you stop on the number line.

> You can rewrite a subtraction equation as an addition equation by using *opposites*.
> • The opposite of ⁻ is ⁺.
> • The opposite of **4** is ⁻**4**.
> • The opposite of ⁻**8** is **8**.

$^-2 - {}^-3 = ?$ **Think:** $^-2 + 3 = ?$

Start at ⁻**2**.
Move **3** units right.   So, ⁻**2** − ⁻**3** = **1**.

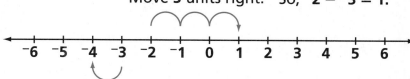

$^-3 - 1 = ?$ **Think:** $^-3 + {}^-1 = ?$

Start at ⁻**3**.
Move **1** unit left.   So, ⁻**3** − **1** = ⁻**4**.

Find each difference. Use the number line above to help you.

1. 5 − 6 ➜ 5 + ⁻6 Start at _____, move **6** units _____. Then **5 − 6** is _____.

2. ⁻3 − 4 ➜ _____ + ⁻4 Start at _____, move **4** units _____. Then ⁻**3 − 4** is _____.

3. 4 − ⁻2 ➜ 4 + _____ Start at _____, move **2** units _____. Then **4 − ⁻2** is _____.

Find each difference.

4. 3 − 7 = _____ + _____ ➜ _____   3 − ⁻7 = _____ + _____ ➜ _____

5. 8 − ⁻8 = _____ + _____ ➜ _____   2 − ⁻5 = _____ + _____ ➜ _____

6. ⁻10 − ⁻7 = _____ + _____ ➜ _____   ⁻10 − 7 = _____ + _____ ➜ _____

7. ⁻3 − ⁻3 = _____ + _____ ➜ _____   6 − 2 = _____ + _____ ➜ _____

You know that subtraction and addition are related. You can use addition properties to help you subtract more than two integers.
  • Rewrite the subtraction expression as a related addition expression. Use properties to add.

$^-3 - ^-1 - 5$ → $^-3 + 1 + ^-5$ → $(^-3 + ^-5) + 1$

$^-8 + 1$

$^-7$

Commutative Property	
The sum is the same if you change the order of the addends.	

$^-5 - ^-5 + 2$ → $^-5 + 5 + 2$ → $0 + 2$

2

The sum of opposites is 0.

Zero Property	
When you add **0** to a number the result is that number.	

Use properties to find the value of the expressions.

8. $^-1 - 2 - 3 =$ _____ $3 + ^-7 - ^-2 =$ _____ $^-1 - ^-3 + ^-4 =$ _____

9. $3 - 5 + 1 =$ _____ $^-1 - ^-7 + 9 =$ _____ $6 + ^-6 - 5 =$ _____

10. $^-2 - ^-3 + 2 =$ _____ $^-1 - ^-7 - 9 =$ _____ $^-6 + 13 - 7 =$ _____

11. How can changing the order of the addends in $^-62 - 18 + 62$ help you find its value more quickly?

☑ **Quick Check**

What ordered pair is being described?   Work Space

12. Start at **(0, 0)**. Go right **2**, then go down **4.** _____

13. Start at **(0, 0)**. Go left **4**, then go up **2.** _____

14. Start at **(0, 0)**. Go down **5.** _____

Add.

15. $7 + ^-3$ _____   **16.** $^-3 + ^-9$ _____

17. $32 + ^-32 + ^-4$ _____

Use properties to find the value of the expression.

18. $^-5 - ^-3$ _____   **19.** $3 - ^-6$ _____

20. $7 - 8$ _____

292 Unit 11 Lesson 6

Problem Solving Strategy: Work Backward

You may need to use the strategy Work Backward to solve some problems.

> **Problem**
>
> Lori is thinking of a mystery number. If she multiplies the number by 3 and then adds 4, the result is 25. What is Lori's mystery number?

---

1 Understand   Try to rewrite what you know in your own words.

- What do you know about Lori's mystery number?

    If I multiply the mystery number by 3 and add 4 to it, the answer is 25.

    What do you need to find?

    _____

---

2 Decide   Choose a method for solving.

- Try the strategy Work Backward.

    What is the result of the operations on Lori's mystery number?

    _____

    What operations did Lori use to get the result?

    _____

---

3 Solve   Organize the information, then solve.

Inverse of addition is _____	Subtract **4**. **25 − 4 =** _____
Inverse of multiplication is _____	Divide by **3**. **21 ÷ 3 =** _____
Mystery Number	_____

---

4 Look back   Check your answer.

Start with 7. Multiply it by 3. Then add 4. What is your result?

_____

Use the Work Backward strategy or any other strategy you have learned.

1. Bruce is thinking of a mystery number. If he divides it by **9** and then subtracts **7** from it, the result is **1**. What number is Bruce thinking of?

Think: What is the inverse of subtraction? Division?

_____

Answer_____

2. Allison bought some cassettes by mail order. Each cassette cost **$7**. There was an additional charge of **$4** per order for shipping costs. The total bill came to **$53**. How many cassettes did Allison buy?

Think: Is the additional charge one amount or many amounts?

_____

Answer_____

3. Bethany left her office and went up **2** floors to work in the library. At lunch time, she left the library and went down **3** floors to the cafeteria. After lunch, she went up **4** floors to the mailroom on the **9**th floor. On what floor is Bethany's office?

_____

4. Jack bought **3** jars of gravy. He used a coupon good for **$0.75** off **3** jars of gravy. He gave the cashier a **$5**-dollar bill. She gave him **$0.68** in change. How much did each jar of gravy cost before the coupon?

_____

5. Amy checked the temperature every hour between **10:00** and **2:00**. At **11:00**, the temperature had risen **1** degree. At noon, it had risen **2** more degrees. At **1:00**, the temperature dropped **1** degree. At **2:00**, it dropped **2** more degrees and the thermometer read **68°** F. What was the temperature at **10:00**?

_____

6. During the month of May, Bob made the following deposits to and withdrawals from his savings account. On May 3, he put in **$65**. On May 8, he took out **$85**. On May 15, he put in **$35**. On May 27, he put in **$49**. At the end of the month, he had **$659** in his account. How much did he have in the account at the beginning of May?

_____

7. On Wednesday, $\frac{1}{2}$ the tickets for a raffle were sold. On Thursday an additional **54** tickets were sold. There were **21** unsold tickets. How many raffle tickets were there in all?

_____

8. In his third game Greg bowled **194**. His score in the second game was **8** more than in the first game, and his score in the third game was **19** more than in the first game. What did Greg bowl in the second game?

_____

Name _____

You can think of multiplication as repeated addition.

- Think of repeated addition to find the product
  of a *negative* integer and a *positive* integer.

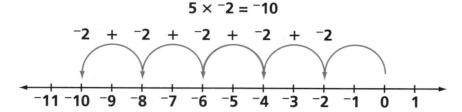

5 × ⁻2 = ⁻10

⁻2 + ⁻2 + ⁻2 + ⁻2 + ⁻2

- The product of a *negative* integer and a *negative*   ⁻5 × ⁻2 = 10
  integer is a positive integer.

Follow these rules when multiplying integers.

The product of two numbers with the **same sign** is **positive.**
positive × positive = positive   3 × 2 = 6
negative × negative = positive   ⁻3 × ⁻2 = 6
The product of two numbers with **different signs** is **negative.**
positive × negative = negative   3 × ⁻2 = ⁻6
negative × positive = negative   ⁻3 × 2 = ⁻6

Circle the sign of each product.

1. 8 × 5   +   –   **2.** ⁻8 × 5   +   –   **3.** ⁻3 × ⁻8   +   –

⁻4 × ⁻5   +   –   6 × ⁻1   +   –   ⁻3 × 8   +   –

1 × 50   +   –   ⁻3 × ⁻9   +   –   3 × ⁻8   +   –

Find each product.

4. 8 × 5 = _____   ⁻8 × 5 = _____   ⁻3 × ⁻8 = _____   ⁻3 × 0 = _____

5. 4 × ⁻5 = _____   6 × ⁻1 = _____   ⁻3 × 8 = _____   0 × 8 = _____

6. 1 × 50 = _____   ⁻3 × ⁻9 = _____   3 × ⁻8 = _____   1 × ⁻5 = _____

7. 7 × 6 = _____   ⁻5 × 7 = _____   ⁻4 × ⁻8 = _____   4 × ⁻9 = _____

8. ⁻11 × ⁻2 = _____   25 × ⁻2 = _____   ⁻16 × ⁻3 = _____   ⁻35 × 4 = _____

9. ⁻11 × ⁻4 = _____   ⁻17 × 3 = _____   15 × ⁻4 = _____   ⁻19 × ⁻2 = _____

Multiplication properties can help you find the product of more than two integers.

Commutative Property

$$^-5 \times 24 \times ^-2$$
$$(^-5 \times ^-2) \times 24$$
$$10 \times 24$$
$$240$$

The order in which numbers are multiplied does not change the product.

Distributive Property

$$3 \times (1 + ^-8) = (3 \times 1) + (3 \times ^-8)$$
$$3 \times ^-7 = 3 + ^-24$$
$$^-21 = ^-21$$

The product of a factor and a sum is the same as multiplying each addend by the factor and adding those products.

Property of Zero

$$^-23 \times ^-16 \times 0 = 0$$

When a number is multiplied by zero, the product is always zero.

Property of One

$$1 \times ^-4 \times 3$$
$$1 \times ^-12$$
$$^-12$$

When a number is multiplied by one, the product is that number.

Find the product. Use the properties of multiplication.

10. $^-4 \times 10 \times 2 =$ _____ $^-43 \times ^-64 \times 0 =$ _____ $2 \times (^-8 \times ^-2) =$ _____

11. $^-5 \times ^-48 \times ^-2 =$ _____ $2 \times (^-8 + ^-2) =$ _____ $^-14 \times 4 \times 1 =$ _____

12. $(2 \times ^-7) + (2 \times 8) =$ _____ $^-10 \times ^-10 \times 33 =$ _____ $^-23 \times 15 \times 0 =$ _____

13. $4 \times 6 \times 50 =$ _____ $(^-3 \times ^-11) + (^-3 \times 11) =$ _____ $^-4 \times 1 \times 38 =$ _____

| Problem Solving |
| Reasoning |

Solve.

14. The temperature in Bob's home was **68°**F when the furnace stopped working. The temperature dropped **5°** every hour. If it continues to drop at this rate, what can you say about the temperature in Bob's home after **6** hours?

_____

Test Prep ★ Mixed Review

15 In a game, Barbara's score was 2. Then she gained 3 points, lost 5 points, and then lost 1 point. What was her final score?

   A $^-3$

   B $^-1$

   C 1

   D 3

16 Isabel's aunt Nina is three times as old as Isabel is. Nina is 30. Which equation could you use to find out Isabel's age?

   F $30 = 3 \times a$

   G $30 \times 3 = a$

   H $30 \times a = 3$

   J $3 + a = 30$

You can use these rules when dividing integers.

The quotient of two numbers with the **same sign** is **positive**.
positive ÷ positive = positive $6 \div 2 = 3$
negative ÷ negative = positive $^-6 \div ^-2 = 3$

The quotient of two numbers with **different signs** is **negative**.
positive ÷ negative = negative $6 \div ^-2 = ^-3$
negative ÷ positive = negative $^-6 \div 2 = ^-3$

Circle the sign of the quotient.

1. $18 \div ^-2$ +   −   **2.** $^-18 \div 2$ +   −   **3.** $^-18 \div ^-2$ +   −

$^-24 \div ^-6$ +   − $66 \div ^-11$ +   − $^-54 \div 9$ +   −

$^-63 \div 9$ +   − $^-9 \div ^-3$ +   − $^-20 \div ^-4$ +   −

Find each quotient.

4. $18 \div ^-2 = $_____ $^-18 \div 2 = $_____ $^-18 \div ^-2 = $_____ $^-3 \div 1 = $_____

5. $^-24 \div ^-6 = $_____ $66 \div ^-11 = $_____ $^-54 \div 9 = $_____ $8 \div ^-1 = $_____

6. $^-63 \div 9 = $_____ $^-9 \div ^-3 = $_____ $^-20 \div ^-4 = $_____ $^-5 \div 1 = $_____

7. $^-21 \div ^-7 = $_____ $25 \div ^-5 = $_____ $^-16 \div ^-4 = $_____ $^-35 \div 7 = $_____

Circle the value of the variable that makes the equation true.

8. $^-24 \div x = 6$ $x = 4$ $x = ^-4$ **9.** $64 \div ^-8 = y$ $y = 8$ $y = ^-8$

$m \div 12 = ^-12$ $m = 144$ $m = ^-144$ $^-55 \div ^-5 = b$ $b = 11$ $b = ^-11$

$45 \div 1 = r$ $r = 45$ $r = ^-45$ $^-72 \div t = ^-9$ $t = 8$ $t = ^-8$

$^-1 \div y = ^-1$ $y = 1$ $y = ^-1$ $g \div ^-3 = 33$ $g = 99$ $g = ^-99$

Write the value of *m* that balances each equation.

10. $^-44 \div m = 4$ $m = $_____   **11.** $m \div ^-6 = 6$ $m = $_____

$^-72 \div m = ^-8$ $m = $_____ $^-80 \div ^-4 = m$ $m = $_____

To find the value of an expression with integers and more than one operation, you must follow the **order of operations.**

Example

$$\frac{(^-5 + 3) \times (^-9 + ^-1)}{^-2}$$

Complete the operations inside the parentheses.
$^-5 + 3 = ^-2$ and $^-9 + ^-1 = ^-10$

$$\frac{^-2 \times ^-10}{^-2}$$

Multiply. $^-2 \times ^-10 = 20$

$$\frac{20}{^-2} = ^-10$$

Simplify. $20 \div ^-2 = ^-10$

Find the value of each expression.

12. $\dfrac{(^-8 + ^-12)}{2}$ _____

$3 \times (6 \div ^-2)$ _____

$(^-4 - 6) \times (9 \div ^-3)$ _____

13. $\dfrac{(^-8 \div ^-2)}{4}$ _____

$\dfrac{^-10 \div (6 + ^-1)}{2}$ _____

$\dfrac{^-4 \times 6 + ^-3}{(9 \div ^-3)}$ _____

| Problem Solving |
| Reasoning |

Solve.

14. The low temperatures this week were as follows: **31°, 18°, ^-5°, ^-2°, 13°, 17°,** and **^-2°.** What was the mean or average low temperature?

_____

15. Kendra received **$5** each day for **5** days for walking her neighbor's puppy. She deposited **$7** in her bank account. Then she divided the remainder of what she earned evenly into **3** envelopes, one marked movies, another marked vacation, and the third marked presents. How much money did she put into the envelope marked vacation?

_____

Test Prep ★ Mixed Review

16 Suppose you are on a number line and you start at ^-2, then jump 5 spaces in the negative direction. Where do you land?

   A 7

   B 3

   C ^-5

   D ^-7

17 You are staying at a friend's house for 5 days. You pack 3 pairs of pants of different colors and 4 T-shirts of different colors. How many different outfits can you make that combine pants and a T-shirt?

   F 12   G 15

   H 18   J 20

Graphing in the Coordinate Plane

You can write a **function** or **rule** that tells how to find ordered pairs. The rule shows how to use one or more operations with a number (*x*) to get a second number (*y*).

- An example of a rule is: **3 + x = y**

  It tells you to "add **3** to **x** to get **y**."

  So when *x* = 2, replace *x* with **2** in the rule to find *y*.

$$\overset{x \quad y}{3 + 2 = 5}$$

- Notice that you can write an ordered pair using the values that you found with the rule:

  x = **2** and *y* = **5**   ordered pair → **(2,5)**

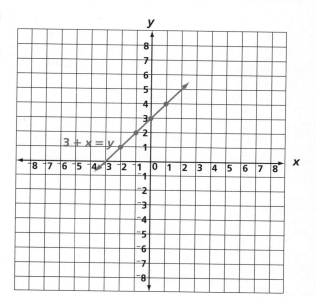

You can use a rule and a table to find other ordered pairs. The table below is called a **function table**. It shows that you start with a value for *x*, then replace *x* in the rule with that value to find *y*.

Rule: 3 + x = y			Ordered Pair
x	3 + *x*	*y*	(*x*, *y*)
⁻2	3 + ⁻2	1	(⁻2, 1)
⁻1	3 + ⁻1	2	(⁻1, 2)
0	3 + 0	3	(0, 3)
1	3 + 1	4	(1, 4)

> Can you see patterns in the table?

If you graph the ordered pairs and connect the points, a line is formed. So you can say that the graph of **3 + x = y** is a straight line.

Complete each function table.

1.

Rule: 2 + x = y			Ordered Pair
x	2 + *x*	*y*	(*x*, *y*)
1	2 + 1		(1,)
2	2 +		(,)
3	2 +		(,)
4	2 +		(,)

2.

Rule: 3 − x = y			Ordered Pair
x	3 − *x*	*y*	(*x*, *y*)
⁻2	3 − ⁻2		(,)
0	3 −		(,)
2	3 −		(,)
4	3 −		(,)

3. Graph the ordered pairs from Exercises 1 and 2 on the grid above. Connect the points. Draw arrowheads on both ends of each figure to show that they are lines. Label each line with the correct rule.

Complete each function table. Then graph the ordered pairs. Connect the points to draw lines. Label each line with the correct rule.

4. Rule: $2 - x = y$

x	$2 - x$	y	Ordered Pair (x, y)
1	2 −		(,)
2	2 −		(,)
3	2 −		(,)
4	2 −		(,)

5. Rule: $x + 5 = y$

x	$x + 5$	y	Ordered Pair (x, y)
−8	+ 5		(,)
−5	+ 5		(,)
−3	+ 5		(,)
0	+ 5		(,)

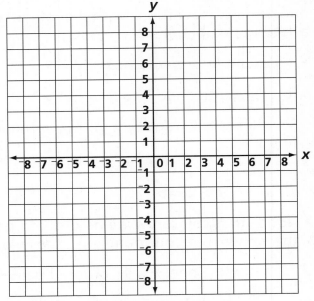

Use this grid for exercises 4–5.

6. Rule: $1 - x = y$

x	$1 - x$	y	Ordered Pair (x, y)
−1	1 −		(,)
0	1 −		(,)
1	1 −		(,)
2	1 −		(,)

7. Rule: $^-2 \times x = y$

x	$^-2 \times x$	y	Ordered Pair (x, y)
−3	−2 ×		(,)
0	−2 ×		(,)
3	−2 ×		(,)
4	−2 ×		(,)

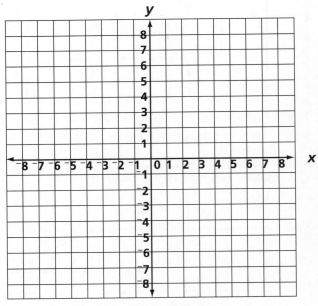

Use this grid for exercises 6–7.

Name _____

You can find the rule for the line that is on this coordinate grid. Follow these steps.

1. Find at least **3** points on the line. Make a table. Write ordered pairs for the points.

(x, y)
(⁻2, ⁻1)
(0, 1)
(2, 3)
(4, 5)

2. Study the pattern in the table. Use words to describe the pattern.

   Add **1** to **x**. Then, **x + 1** is **y**.

3. Write an equation using symbols. **x + 1 = y**.

4. Check the equation. Replace **x** and **y** with the values in the table.

   $x + 1 = y \rightarrow {}^{-}2 + 1 = {}^{-}1$

   The equation is true, so **x + 1 = y** is correct.

Complete the tables for lines A and B. Give the rule in words. Then write the equation for the line.

8. Line **A**

Rule in words: _____

_____

The equation: _____

9. Line **B**

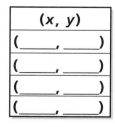

Rule in words: _____

_____

The equation: _____

Complete the table for Line A.
Give the rule in words.
Then write the equation for the line.

10. Line A

(x, y)
(_____ , _____)
(_____ , _____)
(_____ , _____)
(_____ , _____)

Rule in words: _____

_____

The equation: _____

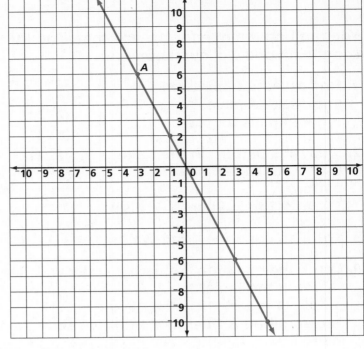

Problem Solving Reasoning   Solve.

11. Tim planted a tree. After **1** year, the tree was **1** foot tall. After **2** years, it was **2** feet tall. After **5** years, it was **5** feet tall. Name **3** ordered pairs that could be used to graph the growth of the tree.

_____

12. How tall would you expect Tim's tree to be in **10** years? _____

✓ **Quick Check**

Find each product or quotient.   **Work Space**

13. $^-8 \times 5$ _____   **14.** $^-28 \div 7$ _____

2 × $^-16$ _____ $36 \div ^-9$ _____

$^-4 \times ^-12$ _____ $^-55 \div ^-11$ _____

Complete.

15. Write an equation for this rule: The first number (x) times **3** is the second number (y). _____

16. The point (**3**, _____) lies on the line of the equation in Exercise 10. Use the graph to complete the ordered pair.

Name _____

When solving a problem, often you have to decide which mathematical operation to use.

In this lesson, you will need to choose the correct operation when solving problems involving integers.

Tips to Remember

1. Understand	2. Decide	3. Solve	4. Look back

- Predict the answer. Then solve the problem. Compare your answer with your prediction.
- Find the action in the problem. Which operation shows the action best: addition, subtraction, multiplication, or division?
- Try to remember a real-life situation like the one described in the problem. What do you remember that might help you find a solution?

Choose the correct operation. Then solve.

1. On Saturday, the lowest temperature was $^-4°$F. On Sunday the lowest temperature was $^-6°$F. Which is the correct operation for finding how much higher the temperature was on Saturday?

  a. $^-4 - (^-6)$ **b.** $^-6 - (^-4)$

  c. $^-4 + (^-6)$ **d.** $^-4 \times {^-6}$

Think: You are comparing two temperatures. Should you add or subtract?

_____

_____

Answer _____

2. The temperature at noon was **0°F**. It dropped **2°F** per hour from noon to **4:00** P.M. Which is the correct operation to find the temperature at **4:00** P.M.?

  a. $^-2 - 4$ **b.** $^-2 + 4$

  c. $^-2 \times 4$ **d.** $4 \div {^-2}$

Think: How many degrees does the temperature drop each hour? What operation does this suggest?

_____

_____

Answer _____

Choose the correct operation. Then solve.

3. Jessica's score was ⁻6 points. In the next game she scored 8 points. What is the correct operation to find Jessica's score now?

    a. ⁻6 + 8   **b.** ⁻6 − 8

    c. ⁻6 × 8   **d.** 8 − (⁻6)

_____

4. Jaime's score was 0. He scored ⁻3 points in each of the next 4 games. What is the correct operation to find Jaime's score now?

    a. ⁻3 + 4   **b.** ⁻3 − 4

    c. ⁻4 × ⁻3   **d.** ⁻3 × 4

_____

5. A football team lost 24 yards over 4 plays. What is the correct operation to find the average number of yards the team lost per play?

    a. ⁻24 × 4   **b.** ⁻24 ÷ 4

    c. ⁻24 + 4   **d.** ⁻24 − 4

_____

6. The temperature was 2°F at midnight. At 3:00 A.M. it had dropped to ⁻1°F. What is the correct operation to find the number of degrees the temperature had dropped?

    a. 2 − 1   **b.** 2 + (⁻1)

    c. 2 × (⁻1)   **d.** 2 − (⁻1)

_____

7. In golf, **par** is the number of strokes it should take to complete a hole. A golfer's score was 4 under par. On the next hole, he scored 2 over par. What is the correct operation to find the golfer's score now?

    a. ⁻4 ÷ 2   **b.** ⁻4 × 2

    c. ⁻4 + 2   **d.** ⁻4 − 2

_____

8. Arnold finished a golf game 5 strokes over par. Lee finished 4 strokes under par. What is the correct operation to find how many more golf strokes Arnold made than Lee?

    a. 5 − (⁻4)   **b.** ⁻4 − 5

    c. 5 × (⁻4)   **d.** 5 + (⁻4)

_____

Extend Your Thinking

9. Look back at problem 3. Suppose Jessica scored the following points in the next three games: ⁻4, 1, ⁻2. What would be Jessica's score now?

_____

10. Look back at problem 6. Suppose that the temperature rose steadily 1°F every hour from 3:00 A.M. until 9:00 A.M. What would be the temperature at 9:00 A.M.?

_____

Name _____

Write the opposite of each integer.

1. 4 _____   **2.** ⁻2 _____   **3.** 551 _____   **4.** ⁻9 _____

Graph the following integers on the number line.
Then order them from *greatest* to *least*. Check students' graphs.

5. ⁻8, 8, 2, ⁻1 _____

-10 -9 -8 -7 -6 -5 -4 -3 -2 -1 0 1 2 3 4 5 6 7 8 9 10

Use the coordinate graph for exercises 6 and 7.

6. Write the ordered pair for each point.

Point A _____   Point B _____   Point C _____

7. Connect the points and extend the line
in both directions.

Write the equation for the line. _____

8. Is (24, 25) a point on the line? Explain. _____

_____

Write each sum, difference, product, or quotient.

9. $5 - 9 =$ _____   **10.** $5 + {}^-9 =$ _____   **11.** $^-5 - 9 =$ _____   **12.** $^-5 - {}^-9 =$ _____

13. $^-5 + {}^-5 =$ _____   **14.** $5 - {}^-9 =$ _____   **15.** $6 + {}^-6 =$ _____   **16.** $3 + {}^-1 =$ _____

17. $7 \times 5 =$ _____   **18.** $^-8 \div 4 =$ _____   **19.** $^-7 \times {}^-6 =$ _____   **20.** $^-3 \div {}^-3 =$ _____

21. $14 \div {}^-7 =$ _____   **22.** $5 \times {}^-1 =$ _____   **23.** $^-16 \div {}^-8 =$ _____   **24.** $0 \times {}^-1 =$ _____

Problem Solving
Reasoning   Solve.

25. The temperature in one city is ⁻2°F and in another city is ⁻9°F colder.

What is the temperature in the coldest city? _____

26. What number added to **75** is **65** and divided by **2** is ⁻**5**? _____

The streets of the town of Brightsville form a grid. Use the grid to answer questions 1 and 2.

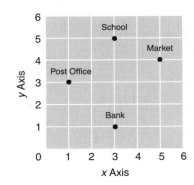

y Axis / x Axis

School, Market, Post Office, Bank

1 Which best represents the coordinates of the school on the map?

A (1, 3)   **C** (3, 5)

B (3, 1)   **D** (5, 4)

2 Which set of directions could you use to go from the school to your house which is located at (⁻1, ⁻1)?

F left 2, down 2

G left 2, down 6

H left 4, down 2

J left 4, down 6

3 The number line is a scale drawing of a street 1 mile long. Suppose you live at point B. The Meliks live $\frac{1}{4}$ mile to the left of you. The Rosens live less than $\frac{1}{4}$ mile to the right of you. Which points represent the Meliks and the Rosens?

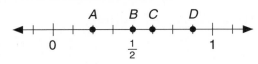

A   B C   D

0        $\frac{1}{2}$ 1

A A, C   **C** C, A

B A, D   **D** C, D

4 Which expression does not have a value of 6 when $n = 3$?

F $60 \div (n^2 + 1)$

G $(6 \div n) \times 3$

H $600 \div (4 \times n - 2)$

J $(6 - n) + (30 \div 10)$

5 Which numbers would you use to complete the table of ordered pairs for the rule $^-5 \times x = y$?

x	y
5	-25
1	-5
0	0
-1	
-3	

A 5, 15   **C** ⁻5, ⁻15

B ⁻5, 15   **D** ⁻5, ⁻25

6 A package of batteries that cost $8.49 was on sale for $6.89. The computer club bought a dozen packages. How much did they spend?

F $101.88

G $89.88

H $82.68

J $71.92

K Not here

7 What is the value of this expression?
$^-4 \times (8 + ^-11) \div 2$

A ⁻36   **C** ⁻6   **E** 6

B ⁻7   **D** 4

Tables of Measures

Metric System

Prefixes

kilo (k)	=	1,000	
hecto (h)	=	100	
deka (da)	=	10	
deci (d)	=	0.1	= $\frac{1}{10}$
centi (c)	=	0.01	= $\frac{1}{100}$
milli (m)	=	0.001	= $\frac{1}{1,000}$

Length

1 kilometer (km)	=	1,000 meters (m)
1 hectometer (hm)	=	100 meters
1 dekameter (dam)	=	10 meters
1 decimeter (dm)	=	0.1 meter
1 centimeter (cm)	=	0.01 meter
1 millimeter (mm)	=	0.001 meter

Capacity

1 kiloliter (kL)	=	1,000 liters (L)
1 hectoliter (hL)	=	100 liters
1 dekaliter (daL)	=	10 liters
1 deciliter (dL)	=	0.1 liter
1 centiliter (cL)	=	0.01 liter
1 milliliter (mL)	=	0.001 liter

Mass

1 kilogram (kg)	=	1,000 grams (g)
1 hectogram (hg)	=	100 grams
1 dekagram (dag)	=	10 grams
1 decigram (dg)	=	0.1 gram
1 centigram (cg)	=	0.01 gram
1 milligram (mg)	=	0.001 gram

Customary System

Length

1 foot (ft)	=	12 inches (in.)
1 yard (yd)	=	3 feet
1 yard	=	36 inches
1 mile (mi)	=	5,280 feet

Capacity

1 tablespoon (tbs)	=	3 teaspoons (tsp)
1 fluid ounce (fl oz)	=	2 tablespoons
1 cup (c)	=	8 fluid ounces
1 pint (pt)	=	2 cups
1 pint	=	16 fluid ounces
1 quart (qt)	=	2 pints
1 gallon (gal)	=	4 quarts

Weight

1 pound (lb)	=	16 ounces (oz)
1 ton (T)	=	2,000 pounds

Area

1 square foot (ft^2)	=	144 square inches ($in.^2$)
1 square yard (yd^2)	=	9 square feet
1 acre (A)	=	4,840 square yards
1 square mile (mi^2)	=	640 acres

Other Measures

Time

1 minute (min)	=	60 seconds (s)
1 hour (h)	=	60 minutes
1 day (d)	=	24 hours
1 week (wk)	=	7 days
1 month (mo)	≈	4 weeks
1 year (yr)	=	12 months
1 year	=	52 weeks
1 year	=	365 days
1 leap year	=	366 days
1 decade	=	10 years
1 century	=	100 years

Counting

1 dozen (doz)	=	12 things
1 score	=	20 things
1 gross (gro)	=	12 dozen
1 gross	=	144 things

Geometric Formulas

Rectangle

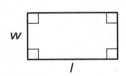

Perimeter:
$P = 2(l + w)$

Area:
$A = lw$

Square

Perimeter:
$P = 4s$

Area:
$A = s^2$

Parallelogram

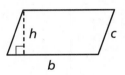

Perimeter:
$P = 2(b + c)$

Area:
$A = bh$

Right Triangle

Perimeter:
$P = a + b + c$

Area:
$A = \frac{1}{2}ba$

Triangle

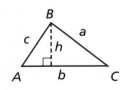

Perimeter:
$P = a + b + c$

Area:
$A = \frac{1}{2}bh$

Rectangular Prism

Surface Area:
$SA = 2(lw + wh + lh)$

Volume:
$V = lwh$

Cube

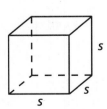

Surface Area:
$SA = 6s^2$

Volume:
$V = s^3$

Glossary

A

acute angle An angle whose measure is less than 90°

acute triangle A triangle whose largest angle is an acute angle

addend A number to be added in an addition expression

adding 0 property Adding zero to any number does not change the number.
Examples: 7 + 0 = 7 and n + 0 = n

addition The arithmetic operation that combines two numbers
Example:
    23 ← addend
  +13 ← addend
    36   sum

algebraic expression (see expression)

altitude (of a plane figure) A segment of a triangle or parallelogram that is perpendicular to the base. In a triangle one endpoint is the vertex opposite the base.

angle A geometric figure formed by two rays with a common endpoint. The angle below can be named either ∠ABC or ∠B.

angle *ABC* or ∠ *ABC*

area A measure of the number of square units in a region or a surface

associative property of addition (also called the grouping property of addition) Changing the grouping of the addends does not change the sum.
Example: (37 + 95) + 5 = 37 + (95 + 5) = 137

associative property of multiplication (also called the grouping property of multiplication) Changing the grouping of the factors does not change the product.
Example:

(25 × 5) × 2 = 27 × (5 × 2) = 270

average (or mean) A measure of central tendency. It is computed by adding all the items of data and dividing by the number of items.

axis (see *x-axis, y-axis*) A reference line on a graph

B

bar graph A pictorial representation of data that uses lengths of bars to show the information

base (of an exponent) The number that is used as a factor when evaluating powers
Example: 3⁴ = 3 × 3 × 3 × 3
The base is 3.

base (of a geometric figure) A side or face in a plane or solid figure

billion The number 1,000 million or 1,000,000,000

C

capacity The maximum amount of liquid that a container can hold

Celsius temperature scale (°C) The temperature scale in the metric system in which the freezing temperature of water is 0°C and the boiling temperature of water is 100°C.

center (see *circle*)

centi- A prefix meaning one hundredth
Example: A centimeter is 0.01 meter.

central angle An angle whose vertex is the center of a circle

certain event An event that will always occur, such as "The sun will rise tomorrow morning." The probability of a certain event is 1.

chord A segment joining any two points on a circle

circle A plane figure that has all of its points the same distance from a given point called the center

circle graph A pictorial representation of data that uses sections of a circle to show the information

cluster Several items of data grouped into a small interval

common denominator A denominator used when adding two or more fractions with unlike denominators. Any common multiple of the given denominators can be used to write equivalent fractions.
Example: Some common denominators of $\frac{1}{2}$ and $\frac{1}{3}$ are 6, 12, 18, 24,…

common factor A number that is a factor of two or more whole numbers
Example: 1, 2, 3, and 6 are common factors of 12 and 18.

common multiple A number that is a multiple of two or more whole numbers
Example: Common multiples of 3 and 4 are 12, 24, 36,…

commutative property of addition (also called the order property of addition) Changing the order of the addends does not change the sum.
Example: 3 + 4 = 4 + 3 = 7

commutative property of multiplication (also called the order property of multiplication) Changing the order of the factors does not change the product.
Example: 3 × 5 = 5 × 3 = 15

compass A tool used to construct circles and other figures

compatible numbers Numbers used to make estimates. They are easy to work with mentally and are close to the given numbers.

composite number A number with three or more factors
Example: 9 is composite, because its factors are 1, 3, and 9.

cone A space figure with one flat, circular surface and one curved surface

congruent figures Figures that have exactly the same size and shape. In congruent polygons, corresponding angles are congruent and corresponding sides are congruent.

coordinate Each number of an ordered pair
Example: (4, 6) has a first coordinate of 4 and a second coordinate of 6.

coordinate plane A grid with number lines used to locate points in a plane

counting number Any of the numbers 1, 2, 3, 4, and so on

cube A rectangular prism whose faces are all congruent squares

customary system of measurement The system of measurement currently used in the United States

cylinder A space figure with two congruent circular bases joined by a single curved surface

D

data Numerical information

deci- A prefix that means one tenth
Example: A decimeter is 0.1 meter.

decimal A number that uses place value to indicate parts of a whole. The decimal point separates the whole number digits from the digits representing parts of a whole.
Example: The decimal

3.67

decimal point

represents the number three and 67 hundredths.

decimal point (see *decimal*)

degree A unit of measure of temperature or of an angle

denominator The numeral below the fraction bar in a fraction. It tells how many parts are in the whole.

diagonal A segment joining two vertices of a polygon that is not a side

diameter A chord of a circle that contains the center

difference The answer to a subtraction problem

digit Any of the symbols used to write numerals. In the base 10 system, they are 1, 2, 3, 4, 5, 6, 7, 8, 9, and 0.

distance The length of a path between two points

distributive property The same answer is obtained whether you add first and then multiply or multiply first and then add.
Example: $3 \times (20 + 7) = 3 \times 20 + 3 \times 7 = 81$

dividend The number that is divided

divisible A number is divisible by another number if there is no remainder when they are divided.
Example: 4, 16, and 640 are all divisible by 4.

division An operation that divides a set into equal sets.
Example:

quotient ➝ 10 R5 ⬅ remainder
divisor ➝ 6)65 ⬅ dividend

divisor The number that is divided by

double-bar graph A bar graph that compares two sets of data by using two bars for each category

double-line graph A line graph that compares two sets of data by using one line for each set

E

edge A line segment that is the intersection of two faces of a space figure

elapsed time A measure of the time that passes between the beginning and end of an event
Example: The elapsed time between 9:30 A.M. and 2:15 P.M. is 4 hours 45 minutes.

endpoint A point at the end of a line segment or ray

equally likely Outcomes of an experiment that have an equal chance of occurring
Example: A spinner is divided into 6 congruent sections. Each section is an equally likely outcome of a spin.

equation A number sentence that says that two expressions have the same value. It may be true, false, or open.
Example: $3 + 7 = 10$ is true; $3 + 7 = 7$ is false, and $3 + n = 10$ is open.

equilateral triangle A triangle with three congruent sides

equivalent fractions Two or more fractions that represent the same number.
Example: $\frac{1}{2} = \frac{2}{4} = \frac{3}{6} = \frac{4}{8}$

estimate To find a approximate solution mentally by using numbers that are close to the original numbers and easy to work with mentally
Example: To estimate $47 + 32$, add the rounded numbers $50 + 30$. The estimated sum is about 80.

evaluate To find the value of an expression

even number A whole number that is divisible by 2

event Any outcome or set of outcomes of an experiment

expanded form A number written so that each digit is expressed as a power of 10 instead of by its position in the numeral
Example:

Expanded forms for 316:

$300 + 10 + 6$
$(3 \times 100) + (1 \times 10) + (6 \times 1)$

exponent A number that tells how many times a base is to be used as a factor.
Example: 3^4 represents the product $\{3 \times 3 \times 3 \times 3\}$ 4 factors

exponent form A number expressed as a power
Example: Exponent forms of 64 are 2^6 and 8^2

expression A combination of numbers and symbols of operation (or grouping) that represents a mathematical quantity
Examples: $(7 + 3) \div 5$ or $6 \times n$

F

face A flat surface that is a side of a space figure

factor A number to be multiplied in a multiplication expression

factor (of a number) A counting number that exactly divides another number
Example: The numbers 1, 2, 3, 4, 6, and 12 are all factors of 12.

factor tree A diagram used to show the prime factors of a composite number

Fahrenheit temperature scale (°F) The temperature scale in the customary system in which the freezing temperature of water is 32°F and the boiling temperature of water is 212°F.

formula An equation that expresses a mathematical relationship
Example: A formula for area A of a rectangle with length l and width w is $A = l \times w$

fraction A number such as $\frac{1}{2}$ or $\frac{3}{4}$ that is used to express a part of a region or set

frequency The number of times an event occurs

function A set of ordered pairs

G

gap A characteristic of data. It is a significant interval that contains no data.

graph A pictorial representation of a data set or equation

greatest common factor (GCF) The greatest number that is a factor of each of two or more numbers.
Example: The greatest common factor of 24 and 30 is 6.

grouping symbol Parentheses or other symbols that indicate the grouping of numbers or terms in an expression

H

heptagon A polygon that has 7 sides

hexagon A polygon that has 6 sides

histogram A type of bar graph that shows frequencies over intervals

I

impossible event In probability, an event that cannot take place, such as "A prime number is also a composite number." The probability of an impossible event is 0.

inequality A number sentence that states that two numbers or expressions are greater than (>), less than (<), or not equal to (≠).
Examples: 3 + 6 < 10 is read "Three plus six is less than 10."
5 + 7 ≠ 10 is read "Five plus seven is not equal to 10."

integer The set of numbers containing all the whole numbers and their opposites

intersecting lines Line that cross each other or that have points in common

interval One of the equal sized divisions on a histogram or other graph scale

inverse operations An operation that undoes the results of another operation. For example, addition and subtraction are inverse operations, as are multiplication and division.

isosceles triangle A triangle with at least two congruent sides

J–K–L

key (of a pictograph) An indication of what a single symbol on the graph represents

kilo- A prefix meaning 1000.
Example: A kilogram is 1000 grams.

least common denominator (LCD) The least number that is a common denominator of two or more fractions. It is the least common multiple of the denominators of each of the fractions.

Example: The least common denominator of $\frac{1}{2}$ and $\frac{2}{3}$ is 6.

least common multiple (LCM) The least number that is a common multiple of two or more numbers
Example: 12 is the least common multiple of 3 and 4.

line A set of points that extends endlessly in two opposite directions

line graph A pictorial representation of data that shows changes over time using line segments

line plot A pictorial representation of a small set of data along a number line. Each data item is represented with an "X" placed above a number on the line

line segment A part of a line that has two endpoints

M

mass The amount of matter in an object. Some units of mass are milligram, gram, and kilogram.

mean The average of a set of data. It is found by adding each item of data and dividing by the number of items.
Example: 4 is the mean of 2, 4, 5, and 5.

median The middle point of the data when they are arranged from least to greatest. If there is an odd number of data items, it is the middle number. If there is an even number of data items, it is the mean of the two middle numbers.
Example: 4.5 is the median of 2, 4, 5, 5.

metric system of measurement An international system of measurement that uses the meter, liter, gram, and degrees Celsius as the basic units of measure

milli- A prefix meaning one thousandth
Example: A milliliter is 0.001 liter

mixed decimal A decimal, such as $0.83\frac{1}{3}$, that ends with a fraction

mixed number A number, such as $2\frac{2}{3}$ that is made up of a fraction less than one and a whole number

mode The number (or numbers) that occurs most often in a set of data. If every number occurs only once, the data has no mode.
Example: 5 is the mode of 2, 4, 5, 5.

multiple of a number The product of the number and any whole number.
Example: The multiples of 4 are 0, 4, 8, 12, 16, . . .

multiplication An operation that expresses repeated addition of the same number
Example: 12 ← factor
           × 4 ← factor
           ‾‾‾‾
            48 ← product

multiplying by 1 property
Multiplying any number by 1 is equal to that number.
Example: $0.3 \times 1 = 0.3$

multiplying by 0 property
Multiplying any number by 0 is equal to 0.
Example: $\frac{1}{4} \times 0 = 0$

N

negative integer A number such as $-1, -2, -3$, and so on that is less than 0

number line A line that has its points labeled with numbers (called coordinates) such as whole numbers, integers, fractions, and so on

number pattern An ordered set of numbers that seems to have a rule or pattern for finding the next number
Example: 1, 4, 7, 10, . . .is a number pattern whose rule is "add 3" to find the next number

numeral A name or symbol for a number

numerator The number over the bar in a fraction. It tells how many parts of the whole are under discussion.

numerical expression An expression that contains only numbers, symbols of operation, and grouping symbols
Example: $(7 + 4) \times 6$

O

obtuse angle An angle whose measure is greater than 90° and less than 180°

obtuse triangle A triangle whose largest angle is obtuse

octagon A polygon that has 8 sides

odd number A whole number that is not divisible by 2

open equation An equation that contains a variable

opposites Two numbers whose sum is 0. They are also called additive inverses.
Examples: 2 and −2 are opposites.

order of operations The rules that define the order in which the operations in an expression are to be evaluated. They are:
1 First work within parentheses
2 Next evaluate powers
3 Multiply and divide from left to right
4 Finally, add and subtract from left to right

ordered pair A pair of numbers used to locate a point in a coordinate plane. The first number is the horizontal distance from the origin; the second number is the vertical distance.

origin The point on a coordinate grid at which the two axes meet. Its coordinates are (0, 0).

outcome A result in a probability experiment

outlier An item of data that is significantly greater or less than all the other items of data

P

parallel lines Two lines in the same plane that do not intersect

parallelogram A quadrilateral that has its opposite sides parallel and congruent

pentagon A polygon with 5 sides

percent A ratio that compares a number to 100
Example: 39% is $\frac{39}{100}$.

percentage The result obtained by multiplying a quantity by a percent

perimeter The distance around a polygon. It is found by adding the lengths of all the sides.

period Each group of three digits seen in a number written in standard form
Example: In the number 306,789, 245, the millions period is 306, the thousands period is 789, and 245 is the ones period.

perpendicular lines
Two lines that intersect to form right angles

pictograph A pictorial representation of data that uses a single symbol or to represent multiples of a quantity

place-value system A system of numeration in which the value of a digit depends on its position in the numeral

plane A smooth flat surface that extends infinitely in all directions on the surface

plane figure A figure whose points are all in the same plane

point A location in space. It is represented by a dot.
 A   point A

polygon A plane figure composed of line segments that meet only at their endpoints. The segments must form a closed figure.

positive integer A counting number such as 1, 2, 3, ... that is greater than 0

power A number that can be expressed using a single base and exponent.
Example: 32 is a power of 2; it is the fifth power of 2.

312

prime factorization Expressing a number as a product of prime numbers
Example: $36 = 2 \times 2 \times 3 \times 3$ or $2^2 \times 3^2$

prime number A whole number greater than 1 that has exactly two factors, itself and 1
Example: $2 = 2 \times 1$

prism A space figure that has two congruent, parallel bases that are joined by parallelograms. A prism is named by the shape of its bases.

probability A number between 0 and 1 used to describe how likely an event is to happen; a measure of chance

product The answer to a multplication problem

protractor A tool used to measure and draw angles

pyramid A space figure whose base is a polygon and whose other faces are triangles that share a common vertex. A pyramid is named by the shape of its base.

Q

quadrant One of the four sections of a coordinate plane formed by the axes. They are numbered counterclockwise starting from the upper right quadrant.

quadrilateral A polygon that has four sides

quotient The answer in a division problem

R

radius A segment from any point on a circle to its center; also the length of this segment

range The difference between the least and greatest numbers in a set of data

Example: The range of the data 2, 4, 5, 5 is $5 - 2 = 3$.

rate A ratio in which unlike quantities are being compared, such as words per minute or feet per second

ratio A comparison of two quantities using division
Example: 3 : 4, 3 to 4, or $\frac{3}{4}$

ray A part of a line that has one endpoint. When naming it, the endpoint is used first.

ray AB, or $\overrightarrow{AB}$

reciprocals Two numbers whose product is 1. They are also called multiplicative inverses.
Examples: 2 and $\frac{1}{2}$ $1\frac{3}{4}$ and $\frac{4}{7}$

rectangle A parallelogram that has four right angles

rectangular prism A space figure all of whose faces are rectangles

regular polygon A polygon that has all sides congruent and all angles congruent

remainder The number that is left over in a division problem

rhombus A parallelogram that has all of its sides congruent

right angle An angle whose measure is 90°

right triangle A triangle whose largest angle is a right angle

rounding a number Replacing an exact number by another number that is easier to use or compute with
Examples: 12,501 rounded to the nearest hundred is 12,500.
4.386 rounded to the nearest hundredth is 4.39.

S

scale drawing A picture or diagram that is exactly the same shape as another but of a different size. Each distance in the drawing is in the same ratio as the corresponding distance in the original.

scale factor The ratio in a scale drawing or other similar figures that compares the scale drawing

dimensions to the actual dimensions

segment (see *line segment*)

scalene triangle A triangle that has no congruent sides

semicircle Half of a circle

sequence Numbers arranged according to some pattern or rule

side of an angle One of the rays that make up an angle

side of a polygon One of the line segments that make up a polygon

similar figures Two figures that have the same shape but not necessarily the same size. In similar polygons, corresponding angles are congruent and corresponding sides are proportional.

simplest form A fraction less than 1 in which the numerator and denominator have no common factors except 1, or a mixed number in which the fractional part is in simplest form
Examples:
$\frac{5}{10} = \frac{1}{2}$ $2\frac{6}{9} = 2\frac{2}{3}$ $\frac{12}{4} = 3$

solve an equation To find the value of the variable (called the solution) that makes an open equation true

space The set of all points

space figure A figure that is not entirely in one plane

sphere A space figure that has all of its points the same distance from a point, called the center.

square A rectangle that has all its sides congruent

standard form A number that is expressed as a base 10 numeral
Example: 3,126 is the standard form of the number three thousand, one hundred twenty-six.

stem-and-leaf plot A way to arrange data by place value. The front digit or digits are called stems, the last digit or digits are called leaves.

Example: This plot shows the following data:

82, 82, 87, 95, 112, 113

```
stem   leaves
  8 | 2 2 7
  9 | 5
 10 | 5
 11 | 2 3
```

straight angle An angle whose measure is 180°

substitution Replacing one symbol by another.
Example: A number such as 5 can be substituted for *n* in the expression 15 ÷ *n*

subtraction An arithmetic operation that takes away a given amount
Example:

$$\begin{array}{r} 345 \\ -122 \\ \hline 223 \end{array}$$ ← difference

sum The answer to an addition problem

surface area The total area of all the faces or surfaces of a space figure

T

term (of a ratio) Either of the two numbers of a ratio

trapezoid A quadrilateral that has exactly one pair of parallel sides

tree diagram A organized way of listing all the possible outcomes of an experiment

triangle A polygon that has three sides

U

unit A fixed quantity used as a standard for length, area, volume, weight, and so on

unit fraction A fraction with a numerator of 1
Examples: $\frac{1}{3}$ and $\frac{1}{7}$

unit price The cost of a single unit of an item
Example: $3 per pound for hamburger meat

unit rate A rate whose second term is a single unit, such as 50 miles per hour

V

variable A letter that is used to represent one or more numbers

variable expression An expression that contains one or more variables

vertex The common point where two sides or edges meet (plural: vertices)

← vertices

volume A measure of the space within a closed figure in space

W–X–Y–Z

whole number Any of the numbers 0, 1, 2, 3, . . .

x-axis The horizontal number line on a coordinate plane

y-axis The vertical number line on a coordinate plane

zero power of a number The zero power of any number that is not zero is 1.
Example: $10^0 = 1$

Symbols

<	is less than
>	is greater than
=	is equal to
≠	is not equal to
n	variable or placeholder
+	plus, addition symbol
−	minus, subtraction symbol
×	times, multiplication symbol
÷	divided by, division symbol
5^4	5 to the fourth power, or $5 \times 5 \times 5 \times 5$
°	degree
(2, 3)	the ordered pair 2, 3
A	point *A*
$\overleftrightarrow{AB}$	line *AB*
$\overline{AB}$	segment *AB*
$\overrightarrow{AB}$	ray *AB*
∠	angle
≅	is congruent to
⊥	is perpendicular to
∥	is parallel to
△	triangle
a : *b*	the ratio of *a* to *b*
%	percent
P(A)	The probability of event *A*
+5	positive five
−5	negative five

314